Women of Hope

Women of Hope

The Story of the Little Company
of Mary Sisters in America

MERRIE ANN NALL

WOMEN OF HOPE: THE STORY OF THE LITTLE COMPANY OF MARY SISTERS IN AMERICA.
© 2005 Little Company of Mary Sisters
Printed in the United States of America.

Library of Congress has cataloged the hardcover edition as follows:
Nall, Merrie Ann
Women of Hope: The Story of the Little Company of Mary Sisters in America
Includes bibliographical references.
ISBN 1-59975-099-6
ISBN-13 978-1-59975-099-6

Published by Little Company of Mary Sisters
9350 S. California Avenue
Evergreen Park, IL 60805

Merrie Ann Nall
Contributing Editors: Abigail Nall and Christina Nall
Design: Lauryn Toczylowski, Gerard Design, Warrenville, IL 60555
Photography: Credits on pages 291 and 292.

"Our love for God and
our companionship with Mary
cause us to search out the lost,
the lonely, the alienated, the sick
in mind, heart, or body,
the dying.

For them, we are messengers of
God's infinite and inclusive love....
We are called ... to be hope...."

(Quote based on the 1999 Constitution of the Little Company of Mary and "A Conversation with Mary Potter," developed by Sister Anita MacDonald, L.C.M., and Sister Mary Scanlon, L.C.M.)

CONTENTS

Foreword

At significant milestones on our journey as Little Company of Mary Sisters, we pause to reflect on all that the Lord has done for us and through us, and more importantly, on what the Lord is yet calling us to be and to do as a congregation. This year, 2005, is such a milestone. It marks our Congregational Chapter, which identified future directions in preserving and enhancing the spiritual heritage of our founder, Venerable Mary Potter.

Mary Potter was a woman of conviction, purpose, and vision. She overcame countless obstacles as she responded to the Holy Spirit in founding a religious congregation devoted to praying for the sick and dying, which became known as the Little Company of Mary Sisters. Although Mary Potter never sent more than two or three pioneer sisters to begin a ministry, word quickly spread of the sisters' distinctive spirituality and compassionate care, first in England and then in other countries.

As the blue-veiled sisters became known, many local young women, who admired their dedication and devotion, joined the congregation. In one of her published works, Mary Potter described their unique vocation: "By uniting themselves with Mary, and by giving all into her hands, the sisters of this Little Company of Mary would bring to the world a way of finding and loving Christ—a 'little' way of simplicity and compassion."

Having experienced the loving care of the sisters as they tended to his wife in Rome, Charles Mair, a Chicago businessman, invited the sisters to the South Side of Chicago where their ministries would be so much needed. Thus, in 1893, Mother Mary Veronica, Mother Mary Patrick, and Sister Mary Philomena began our tradition of caring for the sick and homebound.

We are a compassionate presence in healing ministries in America today because of the faith and courage of those pioneer women who were inspired by the vision of Mary Potter. The commitment and dedication of our sisters since then have not only sustained but also have broadened our vision to include all those suffering in mind, body, and spirit, and have given us the resilience to accept opportunities and meet challenges whenever they occur in our historical setting.

The Chapter deliberations reflect what Venerable Mary Potter envisioned for her congregation: that her Little Company of Mary would be a small group and that her sisters would be joined by others—the "Greater Company of Mary." Mary Potter's vision has been realized in many ways, most recently with the establishment of the LCM Associates program worldwide. Since 1987, here in the United States, more than 180 men and women have heeded our invitation to become companions in our ministry and to assist the sisters in bringing the healing presence of Jesus to those in need.

In the following pages, we invite you to journey with the Little Company of Mary Sisters, from our foundation in 1877 until today. You are the Greater Company of Mary—generations of physicians, employees, auxilians, volunteers, benefactors, and associates—partners in our healing ministry and our shared legacy as we celebrate "Our Journey of Love … Yesterday, Today, and Tomorrow."

— The Little Company of Mary Sisters

Sister Mary Babcock, L.C.M.

Sister Maria Antonieta Benavides, L.C.M.

Sister Sheila Brosnan, L.C.M.

Sister M. Joseph Casey, L.C.M.

Sister Deborah Conley, L.C.M.

Sister Renee Cunningham, L.C.M.

Sister M. Adrian Davis, L.C.M.

Sister Mary Jane Feil, L.C.M.

Sister Gloria Harper, L.C.M.

Sister Marianne Herres, L.C.M.

Sister Margaret Christina Hoban, L.C.M.

Sister M. Terrence Landini, L.C.M.

Sister Jean Marsden, L.C.M.

Sister Kathleen McIntyre, L.C.M.

Sister Virginia O'Brien, L.C.M.

Sister M. Teresa Oleniczak, L.C.M.

Sister Carol Pacini, L.C.M.

Sister Mildred Radziewiez, L.C.M.

Sister Mary John Schlax, L.C.M.

Sister Kathleen Scott, L.C.M.

Sister Catherine Shalvey, L.C.M.

Sister Jean Stickney, L.C.M.

Sister Maura Tangney, L.C.M.

Sister Sharon Ann Walsh, L.C.M.

Sisters of the Little Company of Mary with His Eminence, Francis Cardinal George
75th Anniversary of Little Company of Mary Hospital, Evergreen Park—September 2005.

PREFACE

On this day twenty-two months ago, I began a journey of my own when, for the first time, I met three Sisters of the Little Company of Mary. A week earlier, I had never heard of this religious congregation, did not know who Mary Potter was, and wouldn't have been able to locate Evergreen Park on a map.

But then I received a message from my daughter Christina, who has worked with the Little Company of Mary for several years. She had heard that the sisters were looking for someone to write the history of their community in America and wondered if I would be interested in being considered for this task. Christina thought that my traditional Catholic upbringing, writing skills, and the fact that I had spent eighteen months in religious life made me a "perfect" candidate to write their book. I agreed to meet the sisters, thinking that nothing would come of it.

Within a few days, I was being interviewed by Sister Carol Pacini, Sister Kathleen McIntyre, and Sister Jean Stickney. They were kind and gracious, but almost immediately I felt that I was not the right person for this job. The sisters had mentioned that they liked the way that the histories of the Italian and Australian Provinces had been written, and after quickly perusing both, I knew that my writing style was very different.

Two days later I called Mary Jo May, the project manager, to thank the sisters for their time but to ask that my name be withdrawn from consideration. To my surprise and dismay, Mary Jo said that she was in the middle of composing an email offering me this project. She asked me to take a little more time before making a decision.

Later that morning, as I was trying to get through some proofreading, the thought "Go to Mass today," occurred to me. I dismissed it. It popped into my head a second time, and I ignored it. But when the thought recurred a third time, I reluctantly put down my work and rushed off to noon Mass. The Old Testament reading that day was the story of Moses being called to lead his people out of Egypt and Moses' fear and reluctance. "How can I do this Lord?" he asked, and was told, "I will be with you." The words hit me like a bolt of lightning. When Mass was over, I was shaking because I realized what I had to do. An hour later, I accepted the assignment.

And so began a most unexpected adventure as I learned about Mary Potter's life and work; journeyed to her final resting place in Nottingham; spent weeks in the LCM Generalate archives in London and months poring over logbooks, council notes, and correspondence in Evergreen Park; visited all of the Little Company of Mary hospitals in the United States and the two hospitals they once ran in Argentina; and met with every sister in the American Province—an amazing group of women in a congregation of religious whose charism is praying for the dying, particularly witnessed by their care of the sick. Their dedication, self-sacrifice, and love of God and His people are evident in everything they do.

This book barely scratches the surface of what the Little Company of Mary Sisters have accomplished during 112 years of their presence in America. Their facilities are extraordinary places of hope and healing. But more important than buildings are the sisters themselves, whose gentle hands and compassionate hearts have touched countless lives. The following pages tell their stories, but it is a partial telling at best, set against the backdrop of what was happening within the country in which they lived and in the context of the Church to which they have contributed so much.

While I was working on this book, my pastor, Father Steven Knox, delivered a homily in which he said that when God calls us to do something, He also gives us the grace to do it—not perfectly, but as He wants it done. I pray that this has been true for this endeavor.

Venerable Mary Potter believed that, "Every incident, no matter how small … is recorded by angels above." This history reveals only a tiny portion of the acts of kindness and love done by members of the Little Company of Mary in America for more than a century. Most of the sisters' deeds remain undocumented—remembered only by those who were fortunate enough to experience them—and by God and His recording angels.

Merrie Ann Nall
Eve of the Feast of Pentecost
May 14, 2005

Women of Hope

The Story of the Little Company of Mary Sisters in America

MERRIE ANN NALL

CHAPTER ONE

HOMECOMING

Mass of Celebration honoring Venerable Mother Mary Potter at the Cathedral of St. Barnabas, Nottingham, December 3, 1997.

T he journey home had been a long time in coming. Mary Potter had died in Italy, and during the last decade of her life, her deteriorating health had kept her from returning to England, the land of her birth, and to Nottingham, the city where the Little Company of Mary originated. Two days after her death, she was buried in Campo Verano, a public cemetery outside of Rome.

Several years later, at the request of her community, Mary Potter's remains were moved to a crypt below the chapel of Calvary Hospital at Santo Stefano Rotondo. At the time, her earthly travels seemed to be finished. But events would occur in the waning years of the twentieth century that the Little Company of Mary could not have anticipated when they decided to reinter their founder in the spot that she herself had chosen.

The future of Calvary Hospital, which had seemed so bright a few decades earlier, was now in doubt. The community was aware of the possibility that the hospital could be sold, and the uncertainty of what might happen to the property led the sisters to reevaluate Mother's final resting place. After thought and prayer, they decided that their founder should be brought home to England.

Thus, on a cold and damp night typical of the English Midlands in late autumn, Mary Potter came back to Nottingham for the last time. Her mortal remains were welcomed back to the city and cathedral where her journey of faith began, amid glowing candles held by members of the Little Company of Mary, the religious community she had founded 120 years earlier. This was a solemn yet joyous occasion for the sisters, one that they would celebrate by observing the long-standing Church tradition of keeping vigil, as they prayed throughout the night and watched over the coffin of their cherished Mother in the hush of the darkened cathedral.

On the following day, December 3, 1997, Mary Potter, who had been declared "Venerable" by Pope John Paul II in 1988, was honored by more than a thousand people—the faithful and the curious, everyday citizens and Basil Cardinal Hume, a prince of the Church; by bishops and priests, family members and strangers, and, most devotedly, by her own spiritual daughters, some still wearing the distinctive pale blue veil of the congregation. In the year that marked the 150th anniversary of her birth, her heroic virtue and achievements were recognized at a concelebrated Mass after which she was gently laid to rest within the Cathedral of St. Barnabas. Her tomb, close to the main altar and near the Chapel of

Prelates and LCM Sisters at the homecoming of Venerable Mother Mary Potter, December 2, 1997.

Our Lady, would be easily accessible to all who wished to visit and pray for her intercession.

Considering Mary Potter's wholehearted devotion to the Blessed Mother, which permeated her life and is such an essential part of the spirit of her community, it would have been fitting if the ceremony honoring her had been held on a day dedicated to the Virgin Mary. Less than a week later, the Church celebrates the solemnity of the Immaculate Conception, a feast that was very meaningful to Mary Potter for several reasons: She entered the Institute of the Sisters of Mercy as a postulant on that day in 1868, although ill health soon forced her to return home. On December 8 1872, she solemnly consecrated her life to Jesus through Mary, and two years later, December 8 became "a landmark in Mary Potter's spiritual journey ... one of the most important days of her life"[1] when she realized the significance of the Maternal Heart of Mary and the Virgin Mother's role of advocacy for the dying.

Several other days in December would also have been particularly appropriate. December 15 is the extraliturgical feast of the Maternal Heart of Mary, to which Mary Potter and her community were greatly devoted. The feast of Our Lady's Expectation, observed in England on December 18, recalls the Blessed Virgin " ... as she anxiously awaited the birth of Christ, wondering when He would be born,"[2] and on December 27, the Church honors Saint John, the Beloved Disciple, whose faithful presence at the foot of the Cross embodies the spirit of Calvary that is so distinctive to the Little Company of Mary. Any of these days would have been especially appealing to Mary Potter, yet the celebration of her life occurred on a day that commemorates Francis Xavier, known for his legendary missionary work in the Far East—a saint who seems so unlike her.

From a physical standpoint, the two could not have been more different. Photographs show Mary Potter as a diminutive, gentle-looking woman with a pale complexion and light eyes. A congenital heart condition meant that she was physically fragile, and she endured numerous potentially fatal illnesses including breast cancer and lung hemorrhages. A severe heart attack, tuberculosis, and other debilitating conditions curtailed her travels and much of her physical activity, and by the last years of her life, she was confined to either a wheelchair or a sofa in her room.

Paintings portray Francis Xavier as an intense, dark-eyed, black-bearded Spaniard. His stalwart constitution allowed him to undertake seafaring journeys of thousands of miles while exposed to the blistering sun and bone-chilling rains and to walk barefoot for hundreds of miles preaching and converting—feats that ultimately led to his being named "the greatest missionary since the Apostles."[3]

In contrast to Xavier, who was born into a life of wealth and privilege in sixteenth-century Spain, Mary Potter was raised in a lower-middle class London home where economic conditions deteriorated after her father walked out on the family. Xavier's family fortune enabled him to attend the prestigious University of Paris and eventually teach in one of its colleges. Mary Potter was musically accomplished and able to speak French,[4] but like most women of her time and social standing, she lacked even the opportunity of receiving a formal education.

Their manner of private prayer also differed considerably. Francis Xavier followed the *Spiritual Exercises* developed by his mentor, Ignatius of Loyola, while Mary Potter's special devotion to the Blessed Mother led her to favor a "Marian" approach advocated by Louis Grignon de Montfort.

But a closer look at the lives of the London-born Victorian woman, who founded a community of nursing sisters, and the Jesuit missionary from Navarre, who was part of a Society renowned for its militant defense of the Faith and its intellectual contributions to the Church, reveals some surprising similarities.

Both incurred the censure of others because of their unstinting charity.

Xavier's generosity was described as "impulsive,"[5] while Mary Potter was criticized for her "extravagant benevolence" and "the complete unconcern with which she disposed of her own shoes and clothes [that] drew her mother to despair."[6]

Francis Xavier and Mary Potter also had a particular affection and empathy toward the poor. Xavier is said to have " ... much preferred the company of simple men, and the poorer they were, the better he seemed to like them."[7] Mary Potter voiced comparable sentiments:

> There is something in mixing with the poor which brings us closer to God, and after my return from Rome, and all its grandeurs and graces ... when I went again among the poor, I said, "Life is worth loving" ... and I carried one little thing or another to relieve the sick and brought the love of God into their souls.[8]

Like most Spaniards of his time, Xavier was "notoriously unsentimental,"[9] yet his writings reveal a man of particular gentleness. "In your dealings with all ... be pleasant and cheerful," he counseled. "Avoid stiffness and surliness, for a gloomy face will deter many.... Let your looks and words speak welcome ... and if you have to admonish somebody, do it with love and graciously...."[10]

Those who knew Xavier described his "tranquility of soul, perpetual cheerfulness, and equality of countenance,"[11] and he was said to have " ... reproved ... with so much sweetness and tender love that no one was offended...."[12] The same could be said of Mary Potter. Toward members of her own community, she exhibited a "fierce tenderness."[13] To those who opposed her plan for starting a training school for Italian lay nurses because they saw these women as uneducable, she answered, "Have patience and be motherly to them and they will learn."[14] "Give generously," she reminded her spiritual daughters. "You may have little to give but you can always give a kind word, a kind look, a smile."[15]

The only hardness the founder of the Little Company had within her was her willingness to do battle for the salvation of the souls of the dying. When the eternal welfare of others was at stake, she manifested a distinctly combative edge. " ... [W]e must do violence for the sake of those who are threatened with losing their immortal souls. We must go out onto the battlefield; we must pick up the wounded and anoint them...."[16] Her words evoke an image of the archangel Michael grappling with the powers of darkness and reveal a spiritual militancy in her typical of the Jesuits, whose founder had exhorted them to be "soldiers for Christ."[17]

Mary Potter demonstrated an amazing toughness in one other area of her life. No one could deter her from the spiritual mission to which she believed God was calling her. She responded as valiantly as any warrior. In spite of her physical limitations, she demonstrated unwavering determination and fierce psychological strength as she resisted her mother and family as well as priests and bishops who tried to impede the fulfillment of that mission.

Francis Xavier is known primarily for his preaching, but like Mary Potter, he was devoted to caring for the sick. While waiting to sail for the Holy Land (a trip that never materialized), he worked for two months at Venice's Hospital of the *Incurabili*.[18] Later, on his first voyage to the Far East, one of Xavier's companions recorded that he " ... performed all the functions of a real nurse for the sick, washed them and their clothes, fed them, gave them their medicine with his own hands, and emptied and cleaned the commodes which they used."[19] Mary Potter's initial nursing experience occurred during her first months with the Sisters of Mercy:

> As a postulant, Mary accompanied a professed sister on visitation of the sick.... She learned basic skills of attendance at the bedside of those suffering or dying ... [and] to "care with great tenderness" [for] those who were ill....[20]

Although she ministered to the sick only briefly because of her own poor health, she contributed immensely to the field of nursing. Not only did she found the Little Company of Mary, whose members have been primarily involved in caring for the sick, but she also was responsible for establishing nursing schools that raised the standards of the profession and extended the spirit of her congregation to lay nurses.

In addition to their dedication to the sick, the Jesuit missionary and the founder of the Little Company were especially devoted to the dying. One of Xavier's earliest biographers described his " ... devouring zeal to help the sick and the souls of the dead...."[21] Xavier's respect extended to the mortal remains of the deceased, and firsthand accounts chronicle that he "... carried the bodies of the dead reverently to the graves we had dug for them."[22]

Mary Potter believed that the primary apostolate of her congregation was working toward the salvation of dying sinners:

You know, dear children, the first objective of our foundation is not to nurse, as so many suppose.... Our first object is to model Calvary ... that mystery of grace.... We see Jesus Crucified, shedding his Precious Blood. Our Lady's Maternal Heart pleading by that blood to save souls.... We watch the happy Dismas [the "good thief"] and long to co-operate with our Mother in thus saving souls at the last hour.[23]

And she urged the members to the Little Company to remember:

Our love [for] souls must show itself at all times but especially at the time of their greatest need, at the hour of death.... Either really present, or spiritually by her prayers and compassion, she assists that one and accompanies it to the brink of eternity....[24]

Xavier was "consumed with an insatiable thirst for the salvation of souls,"[25] and his missionary work was primarily one of conversion as he traveled through foreign lands making the name of Christ known. Despite the contemplative inclinations of her soul, Mary Potter, like Xavier, turned out to be a true missionary at heart. Instead of a cloistered life, she and the members of her community went wherever the need was the greatest, and she reminded the sisters, "It is very evident that God wishes us to be occupied with his vast family."[26] When she wrote, "We are not founded ... simply to nurse.... We are founded to extend God's Kingdom on earth...,"[27] Mary Potter was clearly emphasizing the missionary component of her institute. Although her sisters did not "preach" the Gospel in the formal manner of priests, they spread the good news of Christ in more subtle ways:

The presence of the Sisters gave a certain spirit to the people.... [S]eeing in practice ... what the priest preached was more effectual than the sermons themselves. Religion was not then theoretical. They saw it carried out—the sick administered to, the suffering consoled and comforted, the poor fed, and children instructed and the ignorant learned to love our Lord and His Spirit entered into them....[28]

Xavier's missionary efforts are credited for miraculous numbers of baptisms, earning him the title "Apostle to the East Indies." The early members of the Little Company of Mary were also responsible for bringing many to God as they attended to victims who were mortally ill. At times, the only thing they could do was make their patients as comfortable as possible, yet the sisters' gentle spiritual support often meant that "Deathbeds became the place of many conversions...."[29] Their influence must have also affected a significant number of healthy individuals, for church records indicate that from mid-April 1877 (when the sisters began their work in Hyson Green) to mid-1880, the Catholic population increased from fifty practicing Catholics to eight hundred...."[30]

In his homily, the Most Reverend Patrick Dougherty, Bishop of Bathurst, Australia, and one of Mary Potter's primary biographers, reminded those present: "The God of irony never ceases to come up with His surprises." One of those surprises is that the illustrious missionary and the relatively unknown religious with whom he shared his feast day were far more alike than is readily apparent. The lives and the prolific writings that the Renaissance Jesuit and the Victorian religious left behind reveal the common thread that connects them: each loved God above all else and desired to help save souls.

To achieve that goal, the Spaniard traded a life of wealth and privilege for that of an itinerant missionary, and the Englishwoman left a protective yet comfortably predicable home for an uncertain future. By responding unreservedly to God's call, Francis Xavier and Mary Potter were taken places where they never dreamt of going, and they touched the world in ways they could never have imagined on their own.

December 3 may not be a Marian feast, but it was a most fitting occasion on which to celebrate the life of the founder of the Little Company of Mary. It is a day on which the Church recognizes the sanctity of a man who honored the Virgin Mother by bringing countless souls to her Son— the same apostolate to which Mary Potter committed her entire being.

Bishop Dougherty's comment is also apropos in light of the circumstances surrounding the deaths of these two servants of God. Francis Xavier died at the age of forty-six, after contracting a fever on a sea voyage from Japan. Mary Potter survived numerous potentially fatal illnesses as well as two brutal mastectomies performed under primitive conditions that should have killed her. When her loving heart failed in her sixty-sixth year, the frail woman had outlived the stalwart Jesuit by almost two decades.

Francis Xavier and Mary Potter shared one last similarity even after death. For neither of them was their final resting place *final*. Xavier died on December 3, 1552, and was buried on the island of Sancian, off the coast of China. Several months later, his still incorruptible body was moved to Malacca,[31] and the following year, at the request of the Jesuits, it was returned to Goa, the site of his first mission in India. Mary Potter died on April 9, 1913, and was interred in Campo Verano until 1917, when her earthly remains were moved to the burial site she had chosen at Santo Stefano Rotondo. Eighty years would pass before she returned to Nottingham, the place where her ministry first began.

CHAPTER TWO

BEGINNINGS

Venerable Mother Mary Potter founded the Sisters of the Little Company of Mary in 1877.

Perhaps the most remarkable thing about the ceremony that occurred in Nottingham on December 3, 1997, is that this event even took place. Mary Potter should be unknown today, her name long forgotten. She was frail and sickly throughout her life, and her family was neither wealthy nor socially connected. Like most women of her time, she was not well educated. As a Catholic, she was subject to religious and social prejudices since her allegiance was to Rome, not to the Church of England. And because she was born in the middle of the nineteenth century, her gender relegated her to second-class citizenship by a society that severely constrained women's lives and expected them to keep proper homes and defer to their husbands.[1]

Within this milieu, few women achieved distinction during life or recognition after death. Their world was almost always confined to the important but mundane tasks of caring for husbands, children, and households.[2] Given these circumstances, Mary Potter was a most improbable candidate to accomplish much of anything, let alone create a new congregation of women religious who would heal so many lives.

Throughout history, however, some of the most unlikely men and women have been called to do God's work. Saul of Tarsus became Paul—Apostle to the Gentiles. Jeanne d'Arc, a peasant girl, successfully led her fellow Frenchmen into battle. And Angelo Roncalli, an aged and little-known cardinal, surprised the world twice—first, when he was elected pope and then, as John XXIII, when he convened a Council to renew the Church while endearing himself to all as a humble and simple *Papa*. By selecting a fragile and infirm woman who lived under Victorian constraints and in an overwhelmingly Protestant country to found the Little Company of Mary, God again sends a reminder that He sometimes chooses the weak to confound the strong and that often His ways are not ours.

Mary Potter was born in London on November 22, the feast of St. Cecilia, in the year 1847—exactly ten years after an eighteen-year-old princess named Victoria became queen. During her reign, England became the largest empire the world had ever known, encompassing, at its height, one-fifth of the world's land area and one-quarter of its population.

Halfway through the nineteenth century, the Industrial Revolution, which had begun one hundred years earlier, was in full throttle. As more and more people left rural areas for factory jobs, Britain's urban population exploded. London alone ballooned from one million inhabitants in 1800 to more than six million a century later. Most city dwellers lived in horrifying conditions, in slums where overcrowding, filth, and lack of sanitation were the norm, and outbreaks of disease—particularly cholera, typhus, and consumption—were common.

In all the manufacturing centers of England, factories spewed noxious smoke into the air, which all but obliterated the sun, adding to the unhealthy environment. A visitor to Manchester during the 1840s commented, "The town is abominably filthy ... and the water of the river as black as ink...."[3]

This was a century of extremes and contradictions. One-tenth of the population owned nine-tenths of the land. The wealthy led lives of unimaginable privilege; the destitute endured equally unfathomable deprivation. Children as young as five years of age worked in coal mines for up to twelve hours ... almost a quarter mile below ground in almost total darkness."[4] In the 1840s, class distinctions played an overwhelming role in determining average life expectancy. Professional people could expect to live for thirty-eight years, mechanics and laborers for seventeen.[5]

Yet for all the evils associated with the 1800s, this was also a time of hope and optimism and progress. Amazing social and technological changes took place during Victoria's sixty-three-year rule. In 1837, the first year of her reign, every institution of higher learning was restricted to men. By the turn of the century, even Oxford and Cambridge, Britain's most prestigious universities, admitted women.

During the 1850s, the *Englishwoman's Journal* supported the cause of employment of middle-class women as paid professionals in occupations such as teaching (in girls' schools), visiting the homes of the poor, and nursing. The last calling was considered especially noble after Florence Nightingale's groundbreaking efforts to minister to British soldiers during the Crimean War. "Nursing was the one single-woman's profession that the queen felt fitted perfectly with the feminine qualities of tenderness, solace, and healing."[6]

Throughout the nineteenth century, technology combined with human determination to have an immeasurable impact on the lives of Britons, particularly the building of the railways, which was called "the greatest physical achievement carried out by the human race within a comparatively short period of time."[7] In 1841, less than a thousand miles of railway were operating in England. Seven years later, another five thousand miles were open and thousands of miles of track were under construction. Historian R. J. Evans believes that the linkage of England's towns and cities had a profound effect on ideas, standards, and customs as railways "broke down the isolation of the remote rural districts [and] ... closed the gap between the industrial north and the agricultural south. By enabling poor men to travel widely and cheaply for the first time in history ... [the railways] taught them to think and act nationally instead of locally."[8]

At mid-century, the Great Exhibition of 1851 took place. More than anything else, this celebration of technology, conceived by Queen Victoria's husband Prince Albert, captured the forward-looking spirit of the 1800s. This would be the most incredible industrial showcase that the world had ever seen, including more than nineteen thousand exhibits—machines, inventions, and oddities of the era—all housed within a glimmering Crystal Palace composed of 300,000 panes of glass.

Most of the displays were mechanical or relevant to the Industrial Revolution, including a twenty-four-ton lump of coal, the latest Singer sewing machine, a McCormick reaper, an innovative printing press, and the Great Western's broad-gauge locomotive—the latter a most appropriate inclusion, since more than three-quarters of a million visitors (of more than six million) arrived at the Exhibition by rail.[9] Other exhibits illustrated the diverse culture found throughout the British Empire, including massive stone statues and palm trees from Egypt and a stuffed elephant replete with a gold *howdah*, the mode of transportation for the wealthy in India. Prince Albert's dream that this international exposition would promote commerce rather than militarization and serve as a model of peaceful cooperation between nations was not to be realized. Within three years, the Crimean War began, and more than twenty-two thousand British soldiers died—almost eighteen thousand from cholera.[10]

Despite its authoritarianism, this age gave birth to the questioning of almost universally held beliefs. Some thinkers, like Charles Darwin, rejected the Biblical account of creation, proposing instead a theory of evolution. Others, like John Henry Newman, an Anglican clergyman who taught at Oxford, turned to the past wisdom of the Apostolic Fathers to discover truth. He subsequently embraced Catholicism, was consecrated a priest, and influenced numerous fellow Anglican clergymen to do the same.

In this era of gas-lit streets and crinolined ladies, what was "proper" often took precedence over what was practical. On an average day, thousands of coal fires blackened the skies over London by mid-morning, and most in the middle class typically bathed only on Saturday nights because of the nuisance of boiling water. Charles Dickens, the eloquent voice of the Victorian world, became England's most popular contemporary writer, and a handful of London parlors offered patrons a chance to immortalize themselves by means of a new invention called photography. This was the world into which Mary Potter was born.

Neither of her parents was a model of conventional Victorian values. When Mary was just one year old, her father abandoned the family and sailed to Australia, never to be seen by them again. Elizabeth West, a member of the Little Company of Mary who has written a definitive biography of Mary Potter, suggests that as a pawnbroker—an occupation that Victorian society considered quasi-respectable at best—William Norwood Potter may have been involved in a series of economic misfortunes that would have landed him in debtors' prison had he remained in England.[11] But Portsmouth researcher Pamela Fontana, who has investigated the Potter family in depth, has reached a different conclusion. She believes that he left England to escape an unhappy marriage, a theory bolstered by her recent discovery of evidence showing that William Potter "married" a widow in Australia, although he and Mary's mother never legally divorced.[12]

Whatever his reason for leaving, his wife was an atypical Victorian woman with a mind of her own. Mary Ann Potter's headstrong ways strained their marital relationship, and her decision to leave the Anglican Church for Catholicism and to have their youngest son, George, baptized in the Catholic faith, further angered her husband and contributed to their growing alienation. Although William Potter was only nominally a member of the Church of England, he viewed his wife's actions as a personal affront to his position as head of the household.

Mrs. Potter subsequently had their three older sons secretly baptized, but before Mary's birth, she abandoned her deceit. During this pregnancy, she contracted tuberculosis, a primary cause of death at that time. Fearing for her own life and that of her unborn child, she sought spiritual advice from the parish priest at the nearby church in Southwark. He suggested that she consecrate this child to the Mother of God, which she did before Mary's birth. Since her husband had requested a say in naming his only daughter, her insistence that their baby girl receive only the name "Mary," in honor of Our Lady, stressed their already strained relationship.

Adding to his financial worries and marital unhappiness was a situation that caused William Potter to feel an immense sense of family betrayal. His brother Thomas put money into a trust for William's wife and children instead of leaving a legacy directly to him. In William's eyes, the insult was compounded because he was even excluded from administering the trust. West points out that a letter from William Potter's son makes it very clear why his father broke completely with his entire family:

> What estranged him from us was a question of property, for which his brother was trustee on behalf of my mother.... He wrote saying that from that day forward ... we were, all of us, wife, children and brother, strangers to him, and he never broke the silence.[13]

Despite being abandoned by her father, Mary's childhood was surprisingly normal. Her four older brothers adored their blue-eyed, golden-haired sister, whom they affectionately called "Trotty."[14] As the only girl and the baby of the family, she was doted on by her siblings and frequently became the center of attention. Her brother George, closest in age to Mary, wrote:

> At Christmas tide, we children used to go to Christmas parties. I have vividly before my mind a tiny little girl dressed in white with a blue sash, and looking like a fairy. She is placed on a table for her brothers to admire....[15]

William Potter's leave-taking meant that Mrs. Potter could spend an extraordinary amount of time with her baby girl. West points out that "William's departure gave his wife a freedom to establish herself and her children in a manner in which living with her husband had not provided."[16] Her father's absence, however, eventually had repercussions on the family, especially on Mary's future relationship with her mother.

When Mary was seven years old, the Potter family moved from Bermondsey, a poor and often disease-ridden area, to Falmouth Road in Southeast London. Mary enrolled at Cupola House, a Catholic boarding school for girls, where she received the narrow and guarded education typical for young women of the time, learning what was necessary to function in polite society. She was allowed to read the Bible and Shakespeare, but only abridged versions, which excluded anything deemed possibly offensive to a young woman's sensibilities.[17]

Mary was also educated in the Catholic faith at school, and although she fulfilled the essential requisites of daily prayer and Sunday Mass attendance, later in life she acknowledged that she was not an unusually pious child and was even thankful that while at school she had not been "sickened by piety."[18]

At that time, Catholic revivals were common and often specifically targeted children with graphic accounts of the plight of unrepentant sinners burning in the fires of hell for all eternity.[19] Thoughts of suffering souls condemned to eternal damnation affected Mary deeply, and she eventually became scrupulous—ultrasensitive to even the possibility of sin. Her brother George reported his own firsthand experience of his sister's distressing situation:

> ... [S]he was troubled dreadfully with scrupulosity, and this extended to unthoughtup things. Poor Tom! He was very patient with her. At one time, she maintained that no good Catholic could use a frying pan for fish that had been used for meat.
>
> Father Woollett, the navy chaplain, happened to come and Mary put the matter to him. The dear old priest ... uttered only one word, 'Bosh!'[20]

Years later, her own experience of the detrimental effect that such a great fear of sin and punishment could have on the hearts and minds of young children led Mary to write that instead of emphasizing the fear of God, children should learn of Christ:

> ... As the Lord who so loved little children in his arms and would not let them be sent away from him.... Teach them ... about Jesus ... [and] how they are loved, that is the grand point.[21]

She remained at Cupola House for ten years. At the age of eighteen, "because of a period of frail health,"[22] Mary returned to Portsmouth, where Mrs. Potter now lived with her son Thomas. Mary's education was complete—she was prepared for a life of domesticity. According to West, those who knew Mary Potter described her as "... bright, though somewhat shy, possessed of a keen sense of humour, certain stubbornness, impulsive generosity, and little fear."[23]

Even though Mary was no longer a child, Mrs. Potter exercised strict control over her. She refused to allow her to develop friendships with other young women, although she did permit young people to visit for evenings of entertainment. Since her brother Thomas owned the house, he was free to bring home friends, one of whom was Godfrey King, a mathematics teacher. His background and religious inclinations made him acceptable to Mary's mother, who viewed him "… as a model of rectitude and a very holy young man."[24] Mrs. Potter was particularly impressed to learn that Godfrey had spent some time in a Trappist monastery. New research, however, casts doubt on that claim, as there are no records of his ever having been part of that monastic order.[25]

Godfrey King paid increasing attention to Mary, and they developed a close relationship, much of it based on their shared faith. King, a spiritually intense individual, was convinced that Mary's natural gaiety and light-heartedness were evidence of her lack of spiritual depth. He consequently tried to foster in Mary a deeper spiritual life by providing her with a variety of religious books and introduced her to the confraternity of Our Lady, which sought to "combat religious indifference and convert sinners."[26]

The two eventually became engaged, but their relationship was unconventionally proper, even for Victorian times, and it seems to have been based primarily on a mutual religious fervor. Mary would later write that her idea of marriage "[was] to have a house to ourselves and spend our lives in good works; we could be like Our Lady and Saint Joseph."[27] As West points out, "… the fantasy of celibate marriage was … the stuff of daydream."[28] When Mary told her long-time family friend and confessor Bishop Thomas Grant of her plans, he informed her that such a marriage would not be valid in the eyes of the Church[29] and insisted that she break off her engagement.

When she ended her betrothal, Mary found herself at an important crossroad in her life. Never having felt a particular inclination toward religious life, she became increasingly involved in spiritual devotions and charitable actions, but after listening to the advice of both Bishop Grant and her spiritual advisor, she began to think seriously about becoming a nun.

If Mary Potter could have chosen freely, it is likely that she would have entered a traditional enclosed order, such as the Carmelites, to which she was attracted. However, as West notes, "… the reality was that Potter's desire to enter a community of contemplatives was beyond her reach."[30] Contemplative orders were class-restricted, and Mary was living in

Victorian England, which rigidly adhered to class distinctions. She lacked the aristocratic social standing and the dowry required to be a choir member, and did not have the stamina needed to be a contemplative lay sister.

On the bishop's advice, she visited and entered the institute of the Sisters of Mercy of Brighton on December 8, 1868. Her time with this community would be short because of health problems, but the religious formation that she received, which introduced her to "a process of prayer and work that imposed both discipline and structure,"[31] remained with her. She would also incorporate two elements of the Mercy community into her own congregation—their spirit of Calvary and their special devotion to the Virgin Mary.

As a novice, Mary Potter had difficulty praying in the manner expected of Mercy Sisters. Her confessor, as well as her novice mistress, soon recognized that Mary had a religious vocation, but not to the Mercy community. They decided that she should transfer to the community of Assumption Sisters in Kensington, whose semi-enclosure and emphasis on adoration of the Eucharist seemed to better fit her spirituality. Before that could take place, however, Mary Potter's health suddenly deteriorated, and in June 1870, she returned home.

Until her health improved, any possibility of entering another religious community was out of the question. After she recovered, her mother totally opposed her reentry into religious life, stating, "I consider she was given back to me, so God helping me, not again will I part from her."[32] Mrs. Potter's obstinacy in this matter caused her daughter anguish for years.

While she convalesced, Mary became increasingly aware of the mission to which she was being called: to found a religious institute whose members would devote themselves to the spiritual welfare of the dying; a congregation that would mirror the mystery of Calvary. Her maturing spirituality would be "... marked by a strongly contemplative, incarnation and missionary spirit."[33]

When her recovery was complete, she began to teach the relatively few Catholic children in her area. In 1872, after rereading *The Treatise on True Devotion to the Blessed Virgin* by Louis Grignon de Montfort, she became convinced that she should dedicate her entire life to God through his Mother, which she solemnly did on December 8. In the not-too-distant future, she would incorporate the Marian spirituality found in de Montfort's writings into a new institute of religious, which would bear the Virgin

Mother's name.

While praying on October 4, 1874, the Feast of the Holy Rosary, Mary decided that her vocation should have, at its center, devotion to the dying. She later told Monsignor John Virtue, her spiritual director, that she was being called "to rescue from eternal damnation, even at the last moment, the souls of dying sinners."[34] Two months later, on the Feast of the Immaculate Conception, Mary became more fully aware of her mission—that God was asking her to "Honour the Heart of My Mother." She wrote:

> ... It seemed to me that God had given me a wonderfully efficacious means of prayer ... that we should set before Him from out [of] this fallen world, the Mother Heart of Our Lady pleading for her children especially for those who have the greatest need, the dying.[35]

Monsignor Virtue was reluctant to encourage Mary Potter's desire to start her own community since he knew of a group of religious at the Convent of the Agonizing Heart in Lyons who were dedicated to this same devotion. Mary soon discovered that the French congregation differed from what she envisioned. The French sisters were entirely contemplative, and she believed that members of her community should earn their living. In addition, the sisters in Lyons did not have a particularly Marian spirituality, which Mary thought should be a hallmark of her institute.

Mary shared the vision of what she was convinced that God wanted of her in a letter to her spiritual advisor:

> God is present to me, not in his usual way.... He has replenished me with His grace. He has filled me with His love. He has poured His Holy Spirit upon me and told me to live by it, and now I live no longer in myself but he, [the] Lord God, liveth in me.[36]

However, Virtue either failed to acknowledge or refused to see Mary Potter's growing mysticism, which the Church recognizes as "an immediate, personal experience of God that is truly extraordinary, not only in intensity and degree, but in kind."[37] He misjudged her as delusional[38] and forbade her to continue to believe that God was communicating with her in a special way. Mary obeyed him, but this caused her great distress: "Not withstanding that my heart is breaking, there is a certain peace within me which seems to come from Our Lord's helping me suffer what otherwise I could not."[39] In trying to describe what was happening to her, she also wrote:

It could not be explained, the union with God, the joy. The world seemed another world and to breathe of God. I would wonder whether it was not a return almost to the original joy of the unfallen. [40]

When Monsignor Virtue was transferred to Malta in the spring of 1876, Mary needed a new spiritual director. Mary Fulker, a young woman who once worked in the Potter household and with whom Mary was friendly, recommended Father Edward Selley, a priest in her own parish. Mary began corresponding with this Marist priest, who understood her spirituality and devotion to the Virgin Mary. He also supported her desire to form a new religious community which would differ from existing religious orders that made clear distinctions between active and contemplative members. She envisioned an institute in which all sisters would share in the same primary ministry: "... prayer for, and where possible, care of the dying. Its spirit ... was to be that of Calvary."[41] Along with spiritual encouragement, Selley offered Mary practical help by revising and preparing for publication *The Path of Mary*, her recently completed manuscript on De Montfort spirituality.

That May, she met with James Danell, Bishop of Southwark, regarding her future plans, and later detailed the events in a letter to Fulker:

> I saw the Bishop who told me that I might induce others to join with me in devotion to the dying ... we might live [together] under a certain rule.... [42]

Things were finally coming together for Mary Potter. She had both a supportive spiritual advisor and a bishop who was at least somewhat empathetic. What she had not anticipated, however, was renewed opposition from her mother, who wrote to Father Selley: "... my daughter has a singular inaptitude for managing even small financial matters. Soon would a community, which she managed, be in pecuniary embarrassment...."[43] Mrs. Potter also let it be known that she was ill and required her daughter's help. Local priests relayed this information to Cardinal Manning, who entreated Mary to return home to care for her ailing mother.

Within weeks, her hopes were all but destroyed. When her brother Thomas also wrote to Bishop Danell, informing him of the difficulties she was causing her family, the Bishop of Southwark withdrew his tentative support. Mary Potter's difficulties were further compounded when Father

Selley's superiors forbade him to continue as her adviser.

In the midst of such setbacks, she remained amazingly tranquil. Recognizing that God's plan would be accomplished in His time, not hers, Mary Potter wrote, "[T]he one great sign of its being God's work [is] the absence of human eagerness and impetuosity about it."[44]

Her patience was rewarded six months later. In November 1876, she received a letter from Thomas Arthur Young, a wealthy but eccentric resident of Nottingham who had read her book and offered to provide her with both a convent and the money to begin a religious community. Mary's brother George backed this proposal because friends from Nottingham had advised him that the Bishop of Nottingham would likely support Mary's plans to found a religious community there.

As the Potter family gathered together to celebrate Christmas, Mary faced one of the most difficult decisions of her life. Her mother still refused to grant her permission to reenter religious life, and she now had to choose between obeying her mother, something that was expected of unmarried daughters in Victorian society, and following the life to which she believed God was calling her.

Two weeks later, after spending the day in Brighton with her sister-in-law Marguerite, instead of returning home, Mary boarded a London-bound train. She stayed with her brother Henry, and the following day he provided her with both the moral support and the fare she needed for her journey to Nottingham.

On the morning of January 15, 1877, Mary Potter met with Edward Gilpin Bagshawe, the authoritarian and sometimes overbearing Bishop of Nottingham known for his love of pomp and all things Roman. Although Bagshawe seemed cool at first, he had a genuine desire to help the poor, and soon warmed to the idea of a new religious congregation in his diocese.

The earliest days were challenging for Mary Potter and the small group of women who soon joined her. To her dismay, Thomas Young's generous offer never materialized. Consequently, Bishop Bagshawe provided the necessary funds to begin her institute, which became known as the Little Company of Mary. He planned for the sisters to settle in Hyson Green, a poor community two miles from Nottingham whose inhabitants were mainly Irish immigrants who were nonpracticing Catholics.

The property that the bishop chose for the community was a disused and run-down former stocking factory located on Lenton Street. During the following months, Mary worked alongside hired tradesmen to make the building habitable, an experience that was physically exhausting but also enlightening:

> I wonder at the grace God gave to one who certainly over the years of childhood, was still a child—not allowed to go out alone ever at night, ever thought for and kept, as it is said, in a hot house. Here I was, wandering about alone, then sleeping in an old dilapidated place, in the midst of mortar and rubbish of all kinds, with doors that would not fasten, for I remember getting a pickaxe against it to secure it.... I, who had been so delicate and being supposed to need meat two or three times a day, often made my dinner on bread and pork drippings. [45]

As the house slowly took shape, Mary Potter became acquainted with the families living in the surrounding area and visited the sick. On Good Friday, she nailed together two scrap boards to form a Cross for the convent's roof and later wrote, "I painted it myself last night a glorious red. It was Good Friday; you may imagine what I was thinking of."[46]

Even though the living quarters were not yet complete, the chapel and mission of Lenton Street were dedicated to the Maternal Heart of Mary on Easter Monday 1877 in a joyous ceremony presided over by Bishop Bagshawe. Amid a chapel filled with neighbors and roses from nearby gardens, the choir from St. Barnabas Cathedral in Nottingham raised their voices in a *Missa cantata* (sung Mass) accompanied by the sounds of a borrowed organ.

The new Hyson Green community included Mary Potter, Elizabeth Bryan, Mary Eleanor Smith, Agnes Bray, and Edith Coleridge. Mary Potter drew upon her own experience of religious life with the Sisters of Mercy to help the other women, but the community quickly realized just how active a role Bagshawe would have in shaping the institute. According to one of the original members, the Bishop provided a rigid schedule:

> Every hour of the day had its appointed duty, commencing with morning prayers, meditation, and Holy Mass. After breakfast, during which the Imitation [of Christ] or a life of a Saint was read, we went about our works ... there were the sick of the village to visit and tend, the school and mission work....

> We returned to Dinner at which there was Spiritual Reading, then
> after the visit to the Blessed Sacrament, there was Recreation. Then
> followed ... Prayers for the Dying and Vespers and Compline and
> then work again.... Two or three evenings in the week we had
> Benediction of the Blessed Sacrament, but on other days, after
> Matins and Lauds, we made half an hour's Meditation.... On most
> evenings there were classes for the grown-up people, some to learn
> lessons, to read, write, etc., others to be instructed in preparation for
> reception into the Church, and often our evening recreation was
> very short.... From 9 p.m. there was strict silence.[47]

On July 2, the feast of the Precious Blood, the group officially became
a religious congregation. Mary Potter broke with tradition by not having
her postulants dress in bridal gowns to signify becoming "brides of Christ."
She also chose not to include the use of a pall to cover the sisters, which
indicated "not merely a dying to self but incorporation into Christ."[48]
By omitting this symbolic gesture, West believes that Mary Potter showed
that the members of her institute "... [were] not to die to life or the world,
but to become immersed within it. The world was the place where God
was to be encountered...."[49] A simple black dress with a leather cincture
and a pale blue veil comprised the habit of the new sisters.

Within a short time, it became obvious that Bagshawe's vision of
what her institute should be differed greatly from Mary Potter's. Like
many prelates of his time, the bishop looked at the practical utility
that the sisters could provide, including the homes they could visit and
the "fallen-away" souls they could reach out to and bring back into the
fold. With this perspective, he encouraged the sisters to constantly extend
themselves in mission work. He failed to take into account something
that Mary Potter recognized: that in order to bring Christ to others,
each sister needed time and training to develop her own strong spiritual
foundation. She also believed that the spirit, or charism, of the community
was the most essential quality of the institute—even more important
than the work done by its members. On this critical issue and others, the
founder and the bishop were at odds.

Two weeks after the members became novices, Bagshawe removed
Mary Potter from her role as Superior and appointed Elizabeth Bryan in
her place. He named Mary Potter, who was now known as Sister Mary
Angela, as Mistress of Novices, yet he refused to allow her to individually

counsel those in her charge.

Mary Potter had not anticipated the absolute power that Bagshawe would wield over her congregation. Bagshawe had only been a prelate for three years when he encountered Mary, but he was comfortable in his role as bishop, a position that had only come about because of the restoration of the hierarchy in 1850,[50] when twelve English dioceses were created "chiefly from the modern industrial centres—Birmingham, Liverpool, [and] Nottingham...."[51]

The irreconcilable differences between the two ranged from financial matters and the community's underlying mission to what constituted good spiritual training for the novices. To preserve the institute's integrity, the founder would eventually seek relief from Bagshawe's control by obtaining papal approbation. Adding to the difficulty of the early days was the community's lack of financial support. This prompted the bishop to insist that the sisters beg for their living, which West points out "was often a fruitless, demeaning undertaking...."[52]

Despite her congregation's poverty, Mary Potter's generosity was unlimited, as one of her early biographers illustrates:

> ... [O]ne morning, when Mother Philip was going out to visit a poor boy dying of consumption, taking with her some tea and bread and butter, Mother told her to take eggs as well. The few eggs in the house represented the Community's only possible dinner and there was not as much as sixpence in the house to provide more, so Mother Philip remonstrated at giving away what they themselves needed. Mother's answer was: "Do what I tell you, God can provide for us." So Mother Philip went; and on her return was stopped by one of the neighbours, a kindly good-hearted woman, who said "Sister Philip, will you take this to Mother Mary? I have not sent her any eggs for a long time." And she handed Mother Philip a basket full of new-laid eggs. Mother's comment was: "I told you our Lord would never be outdone in generosity."[53]

Mary Potter's magnanimity was all-encompassing. Her generosity touched every aspect of her life and became one of the Little Company of Mary Sisters' most distinguishing characteristics. Ruth Lindsay, who knew Mother for many years, described her as having:

> ... generosity of heart and mind ... of word and deed. [S]he was

one of those rare people who do honestly rejoice at a rival's success and grieve over his failure. If Mother could have prospered her own congregation immeasurably at the expense of one day's detriment to another, she would hardly have realized that there was a choice to be made, so impossible would it have seemed to her to benefit by another's loss.[54]

In the midst of the turmoil created by the bishop's constant intrusions into the internal workings of the community, Mary Potter discovered that she had breast cancer. Her preexisting heart condition precluded the use of anesthesia, so she was completely conscious throughout the operation. In her reminiscences of this ordeal, Sister Cecilia noted that although Mary Potter suffered excruciating pain, she sought to cheer up her horrified witnesses, a memory that would forever remain with those who were present.[55] Six months later, she endured a second mastectomy under similar circumstances.

Her illnesses had at least one positive effect. When the members of the Little Company realized just how close they had come to losing their founder, they put aside their petty squabbles and rallied behind her to reestablish her as the community leader on February 12, 1879. Two days later, the community received notice of the bishop's withdrawal of all financial support.

Faced with the possibility that the fledgling institute would be irreparably damaged if Bagshawe's influence continued, Mary Potter knew that if the congregation's integrity were to be preserved, she needed the Holy See to approve the community's rule. To accomplish this, she had to go to Rome, but for that to happen, she needed the bishop's approval, which he adamantly refused. It was only after continual requests and much prayer that he relented. West notes:

> [Mary] Potter's journey to Rome began with subterfuge. When Bishop Bagshawe gave permission for her to leave Hyson Green and journey to Rome, he did so because he thought her illness and growing physical infirmity were life threatening.... Believing that she did not have long to live ... he gave her permission to leave Nottingham to visit the Eternal City.[56]

Mother [Mary Potter] left England on September 24, 1882, accompanied by Mother Cecilia and Mother Philip. The journey almost killed her. En route to Turin, she suffered a heart attack. She recuperated and continued on toward Italy, but suffered another heart attack, prompting Mother Cecilia to write: "We feared she would die."[57]

The three arrived in Rome sixteen days after leaving Nottingham and stayed with the Sisters of the Good Shepherd. On October 21, they attended a papal Mass and had a private audience with Pope Leo XIII. The silver-haired, saintly looking pontiff had a keen interest in science and was known for his progressive thinking and interest in social issues.[58] He understood and appreciated the contributions that the sisters could offer if they stayed in Italy. After asking for his blessing for themselves and the rule of her institute, Mother mentioned her plans to go back to England and was surprised when His Holiness asked, "*Perche?* Why not remain in Rome? The gates are wide open to you."[59]

She accepted the pontiff's gracious offer, and Mothers Cecilia and Philip soon began to offer home nursing to English-speaking expatriates. The expertise and professionalism of the "English Sisters" contrasted so greatly with the poor quality of care provided by most Italian nurses that the demand for their services forced Mother to write to Nottingham requesting that other sisters be sent to help. West believes that as a result, "care of the sick became the most significant identifier of the institute of the Little Company of Mary ... by those outside the community ...."[60] This tendency to emphasize the work that members of a particular congregation were involved in, rather than its underlying spirit, was typical until the last third of the twentieth century, when the importance of charisms was finally appreciated.

During their early days in Rome, the sisters found themselves shuttling back and forth between residences. They stayed with two different communities of sisters until they found a place of their own in the Via St. Chiara, but its squalor made it uninhabitable. When the Superior of a group of American Franciscan nuns offered to share their convent with the blue-veiled sisters, Mother Potter accepted the hospitality, only to discover that the offer came with strings: the Franciscans were hopeful that the members of the Little Company would join with them as one community. This proposal was untenable to Mother. She had resisted Bishop Bagshawe's efforts to change the focus of the community, and she believed that consolidation:

... would have meant giving up all that the spirit of the Little Company of Mary implied—the great devotions—Calvary, the Precious Blood, the Maternal Heart, the constant intercession for the dying,—all that had been shown ... as forming the interior of [the] Institute, and keeping only what was more or less secondary, the exterior work of nursing. [61]

As their reputation spread, the sisters found themselves in ever-greater demand. In 1884, Bishop Patrick Moran, on a visit from Ireland, requested that members of the Little Company establish a community in Australia. Five members of the Little Company sailed for Sydney the following year. Bishop O'Dwyer of Limerick also expressed his interest in having the sisters work in his diocese in 1885, after hearing about them from Count Arthur Moore, whose wife had been cared for by members of the Little Company after she contracted typhoid fever in Rome. Mother was acutely aware of just how valuable religious were to a diocese, and she sought to accommodate the wishes of bishops who requested members of the Little Company while doing everything in her power to protect her vision of what the institute was meant to be.

When Mother initially decided to remain in Rome, it was unlikely that she realized the Eternal City would become her permanent residence. She returned to England as long as her health permitted, but Italy soon became her second home and the place where many of her hopes would be realized. The Little Company of Mary continued to branch out into new missions—to the United States in 1893 and to the island of Malta the next year. In 1899, the community expanded to Florence and located in the old convent of S. Girolamo, Fiesole, which for several decades had been a Jesuit residence. When Mother visited the new foundation in 1894:

It nearly cost her her life. The winter of 1899–1900 was particularly severe; the dread influenza was ravaging Italy, and the cold was intense, especially in the hills. After Mother had been a short time in Fiesole, she had a severe attack of rheumatic fever. The house was very cold and meagerly furnished, and the hardships and discomfort ... almost proved fatal to a constitution already weakened by illness and fatigue. Nevertheless, she always cherished a special affection for S. Girolamo, not merely for its natural beauty, but chiefly on account of the holy associations of the old Villa ... the first home of the once famous Order of the Hermits of S. Jerome. [62]

Three years later, Mother's dream of building a hospital in Italy came closer to fruition when the Society of Jesus sold her a piece of property that adjoined the ancient Church of Santo Stefano Rotondo. Here she would oversee the construction of a hospital built in the shape of the Cross and aptly named Calvary in honor of the mystery to which she had devoted her life and committed her institute. Rome also became the Motherhouse of the Little Company of Mary and housed a novitiate. On November 30, 1909, one of Mother's greatest wishes came true when the Nursing School of St. Gregory was formally dedicated.

In the following years, Mother became increasingly weak, and near the end of her life was virtually confined to her room. Ruth Lindsay, who had known Mother from childhood, described a scene that was etched in her memory:

> She used to sit, almost upright, upon a couch placed beside a large open window, overlooking the convent garden, and I never remember seeing that window closed. The sun would shine on her eager, loving little face as she talked and fall in soft pools of light over her long, blue veil; the wind would stir the shawl around her shoulders and disarrange the papers on her desk, but she seemed to love them both; certainly, I never saw her shut them out—but then I do not believe Mother ever shut anything or anybody out in the whole of her life.[63]

According to Lindsay, Mother was not strictly beautiful, but her face was surprisingly attractive ...."[64] Most intriguing to her were Mother's eyes, which had a "certain effect of blue distance ... their expression could not be described by the usual metaphor of looking through me *at something*: it was rather as if she looked *through Something* at me."[65]

From the young girl who had wanted someone to love her alone, she had become a far different person, a woman who loved Someone alone with her whole heart and soul. It was said of Mother, "She attended all her life to only one Person under His million disguises. ... She recognized Him under apparently blinding concealments."[66] Her ability to see Christ in others may be the reason why she was so accessible to all who sought her out. "Mother's door was open as wide as her heart, that her children might enter...," wrote Lindsay. Those who spoke with her came away with the feeling that Mother was not just a good listener, although "[she] was always eager to hear, and … wanted to understand exactly…." but that she demonstrated much more—"a purely personal affection for and interest in the teller."[67]

Mother's physical condition continued to deteriorate throughout 1912. Her worsening eyesight forced her to use a magnifying glass to read and to dictate her correspondence. That winter, she suffered from a series of heart attacks, and during Lent was besieged with high fevers.

For sixty-six years, Mary Potter endured a series of conditions and illnesses that read like a medical compendium: congenital heart disease, cancer, scarlet fever, lung hemorrhages, rheumatic fever, tuberculosis, heart attacks. She bore excruciating pain with dignity and offered it to the Lord. But it was now readily apparent that her weakened heart was failing. In her final days, even as she endured intractable pain, Mother sought to console those who were already saddened by her impending death.

Mary Potter's earthly life ended on April 9, 1913. West describes that moment: "It was not an uncommon dying. There was no struggle, no agony. According to eyewitnesses, she gave a small little cry and 'went to Him, whom she loved and for whom she suffered.'"[68]

John Henry Cardinal Newman, England's most illustrious nineteenth-century convert to Catholicism and its preeminent theologian, like Mary Potter, was a Londoner by birth, a Victorian, a prolific writer, and also one of the Church's "Venerable." In his writings, Newman emphasized the importance of suffering and its effect on the soul: "Be sure of this: that if He has any love for you, if He sees aught of good in your soul, He will afflict you…."[69] Newman believed that "nothing short of suffering, except in rare cases, makes us what we should be."[70]

According to Newman's rationale, Mary Potter must have been extremely loved by God. In addition to her lifelong physical pain, she bore the cross of having her family actively oppose her efforts to begin a religious congregation. She patiently put up with priests and prelates who tested her obedience and perseverance by impeding what she knew was God's Will, and was sorely tested by some members of her own community who both inadvertently and deliberately undermined her mission. She suffered the anguish of having to inform her brother Thomas and his wife of the death of their daughter, Marie, a novice in her own institute, and she agonized when her eldest brother, William, who had left the Faith fifteen years earlier, refused the opportunity of receiving the sacraments just before he died. Mary Potter accepted every pain and disappointment out of love for the Lord. And she did so joyously.

Ian Ker, a professor of theology at Oxford and a Newman scholar, asserts, "At the heart of Newman's spirituality is the doctrine of self-abandonment—'a surrender of ourselves, soul and body, to Him.'"[71] Whether or not Mary Potter was familiar with Newman's writings, she agreed with his conclusions. In 1885, she urged the sisters "... to suffer all for the love of Jesus, to keep happy though sick and suffering, to hide from others any pain of mind or body you may feel, to have a smile and a kind word for all, to do all the acts of charity possible...."[72] This was not just motherly advice to her spiritual daughters. Without even being aware of it, Mary Potter had described the way in which she had lived her entire life.

Those who paid their last respects to "*la santa Madre*" loved her for that. "She was extremely prone to tiny acts of kindness...."[73] and had indelibly touched the lives and hearts of small children and powerful members of the Curia, hardworking laborers and distinguished professionals, titled nobility and ordinary folk who, in her eyes, were never ordinary. Mother's death was a time of tears, but also a time of joy for the members of the Little Company of Mary. Their founder's earthly struggles were finally over, yet her spiritual presence would remain to guide them in their continuing mission.

CHAPTER THREE

INTO AMERICA'S HEARTLAND

America's Midwest became home to the first LCM Sisters in 1893.

During the last week of April 1893, three members of the Little Company of Mary set out on a journey that would eventually touch countless lives and have far-reaching effects on the future of their own religious community. Like millions of other Europeans in the last decade of the nineteenth century, they embarked on a transatlantic voyage that would take them to America.[1]

The blue-veiled trio became part of history as they were counted among those who participated in "the greatest expansion and development of Catholicism that took place in the Northeast and Great Lakes regions."[2] It resulted in a ninety-two percent increase in the Catholic population of the United States—from just over six million in 1870 to twelve million in 1900. During the mid-1800s, Catholics comprised only five percent of the U.S. population, but by the turn of the century almost one of every five Americans was Catholic, making Catholicism the largest religious denomination in the United States.[3]

For Mother M. Veronica Dowling, Mother M. Patrick Tuohy, and Sister M. Philomena Haslem, the first members of the Little Company of Mary to bring their founder's vision and apostolate to the New World, coming to America not only became a portion of their own life's story, but also marked a new chapter in the history of the congregation.

The growth of the Little Company of Mary from its first days in Nottingham only sixteen years earlier was certainly astonishing. In less than two decades, the sisters could be found working in Italy and Malta, in Australia and South Africa. What is most striking is that each new site of their endeavors was not the result of the community's desire to expand, but rather a response to the wishes of others, from Leo XIII's invitation to Mary Potter and her companions to remain in Rome and the requests of bishops who wanted the sisters to work in their dioceses, to individuals whose lives the sisters had somehow touched, and who, in return, wished to extend their healing presence to others.

The American connection came about because of the efforts of Charles A. Mair, a wealthy Chicagoan who was vacationing in Italy with his wife, Cornelia, in 1889. While in Rome, she contracted typhoid, an acute, life-threatening illness often caused by bacterial contamination of food or drink.[4] When Mair heard of the superb care offered by the "English Sisters," he asked them to help his wife, who was suffering from persistent, high fevers. Mother Agnes could do little for Mrs. Mair except

The Kaiser Wilhelm II conveyed the first blue-veiled sisters from Genoa to New York.

Ship's passenger list. The names of Sisters Veronica, Patrick, and Philomena occur midway down the page; their "calling or occupation" was recorded as "nurses."

ease her discomfort. Cornelia Mair eventually succumbed to the illness, but her husband was so grateful for the loving care she had received that he resolved to bring the Sisters of the Little Company to the United States. Mother put his offer on hold until such time when she felt that her community could spare several sisters for this new mission.

In a September 1892 letter addressed to "Reverend and Dear Madame," Charles Mair informed the founder of the Little Company of Mary:

> [I] have today, had my interview with Archbishop Feehan to ask his permission for your Order to enter this Diocese and his approval of my enterprise in bringing your Sisters out. His Lordship was very glad to give his endorsement and approbation.... [I] told him of your work in Rome and Florence and Sydney. He asked what means

you had for support. I answered, "… none but contributions and such pay as those nursed choose to give." The field is great here and I have no question whatever as to the success of the venture.

I will undertake bringing such Sisters from England to Chicago, as you consider wise and proper to send. I would rent a house for their comfortable maintenance for such time as they need and until they have been long enough established in Chicago to decide which is the most suitable quarter for a permanent establishment.… I shall furnish the house simply, supply articles needed for the room set apart as a Chapel, supply fuel and food until the Sisters get on their feet.…[5]

The following month, Mair sent a follow-up note:

All Chicago will be absorbed in greeting the company strangers for the year to come [i.e., visitors to the World's Fair], and we shall naturally have a great field for your good and devoted nursing Sisters. From what I [have] learn[ed], the German Nursing Sisters are now practically engaged in the work of their Hospital of St. Elizabeth all the time and in this great city we have not a single Catholic Nursing Order available to do the work you undertake in the houses of the poor.…[6]

In the spring of 1893, the Little Company of Mary received its final approval from Pope Leo XIII, and Mother decided that the time was right to respond to Mr. Mair's generous offer. Part of the oral tradition of the community is a story that the sisters tell regarding how the founder determined which of the three sisters chosen to go to America would be best suited to undertake the difficult task of leading the new foundation. Mother is said to have devised a simple but ingenious test. Each sister was to sip a cup of tea into which a touch of salt was added. Mother believed that whoever questioned the taste had the strong character and common sense that the office required.[7]

Dublin-born Mother M. Veronica Dowling, who had entered the Little Company of Mary in 1883 and made final vows in 1888, passed Mother's test with flying colors and was appointed as the first Superior of the American foundation. The founder's decision to appoint Mother Veronica was a solid vote of confidence in a daughter who had endured a great deal when she was the first Superior of St. John's Hospital in Limerick. While in that position, Mother Veronica had incurred the wrath of Bishop O'Dwyer. West points out, "O'Dwyer's despotism provided much heartache for the first superior [Mother Veronica]"[8] and the bishop had unjustly accused Mother Veronica of numerous failings including "disruption, disobedience, and negligence."[9]

The founder of the Little Company of Mary, who knew her daughter Veronica well, recognized that the bishop's charges were without merit. In a heartfelt yet frank letter written from Via Sforza, Mother attempted to console her suffering daughter:

> God bless you again and again, my poor child, or rather my happy child. You could not have a greater sign of being one of the Little Company of Mary on Calvary. You have suffered as others before you. You could scarcely believe how old Sisters have suffered from calumny. How can we be on Calvary without being condemned, and sometimes by our own?
>
> I remember well one time, M. Cecilia was going to have an operation, and we put her for quietness in a cottage we had near.... Well, the talk went about ... that she was going to have a baby. So much so that when I had to have my operations I had them ... and even showed some poor women who came up (to convince them) where my breast had been taken off.
>
> Ah, my child, do not trouble. St. Ignatius said his order would cease when it ceased to be persecuted. In the Little Company of Mary, individual members seem to suffer, one or the other.... You are more my child than ever.... It is well you wrote openly. Always do, to whoever might be in my place. All mothers might not know [you] as much as your loving mother. Mary[10]

In an undated letter to Mother Veronica, written either late in 1892 or early in 1893, Mother counseled:

> Now prepare for the work God has been preparing you Himself for. Go in God's name to that new spot on earth.... [B]e Our Lady's little instrument in the New World. We have indeed thought and prayed about you and your assistant, and ... we finally decided that Sr. M. Patrick and yourself would be one in spirit, and union in the Superiors is so edifying in a house.... You will be a good Mother. Sr. Philomena is glad to go with you. Your loving mother, Mary[11]

The trio left Rome on April 24, accompanied by the blessings of the Holy Father and their Mother General and with the prayers of their fellow sisters. Mothers M. Philip and M. Cecilia traveled with them to Genoa, the nearest port city, 467 kilometers (290 miles) away. After attending Mass on April 26, the feast of Our Lady of Good Counsel, the sisters boarded the S.S. *Kaiser Wilhelm II* [12] bound for New York, and, with tears in their eyes, watched Mother M. Cecilia and Mother M. Philip "as they stood on shore waving their handkerchiefs till they became lost in the distance."[13]

On shipboard, they were soon befriended by a number of fellow passengers, including a married couple named Ritchie, one of their friends, and Thomas Joseph Dowling, the Bishop of Hamilton, Ontario, who along with his chaplain had just completed a pilgrimage to the Eternal City and to the Holy Land. The Limerick-born prelate and the new American Superior soon discovered they had a great deal in common. Not only were they both of Irish heritage, but they also shared the same last name. The group enjoyed each other's company until the ship encountered rough water after reaching Gibraltar. Describing their ordeal, Mother Veronica wrote

> As we lost sight of the grand old rock, the steamer got into what the sailors call an "ocean swell" and now began our troubles! [N]early all on board became as sick as the proverbial "dogs" and for nine days, were unable to leave our cabin. The steamer rocked so that everything was dashed from side to side. Fortunately, Sr. M. Philomena did not suffer at all from seasickness.... The only one who rejoiced in perfect health, spirits and appetite was the Bishop's chaplain who made all the fun he possibly could out of our deplorable condition, telling the Bishop he thought he ought to get holy oils and anoint poor M. M. Patrick! However, we got into smooth water as we neared our journey's end, which was a relief. [14]

The ocean crossing took fourteen days. On May 9, the *Kaiser Wilhelm II* steamed into New York Harbor and past the welcoming Statue of Liberty:

> We had Mass ... on board for the last time. Shortly after, the Tender drew up and we received a most cordial letter of "Welcome to America" from our good benefactor Mr. Mair ... telling us his agent would meet us when we landed, which he did—handing us another

State Street, Chicago, May 1893. The street is decorated for the Columbian World Exposition. (Courtesy of the Chicago Historical Society)

letter from Mr. Mair, with our tickets to Chicago ... but it was about 1 p.m. when we got our luggage from the boat. It would not be possible to continue our journey that day.[15]

After attending early morning Mass on Ascension Thursday, they boarded the train for Chicago. On the following evening, Friday, May 12, they arrived in Chicago, America's second-largest city with a population of one million. By the late 1800s, Chicago had become the commercial hub for grain and livestock after the railroads linked the east and west coasts, and as the city's manufacturing sector continued to grow, thousands left small prairie towns and family-owned farms for a chance at what they hoped would be a better life. In addition, between 1880 and 1890, the city's foreign-born population nearly tripled from more than two hundred thousand to almost six hundred thousand.[16]

Chicago was quickly rebounding from the Great Fire of 1871, which had reduced more than eighteen thousand buildings to ashes, destroyed two hundred million dollars of property—one-third of the entire valuation of the city—and left almost seventy-five thousand residents homeless.[17] "What the fire could not touch was Chicago's most important feature, its location, which made it more accessible than any other place on earth to resources and markets throughout the globe at the very time when America was taking over world leadership in industrial enterprise."[18]

The makeup of Chicago (as well as the Catholic Church in the United States) during the last decade of the nineteenth century reflected the face of recent immigration. The heavy concentration of Irish and German immigrants was slowly giving way to newcomers from many other countries, including Poland, Italy, Sicily, Serbia, Croatia, Hungary and Lithuania.

When Mother Veronica, Mother Patrick, and Sister Philomena arrived in America in 1893, the United States was in the throes of another wave of nativism, an anti-immigrant reaction on the part of some Americans. During the 1830s, Protestant nativists began focusing their attacks on Catholic immigrants whom they perceived to be ignorant, superstitious, and priest-dominated—characteristics they saw as incompatible with a republican form of government.[19] Midway through the nineteenth century, this feeling intensified because of the mass influx of Irish during and after the Great Famine. Anti-Irish sentiment grew, and it was not unusual to see "No Irish Need Apply" signs in establishment windows.

The pioneering members of the Little Company of Mary appear to have escaped the nativism that was prevalent for several reasons. As religious, they would have been treated with a certain degree of respect by almost all Catholics and even by a considerable number of non-Catholics. More importantly, as nurses, they quickly earned the admiration of others by their tireless and courageous efforts to provide whatever care was necessary. The sisters assumed tasks that most people were either untrained for or had no desire to undertake, even endangering their own lives by caring for those with infectious diseases. The pervasive negativism toward newcomers eventually culminated in the creation of the Immigrant Restriction League in 1894, which greatly limited the number of immigrants entering the United States.

Such was the world they encountered when they reached Chicago and were greeted by Mr. Mair. He had arranged for them to stay at a nearby convent until their new house became habitable, but their train had arrived too late for them to go to the convent that evening, so he drove them to the Auditorium Hotel for the night.

The next few days were a period of adjustment for the new immigrants:

Charles Mair's generosity was primarily responsible for the first LCM Sisters coming to the United States.

We were all three very sick after the voyage and the Good Shepherd nuns used green tea. The look and flavor of green tea we were unaccustomed to and it made us sick. So one day as were coming on to work, one of us suggested [that] it would be a good thing to buy a spirit-lamp and as we had some of our own dear black tea, we could make a cup and we felt sure it would cure us.... [W]e bought the lamp and worked ... all day thinking of the nice cup of our own tea we would have in the evening. About 3:30, the usual hour, we made the tea and went to the cupboard for the cups ... and it was only then it dawned upon us that we had no cups.... [W]e thought we could ... drink it out of the pot we cooked it in. When again we were confronted with another calamity, we found we had neither sugar nor milk. Mother Veronica bethought of a few lumps she laid somewhere and hunted them up and then there was no help for it but to drink it out of the pot—black and all the tea leaves swimming 'round in it as we passed it round from one to another like the loving cup—and though it did not taste to our liking, we made merry over it—for these were the good old days that are gone.[20]

Their new home would be a small cottage located at 4124 Indiana Avenue. In a letter to Mother Catherine, Mair explained, "The impossibility of renting any suitable place in [a] good location has forced me to secure the 1-1/2 story frame cottage...."[21] The "impossibility" may have been due to the opening of the Columbian Exposition, which coincided with the sisters' arrival. A more intriguing question surrounds the condition of their new "home," of which Mother Veronica provided some detail:

> After breakfast, Mr. Mair came and took us by the elevator train to the convent on 49th Street. Here we were received with loving welcome and made to feel quite at home. Mr. Mair gave us the key of our little house and said it was about a mile from this convent, remarking what a strange coincidence that we should arrive in Chicago on the 12th of May. That very day, four years ago, M. M. Agnes came to nurse his dear wife in Rome. That afternoon we went to see our future home. The last occupants had not long left and the place looked most deplorably dirty—inside and out.[22]

Since their benefactor was so solicitous toward the sisters, it is puzzling that he would provide them with a house in such a dilapidated state, but this may simply have been an unforeseeable circumstance caused by its previous tenants. Whatever the reason, history seemed to be repeating itself because Mary Potter had encountered a similar situation at the run-down stocking factory in Nottingham and the congregation's first house in Rome also turned out to be uninhabitable.

Mother Veronica chronicled their busy days as the sisters prepared to move into their new house: "We stayed for three weeks at the Convent of the Good Shepherd on 49th and Prairie and every day we came here to clean and scrub and try to get things in order. One can hardly believe all the little things that have to be got and fixed in a house when you only have the bare walls."[23]

Everyday situations presented challenges for the trio, even the American way of catching a streetcar:

> [B]efore we came here we were accustomed to cars stopping anywhere.... [W]e thought we were very obliging to go to a crossing or cross street, but we invariably stood at the wrong place and fully expected the cars to stop for us.... They never did, of course, but sometimes an obliging conductor would wait while we crossed ... at other times, although we gave the signal we wanted to get on the car—they took no notice of us, but dashed past. We wondered what could be the matter and thought to ourselves, nuns are not in the habit of going in public cars—and they must think we are not right and do not want to be bothered with us.... [O]ne day a little girl came out of a house and said, "Sisters, when you want to get on the

cars, you must cross the street, for they are not allowed to stop at the near side." Then it was we saw our mistake.... [W]e often think since how kind the men were to call us and wait for us....[24]

As the sisters settled in and prepared to begin nursing, all three experienced the frustration of having to relearn simple domestic tasks that usually would have been second nature to them:

The stove was not set in place until the 30th ... and one of our numbers who thought herself very capable of making fires and cooking went to work to light it. We were so busy, she had to do it all by herself and she did it and it went out.... She lit it again and it went out again.... Well, that happened five or six times and every time she came for sympathy to the other two, who ... could only say, "Oh, I wonder what ails it," ... [since] we felt we were not half as knowledgeable about fires as the sister who was making it. After a few more trials and failures, we came to the conclusion there was something wrong with the coal and one of us went to borrow coal.... One neighbor said she had none and another said her coal was the same as ours and she had no trouble.... She guessed there was something wrong in the way we "fixed it." So she came and "fixed it" herself and in less time than it took me to write about it— she had a blazing fire. It appeared [that] we did not put enough wood in and it always went out before the coal had time to light.... [W]hen we saw how easy it was ... we slipped out of the kitchen, feeling very small indeed.[25]

Just two weeks after taking possession of their house, the sisters managed to make it presentable enough to have Mass celebrated there, although this required extraordinary effort:

Father McGavie came and blessed the house and as he since told us, he thought to himself, they will be in a nice mess tomorrow, for although we were making progress, the place did not look like it. There were heaps of shavings and boxes opened and straw strewn about and papers thrown here and there and ladders and tools everywhere, but we stayed up all night and the morning found order reigning supreme.[26]

The American apostolate, which began that spring, resembled the work of the first members of the community in Hyson Green, as the sisters traveled from home to home, not only providing nursing services but also caring for children, preparing meals, and helping with household tasks. Several months later, three more sisters from Hyson Green joined the Chicago group: Sister Mary Evangelist Tuohy, Sister Mary Laurence Delaney, and an unnamed novice who eventually left the congregation. Upon first seeing the additional members, one of the pioneering group wrote, "We welcomed them as though we never saw a sister before."[27] Throughout the summer the sisters took on nursing cases, and according to Mother Veronica, "All were busy."[28]

When the first members of the Little Company of Mary arrived in Illinois, Chicago was experiencing a pivotal moment in its history as it hosted the World's Columbian Exposition of 1893. The event, commemorating Columbus's discovery of the New World four hundred years earlier (but one year late), was meant to showcase the progress that had occurred in America since that time, much in the same way the Great Exposition of 1851 had captured the forward-looking spirit of Victorian England forty-two years earlier. The Columbian Exposition—the last, and by many accounts, the greatest World's Fair of the nineteenth century—also "… marked Chicago's appearance on the world stage. Not only did the world take notice of Chicago, but Chicago left its mark on the world."[29] London might have had its Crystal Palace, but now Chicago took center stage with its much heralded "White City," so called because the Fair's fourteen "great" buildings, designed in the Beaux-Arts style, were covered with gleaming white stucco.

Set on 633 acres within Jackson Park, this Exposition positively redefined the country, which was experiencing difficult social changes as it shifted from being a predominantly agricultural nation to a primarily industrial one. As visitors stepped through gates, the harsh realities of late nineteenth-century life could be left behind: the smallpox, consumption, cholera, and scarlet fever that were rampant in Chicago's unheated, unventilated tenements; the "sweatshops" where immigrant workers, including children, toiled for up to sixteen hours a day; the recent violence of labor strikes; and the fact that America was in the midst of a major economic depression.

Unlike the real Chicago, where factories and freight yards were engulfed in clouds of gray smoke, the White City presented a utopia where immaculate streets led to magnificent classically designed buildings

View of the "White City," as the Columbian World Exposition of 1893 became known. (Courtesy of the Chicago Historical Society)

surrounded by greenery and water. The Fair's exhibit halls housed all sorts of wondrous inventions: Thomas Edison's kinetoscope showed "moving pictures," and the telephone must have seemed like magic. And, of course, there was electricity. An entire building was devoted to this amazing invention, prompting one British historian to comment, "Perhaps the portion of the World's Exposition which America is far ahead of all in competition is the Palace of Electricity; here she is seen in her natural splendour, eclipsing by her dazzling light every other nation."[30]

More than twenty-seven million visitors (almost half the population of the United States in 1893) from all over the world took in the sights. The Manufacturers and Liberal Arts Building, the largest building in the world at the time, towered nineteen stories above the fair grounds and displayed all sorts of items: Tiffany stained glass and Remington typewriters, the University of Chicago's seventy-ton Yerkes telescope, and Bach's clavichord. People waited in line to ride the Fair's most popular attraction, a wheel invented by George W. Ferris. A million and a half attendees paid an additional fifty cents (the cost of admission to the fair) to sit on a plush seat in one of the wheel's thirty-six wood-paneled cars for a twenty-minute spin, which was especially spectacular after dark when thousands of incandescent lights were switched on.

Along with elements of "high culture," the Columbian World

Exposition also featured diverse entertainments in its Midway. Visitors could watch the hootchie-kootchie antics of "Little Egypt," tap their feet to a catchy rhythm of something called "ragtime," sip a nose-tickling beverage made of carbonated water and flavoring, or sample a popcorn, peanut, and molasses confection introduced at the fair, which later became "Cracker Jack®."

The Exposition lasted for only five months, from May to October 1893, but the technology it introduced to the public, which seemed incredible at the time, steadily became part of the lives of almost all Americans within a few decades, and changed the landscape of American life forever.

It is not surprising that there is no mention of the sisters ever attending the Exposition, for at that time it would have been unseemly for "nuns" to partake of such entertainment. But Mother Veronica did record that the community enjoyed the company of a number of guests who visited them that summer because of the World's Fair—including the Bishop of Nottingham's niece and her husband and Mr. and Mrs. Ritchie, who had been the sisters' shipboard companions en route to America. In addition, the Little Company of Mary nursed a young Irish-Argentine woman who had come to Chicago for the Exposition. Mother Veronica made note of this case, which would have unexpected consequences for the American foundation two decades later:

> [O]ne afternoon, a priest came who wanted a sister to nurse a young lady who was [a]board the ship with them.... She was traveling ... and was taken worse in Chicago.... Mother Veronica and Sister M. Laurence were with her when she died. Her name was Mary Morgan, daughter of Mrs. Morgan, San Antonio, Buenos Aires.... She and her sons ... called here often during their short stay in Chicago.... They returned to their home after speaking words of gratitude to the Little Company and promised not to forget them. [31]

During their first winter, the frigid Midwestern temperatures and accompanying ice and "piles of snow" were particularly difficult for the sisters who were used to the more temperate climates of England and Ireland. Mother Veronica wrote:

> We could not believe it could be so cold.... [W]hen Mr. Mair spoke about a furnace and how necessary it was [that] we should have one or

we could not keep warm—we tried hard not to get one. We thought we would not be cold and with a fire in the grate we would be very comfortable—but he knew better and put a furnace in and sure enough we were nearly frozen, even with the fire … and the furnace.[32]

The community also had a scare when Sister Laurence, who was caring for a patient with typhoid fever, contracted the disease herself. Fortunately, she had a mild form and made a complete recovery.

The first year in America had been momentous for the pioneering members of the Little Company of Mary. In the waning months of 1893, the sisters became aware of a change that affected their neighbors and themselves, which was later chronicled by urban historian Richard Wade:

> The year 1893 was one of ambivalence for Chicago. It began with excitement—the opening of the World's Columbian Exposition … it ended in despair—a deep depression gripped both city and nation. Inside the Exposition grounds all was glitter, gaiety and the celebration of progress; outside, sullen men shuffled the streets, slept in parks, and bitterly faced a bleak future.[33]

The nation's worsening economy meant that some of the poor families for whom the sisters provided nursing care found themselves in even worse straits. Consequently, payment for their services was often delayed or lessened, and sometimes the sisters received nonmonetary remuneration such as food or work provided for them.

Four months later, devastating news hit the community. Mother Veronica was diagnosed with breast cancer. Mother (Mary Potter) wrote to her, "God bless my child. I am sure you have suffered and suffered well. I have felt so much for you…. I do not know if it will be any comfort to you to know that your disease must have been just the same as your mother's."[34] The operation was performed at the convent. It initially appeared to be successful, but the tumor recurred two months later.

In August of 1895, two more members of the Little Company, Sister M. Rosarii Hassett and Sister M. Barbara Crowe, left Hyson Green for Chicago. Their arrival could not have come too soon, as Mother M. Patrick was suddenly felled by typhoid fever contracted from a patient whom she was nursing. While recuperating, phlebitis set in, and for a time it appeared that she might not survive. Mother Veronica cared for her while she recovered, even though she herself was quite ill.

On October 13, 1895, Sister M. Philomena and Sister M. Evangelist became the first sisters to make their final vows in America. They did so in the presence of Patrick Augustine Feehan, the first archbishop of Chicago. The prelate, who had held Chicago's highest ecclesiastical office for fifteen years, had been described as possessing "a sense of highly cultivated power tempered with exquisite gentleness ... look[ing] every inch a prince of the church...."[35]

Mother Veronica mustered all her strength for this special day. She had given the retreat for the sisters, and according to those who were present, "was here, there, and everywhere on the day of Profession." This would be her final endeavor because "... a few days later, she lay down, never to rise again."[36] Mother Veronica lingered until March 4, when she went to the Lord. On June 1, 1896, Mother Patrick was appointed as her successor.

The congregation's founder assured Mother Patrick that she understood the burden that this role thrust upon her. "God bless you my child who now has the extra blessing upon her of obedience as Superior of the Little Company of Mary in America. You will never be so light-hearted again, my Paddie," she wrote.[37] In subsequent correspondence, the founder of the Little Company of Mary expressed her sorrow for the loneliness that Mother Patrick was feeling since Mother Veronica's death. "I do hope the two new sisters who will be with you in the autumn will be a comfort.... I suppose I cannot fathom your loss and how you miss her...."[38]

Six months later, Sister M. Bon Consilio Sullivan and Sister M. Elizabeth Ryan arrived from Limerick, bringing the number within the Chicago Foundation to eight. The small cottage had quickly become too small for the growing community, but even Charles Mair was temporarily unable to help them. Following the Depression of 1893, the country experienced a time of financial difficulty, "one of the worst in American history, with the unemployment rate exceeding ten percent for half a decade. Multiple factors contributed to the economic downturn including "Storms, droughts, and overproduction ... [which] had reversed the remarkable agricultural prosperity and expansion of the 1880s...."[39] In addition, a panic, which began with the financial failure of the Philadelphia and Reading Railroad in January 1893, quickly spread ... eventually causing five hundred banks and over fifteen thousand businesses to declare bankruptcy.[40]

An entry in the sisters' logbook halfway through 1896 indicates that their benefactor was one of the countless Americans affected by the Depression:

[O]ur little chapel can accommodate only a few people and we expect an increase in our community and we have no place for them to sleep. The cry of hard times is heard all over Chicago and more than once Mr. Mair thought it wiser not to spend so much money....

In Nov. 1896, Mr. McKinley was elected President—and though we did not know it, the building of our convent rested on that fact, for confidence was in a manner restored and people with money felt more secure and began to spend it more freely.[41]

Believing that better times were at hand, Mair contributed eight thousand dollars toward a new chapel. Construction began in December, requiring that the house be moved toward the back of the property: "All the sisters were careful to note when and what hour the house would be moved and nearly all were home on time. It was moved while we were having tea and if we did not know what was happening, we would not have noticed—it glided like a train...."[42]

Charles Mair laid the cornerstone on December 3, 1896. Fortunately, the winter of 1896–1897 was unusually mild, so construction was able to continue unabated. Six months later, on May 31, 1897, the chapel was dedicated in honor of the Maternal Heart of Mary and to the memory of Cordelia Mair on the eighth anniversary of her death. After the chapel was blessed and consecrated, the Blessed Sacrament was removed from the old tabernacle. The sisters, garbed in white cloaks and bearing lighted candles, led the way, followed by Father Riordan of nearby St. Elizabeth's, who carried the Eucharist. Mother Patrick recorded the emotion felt by the sisters that day:

It was very touching, but to the first sisters, a feeling of loneliness, mixed with joy pervaded their feelings. The little sanctuary in the first and old house was such a sweet spot—and when one looked at it, it brought to mind our first days and labours of love, making the first home for Jesus of the Little Company of Mary, and she [Mother Veronica] who took such an active part ... with every little detail of that little altar and chapel....[43]

The gladness of that day would contrast starkly with what lay ahead in the upcoming weeks when thirty-four-year-old Sister M. Elizabeth became the third victim of typhoid fever, contracted while nursing. Her symptoms lessened after six weeks, but she was obviously very ill. She died one week later, but not before making her final vows on her deathbed. Many who attended her funeral Mass had been nursed by her and were moved to tears. Even her fellow sisters were shaken by her sudden and unexpected death. After she was laid to rest in Calvary Cemetery next to Mother Veronica, one member wrote, "The bell tolled to express our respect for our dear Sister...."[44]

Not long afterwards, Sister Bon Consilio was hospitalized in a sanitarium in St. Louis and eventually returned to the community in Nottingham, which was also her home. Although the two sisters from Limerick were part of the American community for only a short time, the number of members in Chicago remained at eight when Agnes Killeen and Esther Merriman, both from Chicago, became the first two postulants of the Little Company of Mary in America. They were sent to Rome for their novitiate, and on April 26, 1898,[45] received the habit and their religious names: Agnes was given the name Sister M. Veronica and Esther, Sister M. Patrick—the names of the first two Mothers of the Chicago Foundation. The following year, Mother Patrick wrote, "We have many applications for membership, but for one reason and another, we do not think them fit or suitable subjects, and we do not receive them."[46]

On Holy Saturday 1898, Charles Mair again demonstrated his generosity by canceling the remaining $700 debt on the chapel, and he and his new wife signed the deeds over to the Little Company of Mary, making the parcel of land in Evergreen Park "the first piece of property owned by the community in any part of the world...."[47]

In a heartfelt letter, Mother M. Patrick acknowledged, "We can liken you to the good rich man Joseph of Arimathea who gave our Lord a sepulcher new and undefiled—you have given us a new and unencumbered abode where year after year, those sacred mysteries will be commemorated...."[48]

This was a hectic time for the nascent community. With the exception of one sister who remained in the convent, the sisters' days were completely occupied with the care of the sick. "[W]e were only six Sisters and we needed one hundred to meet the demands for their care. The cases were so urgent that nearly all the time during the day, I was alone in the convent—all the Sisters being out. When in, they keep strict rules and are very edifying and when out, they are full of charity...."[49] Under Mother Patrick's care, the fledgling group attempted to maintain the delicate balance between the active and contemplative elements of religious life in accordance with their founder's belief that regardless of the demands of an active apostolate each sister pay close attention to the care of her spiritual life by allotting time for silence, prayer, and recollection.

Mother Patrick was sensitive to the effects that Sister Elizabeth's untimely death had had on her little congregation. She subsequently arranged for two sisters at a time to spend eight days at the country house belonging to the Sisters of Mercy, which gave them a break from their nursing duties, a change of scenery, and time to regroup.

The year 1899 began with two significant events. On January 22, Pope Leo XIII promulgated *Testem Benevolentiae Nostrae*, an encyclical addressed to James Cardinal Gibbons of Baltimore that condemned "Americanism," a heresy that advanced the idea that "the Catholic Church should adjust its doctrines, especially in morality, to the culture of the people."[50] The pope had sent a message to the bishops of America, lest it appear "that there are some among you who conceive of and desire a church in America different from that which is in the rest of the world."[51] This papal proclamation had a significant effect on the way Rome looked at the United States and particularly at the American concept of religious freedom both then and throughout the twentieth century.

The second event had a more immediate impact on the community. Two additional sisters arrived from Limerick months after enduring a stormy ocean voyage during a winter that was unusually severe. All in the Chicago Foundation already knew Sister Bernadette O'Neill; the other [Sister Lucy Ambrose] was "a surprise." The two new members were greatly welcomed, for the Chicago sisters were quite overextended. "We are always very busy—our cry is still—work for one hundred and we are only eight. The more [that] the Sisters are known; the more they are sought after.... [T]hey are a great help to doctors and patients, besides looking after the souls of their charges."[52]

During these early years when nursing was done in their patients' homes, the sisters' time as a community was limited and precious. On Friday evenings, the sisters themselves returned home for Stations of the Cross, Chapter, and confession. They eagerly looked forward to letters that arrived during the week, as Mother Patrick recorded, "[W]e are all united in unison of soul and body with our other sisters all over the world. We seem to know one another thoroughly, though we never saw a great many of the writers."[53] She was well aware of the sisters' need to recoup from the long hours of nursing because of the physical and mental toll it took on them. "I like to encourage as much as possible the happy moments, for the sisters need lightening [of] their spirits...," she wrote. "After supper, all are off again, on-duty bound, with serious faces and gaiety put in their pockets until they next meet, which is usually on Sunday for Benediction and supper."[54]

The century was coming to an end, but the mission of the Little Company of Mary in America was just beginning. The number of sisters in the Chicago Foundation would remain relatively small for some time, but their presence would touch an ever-increasing number of lives. Mother Patrick's words, "the more the Sisters are known, the more they are sought after" rang true and prophetic. Before long, the community would find itself inundated with requests both by individuals who personally needed their help as well as by numerous prelates who quickly recognized their invaluable worth.

CHAPTER FOUR

A BLUE VEIL AMONG
DIAMONDS AND PEARLS

*Bertha Honoré Palmer, the grande dame of Chicago society, turned
to the Little Company of Mary during a time of need. (Courtesy of
the Chicago Historical Society)*

At the turn of the century, the United States had almost fully recovered from the self-inflicted wounds caused by the Civil War and was on the verge of becoming a world power. A year later, Theodore Roosevelt was in the White House. The former Rough Rider of the Spanish-American War, a heroic, larger-than-life figure who wore rimless glasses and sported a bushy mustache, had become the youngest of U.S. presidents after the assassination of William McKinley in 1901.

The Little Company of Mary had been in America for seven years. During that time, the English-born congregation, composed almost entirely of Irish sisters, kept a logbook of their activities and important events, much of which forms their present history. In July 1899, however, the book's entries abruptly ended. The next recorded event is dated June 6, 1925.

Except for a handful of documents and some correspondence between the Motherhouse in Rome and the sisters in Chicago, there are almost no written accounts chronicling what the sisters were doing or how the foundation was changing for more than a quarter of a century. One exception is an account written sometime between 1930 and 1951 by Sister M. Dunstan Kelleher, which tells of the unusual circumstances that brought her own Superior, Mother M. Stanislaus Madigan, to America.

Early in the 1900s, the Little Company of Mary still provided home nursing. The majority of their patients were hardworking yet relatively poor Chicagoans, but Sister Stanislaus's story involved one of the city's most prominent families.

In 1871, twenty-one-year-old Bertha Honoré, the daughter of a wealthy and influential Louisville family which moved to Chicago when Bertha was six, married forty-four-year-old Potter Palmer, Chicago's premier real estate magnate. The couple soon became Chicago icons. Potter Palmer had established a very successful dry goods business in Chicago in 1852, which later merged with an emporium run by Marshall Field. The establishment became Marshall Field & Company in 1881— Chicago's most famous department store. He also built the Palmer House, one of the city's landmark hotels, as a wedding gift for his young bride.[1] In addition to helping make State Street the retail center of the Midwest, Palmer and his wife were "key figures in the development of Chicago's Gold Coast as well as Chicago's Loop."[2]

One month after their marriage, the Great Chicago Fire reduced "...

his labors [to] an intensive heap of ashes,"[3] wiping out the thirty-two buildings he owned in the city. His new bride convinced the insurance companies to lend her husband $1,700,000 to start over—"the largest single loan made in the United States to that time."[4]

In addition to her social prominence, Bertha Palmer became known as a supporter of suffrage and higher education for women and "gained national and worldwide fame when she was appointed president of the Board of Lady Managers of the upcoming World's Columbian Exposition."[5] The fair's original plans did not include any exhibits featuring the accomplishments of women, but under Mrs. Palmer's leadership, a group of women created the Women's Building, designed by Sophia Hayden, one of the few female architects in nineteenth-century America.[6] It included exhibits from women in every state and forty-seven nations, including paintings by Mary Cassatt, a library of seven thousand books written by women, and even the Queen of Italy's handmade lace, as well as women's inventions such as portable dish-heaters and mechanical dusters.[7]

"Much of the success of this huge project was the result of the commitment of Bertha Honoré Palmer … [who employed] … the strategy of displaying the achievements of women in an impressive building that was part of an event designed to capture the attention of the entire world."[8] At the Opening Day ceremonies, Mrs. Palmer, "whose diamonds radiated an almost palpable heat,"[9] remarked, "Even more important than the discovery of Columbus, which we are gathered together to celebrate, is the fact that the general [i.e., federal] government has just discovered women."[10]

That such a legendary Chicago family would have turned to the Little Company of Mary for assistance makes for a wonderful story, but it could not have happened as written by Sister Dunstan: "Way back in 1905 … [Sister Stanislaus] was assigned … to a very peculiar case—to accompany the body of Mrs. Potter Palmer back to Chicago [from Italy]."[11] The *Chicago Tribune's* front-page coverage of Mrs. Palmer's death shows that Mrs. Palmer died in 1918, not in 1905. Moreover, she passed away at her summer residence in Sarasota, Florida, not in Europe. What appears to have occurred is that either the passage of time blurred Mother Stanislaus's recollections, or Sister Dunstan inadvertently misreported the details.

> **MRS. ELIZA M. HONORE DEAD.**
>
> **Mrs. Potter Palmer's Sister-in-Law Succumbs to Typhoid in Italy.**
>
> *Special to The New York Times.*
>
> CHICAGO, Jan. 23.—Mrs. Eliza M. Honore, wife of Harry H. Honore, Jr., daughter of J. Russell Jones and sister-in-law of Mrs. Potter Palmer, died to-day in Florence, Italy, after a long attack of typhoid fever.
>
> Mrs. Honore was thirty-seven years old and had been married thirteen years. She was born in Chicago, but received most of her education in Brussels, where she studied for eight years. She is survived by two sisters and a brother—Miss Rose Jones, Mrs. A. E. Dyer, and D. C. Jones. Mr. and Mrs. Honore had lived in Highland Park for several years.

On January 24, 1902, The New York Times carried the above death notice on its front page.

According to the original logbook from Florence, Italy, Sister Stanislaus did not come to America in 1905. She was assigned to the United States at the end of January 1902.[12] That three-year discrepancy holds the key to what actually happened and makes possible the reconstruction of the improbable yet providential events that led Bertha Honoré Palmer, the most prestigious woman in Chicago, to turn to the Little Company of Mary.

In August of 1901, Mrs. Palmer's brother, Harry [Henry Hamilton] Honoré, Jr., his wife, Eliza, and her sister, Rose Jones, left Chicago for Europe, where they planned to spend a year traveling for his health.[13] While in Florence in early December, thirty-seven-year-old Eliza contracted typhoid fever.[14] She seemed to be recovering,[15] but her condition suddenly worsened, and she died on January 22, 1902. The following day, the Little Company of Mary in Florence received a request from Bertha Palmer to have one of their sisters accompany Mrs. Honoré's remains back to the States and to assist Mrs. Palmer's brother and his sister-in-law on their journey.

There is no evidence that Eliza Honoré was ever cared for by the Little Company of Mary, so it is unclear why Mrs. Palmer turned to the congregation for help. Although her family attended the First Christian Church, Bertha's education was very Catholic, from her first days at

Chicago's St. Xavier's Academy to its completion at Georgetown's Convent of the Visitation. Consequently, she was familiar with the Catholic faith and ritual and had developed a great respect for Catholic sisters.[16]

Bertha Palmer may have been familiar with the "English Sisters" after her husband became ill while traveling in Egypt in 1899. She had rushed him to Rome for medical treatment,[17] and since most of sisters' patients were either English-speaking expatriates or visitors from England and America, it is quite possible that the Little Company of Mary provided his nursing care while he recuperated at a nearby villa. Or she might have heard of the Little Company of Mary through [Raphael] Merry del Val, then a monsignor, who was a friend/adviser to Mother [Mary Potter].[18] After he recovered from his illness, the Palmers had a private audience with Pope Leo XIII, then "... toured the Vatican Gardens and were shepherded around by Merry del Val, who was already well known to Mrs. Palmer"[19] because he had been friends with Bertha's sister Ida and her husband years before in Vienna.[20]

However it was that she knew of the "Blue Nuns," Mrs. Palmer contacted the sisters in Florence asking for their help and purchased a roundtrip boat ticket for one member of the community. Twenty-seven-year-old, Irish-born Sister M. Stanislaus (originally Katie Madigan of County Clare) was assigned to "take care of the Potter Palmer family until all arrangements were completed in Chicago, then ... go to the convent of the Little Company of Mary at 4130 Indiana Avenue and spend ... three months there before returning to Italy."[21]

She arrived in Chicago in early February 1902 and stayed with the Palmers at their English Gothic-style mansion on North Lake Shore Drive[22]—a residence known throughout the city as "the Palmer castle." "No private home in Chicago's history was so much discussed,"[23] not just because the edifice was so costly (its 1885 million-dollar price tag equates to about twenty-one million dollars in 2005), but because of its sheer magnificence: the ballroom rose forty feet high, the dining room easily seated fifty, the house was filled with magnificent carvings, Tiffany glass chandeliers, Venetian mosaics, fine Chinese porcelains, and "the first Louis XVI salon to be seen in Chicago."[24]

In her account, Sister Dunstan recorded, "Many times have I heard [Mother Stanislaus] describe her time spent in the Potter Palmer house. It was a mansion ... a showplace ... [and] resemble[d] an art gallery

The renowned Potter Palmer mansion on Chicago's Lake Shore Drive became home for a short while to Sister M. Stanislaus. (Courtesy of the Chicago Historical Society)

rather than a private home."[25] Her assessment was accurate, but the blue-veiled sister would not have recognized much of the art surrounding her since many of the works were done by a fairly new and unknown group of French painters—Monet, Renoir, and Manet—whose style Mrs. Palmer greatly admired. When she bought these works in the early 1890s, she was "very much criticized for throwing her money away,"[26] but after her death, the Palmer family's donation of fifty-two of these paintings to the Art Institute of Chicago, made its Impressionist Collection one of the finest in the country.

According to Sister Dunstan, when Sister Stanislaus spoke of the days during which she stayed with the crème de la crème of Chicago society, she recalled:

> ... the friends of the Potter Palmers—the "Who's Who" in Chicago at that time—their meetings there, the parties—the magnificent gowns and jewels worn—the laughter and dancing in the ballroom, while ... taking a good many peeks from the staircase above ... [of] thoroughly enjoy[ing] every minute of it, [yet still] thinking how soon she would leave it all and get back to Rome and dear old Fiesole and Florence.[27]

But Providence had something else in store for her. Not long after she arrived in the United States, the Chicago Foundation received the following telegram: "Sister M. Stanislaus is to remain in the Chicago house until further notice."[28] The following month the Generalate Council in Rome appointed her as the new assistant Superior. [29]

Thus, the 1902 death of an American woman in Florence brought together two women whose lifestyles could not have been more different. The young Irish nursing sister, who wore the pale blue veil of the Little Company of Mary, lived a life committed to God through quiet service to ordinary and often poor families. The middle-aged Chicago socialite, whose signature necklaces included a "seven-strand collar of 2,268 pearls"[30] and a choker comprised of more than one thousand diamonds,[31] enjoyed a life of leisure and a circle of friends that included presidents and royalty. Yet in Mrs. Palmer's time of personal tragedy, a Little Company of Mary Sister bridged the gap by bringing healing comfort to "The Queen of Chicago society,"[32] something neither her wealth nor power could provide.

Sister Stanislaus remained in America for fifty-nine years. She served as Novice Mistress, assistant Superior, and Superior of two foundations, and oversaw the opening of a novitiate, a nursing school, and hospitals in Illinois and Indiana. "Mother Stanislaus," as she was later called, returned to Italy only for council meetings. She never again served in either her beloved Fiesole or Florence.

Bertha Honoré Palmer died of pneumonia at the age of sixty-three, having survived her husband by thirteen years. Today, they "rest in splendor underneath rows of imposing Doric columns"[33] within the largest mausoleum in Graceland Cemetery, which has earned the title of "home to Chicago's most illustrious dead."[34] Mother M. Stanislaus returned to the Lord in 1961 at the age of eighty-seven.[35] Her mortal remains are buried in St. Joseph Cemetery in Jasper, Indiana, along with five other members of the Little Company of Mary, whose modest graves, like their lives, are marked by the simple sign of the Cross.

CHAPTER FIVE

NO LONGER
MISSION TERRITORY

Photo of Mothers and Sisters present at the First LCM General Chapter in Rome (May 1914). Mother M. Patrick, representing the sisters in America, is on the far left in the second row. Mother General M. Hilda Potter (niece of Mother Mary Potter) is second from left in the first row.

The sisters in the Chicago Foundation continued to establish their reputation as excellent nurses throughout the first decade of the twentieth century. Seventeen years had elapsed since the first three members of the Little Company of Mary had arrived in the city, and during that time the congregation had increased in size and had touched the lives of thousands of Chicagoans. The high regard in which the sisters were held is evident in a letter that the Superior of the community received from Dr. John Dill Robertson, the owner of Jefferson Park Hospital, in May 1910:[1]

> I am writing to you in regard to the Jefferson Park Hospital located at the corner of Monroe and Loomis Sts. ... a hospital connected with Bennett Medical College with which Loyola University has recently affiliated.... The capacity ... is about fifty beds. It is a three-story building ... and in first-class repair ... has a nice lawn around it and the overlook over the park is beautiful.... It has a training school with thirty nurses.... In order that the hospital might be conducted by the Sisters, we are willing to sell it together with all equipment ... for $40,000. It cost us nearly $50,000. The net profits from it now are $6,000 a year. I would be pleased to make an appointment and meet you any time, if you so desire to inspect it.[2]

Two weeks later, the Reverend Henry S. Spalding, S.J., Regent of both Loyola University's School of Medicine and Law School,[3] sent additional information about the hospital to Mother Patrick on stationery still embossed with the name of St. Ignatius College, although the school officially had been renamed Loyola University Chicago the year before.[4] "The building is centrally located at the edge of one of the small parks of the city," he explained. "The place is an ideal one...." He ended the letter with a piece of advice: "If you have any intention of securing a hospital in this city, this opportunity will certainly not offer itself again." [5]

A few days afterwards, Dr. Thomas Crowe, the Irish-born County physician of Chicago[6] who had assisted in organizing Loyola Medical School[7] provided some additional input:

> Enclosed you will find a synopsis of the hospital I spoke of to you....
> I may add Fr. Spaulding [sic] is very enthusiastic about your getting control of [the] hospital.... The advantages would be great on both sides since we intend to establish the leading medical school in

Letter from Dr. Thomas Crowe to LCM Sisters in Chicago. He hoped that the sisters would buy the Jefferson Park Hospital in 1910.

America in Chicago and … the introduction of a new era in the teaching of medicine in this country … and affiliated with Loyola and an integral part of Jesuit progressiveness, it seems but meet that we should have the <u>one order</u> of sisters with us who <u>thoroughly</u> understand[s] nursing and all its details.[8] [underlined in original letter]

The offer was tempting, but beyond the reach of the seventeen-year-old Chicago Foundation. And even if the community had been in a financial position to avail itself of the opportunity, the sisters would probably have been somewhat hesitant to buy the hospital precisely because of its location. Some years earlier, their founder had cautioned members against competing with other congregations of nursing sisters, and three of Chicago's fourteen Catholic hospitals—St. Anthony's, Mercy, and St. Joseph's—were quite close to Jefferson Park Hospital.[9] When the Little Company of Mary established its own hospital two decades later, the facility would be miles away from downtown Chicago and distanced from any other community of nursing sisters.

The U.S. Catholic population in 1910 had grown to well over fourteen million[10]—an increase of almost four million from only ten years before. Pope Pius X removed the Church in the United States from the jurisdiction of the Congregation for the Propagation of the Faith in 1908, meaning that "America was no longer regarded as missionary territory."[11] The Catholic Church in the United States had come a long way from Colonial times, when Catholics were persecuted by fellow colonists who had fled to America in search of their own religious freedom.

Historians have described the years between 1898 and 1914 as an era that offered "the promise of unlimited progress—the rapid development of the automobile, the proliferation of telephones, the increasing use of electricity, and the invention of the airplane seemed to confirm the promise."[12] Life was becoming easier for many Americans as an ever-increasing number of "modern" conveniences became part of their lives. Women still wore long dresses, but the "hobble skirt," so-called because its narrow design forced its wearer to take tiny steps, was coming into vogue. Movies had become the latest rage, ragtime music was popular, and more Americans than ever were buying cars. Life expectancy was 48.4 years for men and 51.8 years for women, and only one marriage in a thousand ended in divorce.[13]

By the second decade of the twentieth century, America looked and felt quite different than it had at the turn of the century. The United States was now the most industrialized country in the world. Labor unions continued to grow as workers became increasingly unhappy with working conditions, and there was still no federal legislation to prevent or limit the hours that children could work in factories, mills, and mines.[14]

War broke out in Europe in 1914, following the assassination of Archduke Franz Ferdinand, heir to the Austrian throne. That same year, Pius X died, and the cardinals, mindful of the diplomatic talents of Giacomo della Chiesa, elected him as successor. Benedict XV, as he was known, understood the necessity of maintaining strict neutrality, which he did so skillfully that the "Allies called him pro-German [and the] Germans called him pro-Ally."[15] In 1914, the pontiff proposed the idea of a general Christmas truce to end what he called "the suicide of Europe,"[16] and although his plan was not implemented, he was able to get disabled prisoners exchanged through neutral countries and have sick and wounded prisoners sent to neutral countries to recuperate.

The United States resisted entry into the conflict by maintaining a neutralist position until 1917. In January of that year, the German government notified President Wilson of the resumption of unrestricted submarine warfare, a policy that had led to the torpedoing of the *Lusitania* two years earlier. The British liner had sunk off the coast of Ireland with a loss of about twelve hundred lives, one hundred eighteen of which were American. On April 6, 1917, after the sinking of five U.S. vessels and following the British interception and decoding of the Zimmerman telegram, (a dispatch from Arthur Zimmerman, the German state secretary for foreign affairs, to the German minister in Mexico City, telling him to advise the Mexican president that "if the United States went to war with Germany, Germany would form an alliance with Mexico ... enabling Mexico to get back its 'lost territories'"[17] [i.e., Texas, New Mexico, and Arizona]), the President asked Congress for a declaration of war, "to make the world safe for democracy."[18] During America's nineteen-month involvement "over there," fifty-three thousand Americans died in battle; more than sixty-three thousand succumbed to disease. [19]

In 1917, Benedict XV promulgated a new code of Canon Law. This ecclesiastical legislation codified and extended the restrictions toward all congregations of active Catholic religious women set forth by Pope Leo XIII earlier in the century. As Elizabeth West points out, it had numerous detrimental effects, including negating the charism of a religious congregation, which gives a particular community its unique spiritual identity and mission in the Church. It also imposed strict limitations on the sisters' work and behavior, which "... thrust women [religious] back into a role [of] ... childlike dependency."[20] Since Mary Potter's community originally embodied both missionary and apostolic elements, and this legislation essentially did away with those components of the congregation, "the effect ... was to alter the shape of the institute."[21] In the eyes of the Church, the Little Company of Mary was seen simply as a nursing community without its distinctive spirituality and unique charism. Almost fifty years would go by before the value of those elements would be recognized, and a new Code of Canon Law affecting religious life would not go into effect until 1983.[22]

The sisters were able to pay off the mortgage on their home and three adjacent properties on Indiana Avenue in June 1917 because of a ten thousand dollar bequest left by the late Charles A. Mair. His gift enabled the Chicago Foundation to be "free of debt or incumbrance [*sic*] of any kind."[23] The following year, the committee proposed:

> To place at the disposal of the Government under the patronage of the
> Knights of Columbus for the time being, the property known as
> 4116, 4120, 4126 Indiana Avenue, for the use of wounded Soldiers
> and Sailors or the sick of the Army, as they saw fit, the sick and
> wounded to be nursed by the Sisters of the Little Company of Mary.[24]

According to the corporation minutes, "the motion was carried with
enthusiasm."[25] The government never took the sisters up on their offer
because five months later, on November 11, 1918, the "war to end all
wars" ceased with the signing of the armistice in France. Peace in Europe
would last a little more than two decades.

That same year, a virulent influenza swept through much of the
world, killing almost one hundred million people—more than five
hundred thousand in the United States. The "Spanish flu," as it was called,
received its name "because only Spanish newspapers were publishing
accounts of the spread of the disease."[26] All other countries imposed
some form of censorship to avoid causing panic. New research shows that
the flu did not originate in Europe, but probably began in Haskell
County, Kansas, quickly reached a nearby army camp, and moved east
with American troops. After being carried overseas, the initial virus,
which was fairly mild, mutated into a deadly strain, and was brought
back to the United States by returning servicemen.[27] As the soldiers
arrived home, "the epidemic hit the East Coast ports like wildfire."[28]
In October 1918, the flu was declared an epidemic in Chicago. During
one week alone (October 8-14), 11,239 cases were reported in the city
resulting in 1,461 deaths. [29]

An Illinois newspaper reported:

> City and State Health authorities were to meet here today to give
> their final decision on the question of the closing of churches,
> saloons, cabarets, schools, pool rooms and ice cream parlors as a
> result of influenza. An order closing theaters and movie picture
> houses went into effect yesterday through-out [sic] Illinois.

> During the last 24 hours, there were 317 deaths in Chicago alone,
> due to the epidemic ... [and] 2,221 new cases reported in the city.
> According to reports compiled by Dr. C. St. Clair Drake, State Health

Commissioner, the disease has affected 300,000 persons in the State of Illinois. [30]

Although the Illinois Superintendent of Public Health had privately recommended that all places of business be closed for a time to save lives, "Chicago Public Health Commissioner John Dill Robertson violently rejected that suggestion as unwarranted.... He later explained, 'It is our duty to keep the people from fear. Worry kills more people than the epidemic.'"[31] His seemingly preposterous statement was partially accurate. According to historian John Barry, "Fear really did kill people. It killed them because those who feared would not care for many of those who needed but could not find care, those who needed only hydration, food, and rest to live."[32]

Not surprisingly, the blue-veiled sisters were intrepid in the face of an epidemic in which "young adults, the healthiest and strongest part of the population, were the most likely to die."[33] The sisters undoubtedly provided nursing to many flu victims, although they only recorded one particular case. An Indiana teacher named John Tierney traveled to Chicago to get help for a relative who had come down with the influenza. How Tierney heard of the Little Company of Mary is unknown, but he spoke with Mother Patrick, who responded to his request by sending Sister Rosarii Hassett to care for his cousin, who eventually recovered.[34] The Spanish flu indirectly had one long-lasting effect on the community. Two decades later, John Tierney remembered the excellent care and kindness provided by the congregation and reached out to the sisters for assistance in his own life. They responded a second time and established a community-altering connection that would eventually result in their presence in San Pierre, Indiana.

Despite the sisters' close contact with "the plague," as it was called, not one member of the Little Company of Mary in Chicago succumbed to the deadly disease. The Spanish flu, however, did impact the community in a roundabout way. A former member, who had been granted secularization (dispensation from her vows) in the spring of 1918, died of influenza that October in a public hospital. The sisters saw to it that the woman, formerly known as Sister Mary Dismas, was buried in the consecrated ground of the lot belonging to them at Calvary Cemetery.[35]

The early 1900s had been years of unexpected growth for the

Document (1922) from Rome regarding the division of Provinces. Another thirty-three years would elapse before America became a separate Province.

American Catholic Church because of large numbers of Catholic immigrants from southern and eastern Europe. By 1918, however, a big change had taken place. Historian Charles Shanabruch believes "World War I was a watershed for the Catholic Church in Chicago, as the immigrant Church assumed a new identity, American Catholicism. [Now] [t]he majority of the Catholic constituency was American by birth, and the decline in immigration, due to the war, ensured continuance of this fact." [36]

On June 20, 1921, Mother M. Stanislaus was appointed as Superior of the Chicago Foundation. [37] The following year, the Sacred Congregation for Religious, which oversaw the workings of all religious congregations, notified the Council in Rome that the Little Company of Mary had to divide itself into provinces. It had been suggested to the sisters that the houses in Ireland and America form one province, but the Council decided to "lay before His Eminence the Cardinal Vicar, the difficulties with regard to ... [this] scheme...." [38] Council members objected to "the impracticality of making an Irish American Province, on account of the great distance between America and Ireland, which would render communication difficult [and] make it almost impossible to have the annual visitation on account of the great expense," and felt that such partition "would also divide the Irish Sisters in England from those in Ireland, and cause fresh discontent and dissension." [39]

In August 1922, Mother General M. Hilda Potter sent a Translation of a Decree from the Sacred Congregation to Mother M. Rita Carroll (in South America), informing her that the Little Company of Mary had been divided into Provinces, and added:

> ... though we had not expected [this] quite so soon, [it] is what would eventually have taken place in a Congregation that has spread so widely as we have.... For you and the Sisters in Chicago, there will be no change at all for the present.... [U]ntil you grow much bigger, you [will] remain as you are, detached from any Province and subject to the Mother House [sic] only. I think that part of the decision will please you all, as it certainly pleased dear Mother Patrick....
>
> All the Provinces will have special titles of their own, for as far as possible we want to leave nationality aside, and be as ever "One in the Heart of Mary our Mother...."
>
> The American Houses must begin to grow now, so that later on you will become another of Our Lady's Provinces....
>
> [T]here is a great deal to be done before the Provinces are properly started in working order. Will you pray earnestly ... that all may turn out well, for God's greater glory and for the good of dear Lady's Little Company all over the world? [40]

Several decades would elapse before the hope for an American Province became a reality, but as the Little Company of Mary reached its thirtieth year of service in the United States, the number of American-born sisters was slowly increasing. Between 1909 and 1925, ten American women joined the community,[41] which only a few years before had been composed almost entirely of Irish-born sisters.

Four years before the first sisters arrived in the United States, Mother [Mary Potter] had written of her hope that her daughters would serve in America:

> I have promised a sister ... for a sick lady to return with her to America in September. She does wish [that] we could be established there. I think with so many wishing it and the evident need there is, it might be arranged in the course of time.
>
> A House in America would be a great help to the whole Community

in many ways, and I think our simple, free spirit would suit the Americans....[42]

Since vocations continued to increase, it seems that she had been right—the simple, free spirit of the community was appealing to Americans. However, once the United States was no longer mission territory, a set of stricter ecclesiastical rules took effect. The Motherhouse also sent additional regulations which mandated that "the temporarily professed novices [are] to go to Mercy Hospital until final vows [and] novices must make their vows on the day they are due." The sisters were also reminded that "Novices are to be separated entirely from the Professed,"[43] something that had not been strictly observed in the community's earliest days.

By their third decade in Chicago, the congregation had become more established and well known. The ever-increasing number of sisters reached out to more and more people, and not just through nursing, as a document dated 1923 illustrates:

> ... all [LCM Sisters] visited the poor and also sick families [and] brought them food and Sister Barbara made dresses and suits for the children making their First Holy Communion. When the neighbors knew [the sisters] were taking care of the sick, the good news spread to Chicago and other places. Well they had meetings on account of the ... [hope] that if the L.C.M. would build a hospital they could take care of 5 & 6 patients at a time, instead of being in a poor home for several days. [44]

After years of struggling financially, the congregation received sizable bequests from the widow of Charles Mair and from the estate of Florence Lewis,[45] which provided a portion of the capital necessary to begin planning for the realization of one of their dreams.

The greatest change in the Little Company of Mary's apostolate since the sisters' arrival into America's heartland was about to take place. Their days of home nursing were coming to an end, but a new phase of their mission was about to begin. Within a few years, the community would relocate to Evergreen Park, a relatively unknown village southwest of Chicago, where the sisters would begin to care for patients in a hospital that would bear their name—a hospital that they could truly call their own.

For several decades, a small cottage on South Indiana Avenue, served as the LCM Sisters' first convent in America.

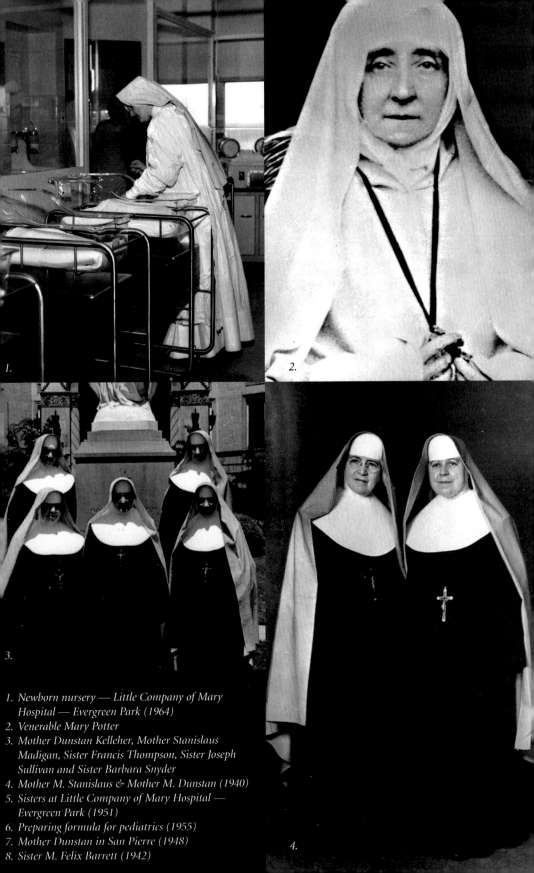

1. *Newborn nursery — Little Company of Mary Hospital — Evergreen Park (1964)*
2. *Venerable Mary Potter*
3. *Mother Dunstan Kelleher, Mother Stanislaus Madigan, Sister Francis Thompson, Sister Joseph Sullivan and Sister Barbara Snyder*
4. *Mother M. Stanislaus & Mother M. Dunstan (1940)*
5. *Sisters at Little Company of Mary Hospital — Evergreen Park (1951)*
6. *Preparing formula for pediatrics (1955)*
7. *Mother Dunstan in San Pierre (1948)*
8. *Sister M. Felix Barrett (1942)*

5.

6.

7.

8.

CHICAGO Sept 8th 1892

Revd & Dear Madam

You have doubtless wondered at my silence, and thought that I had forgotten the very important matter on which Mother Philip & Mother Catherine visited me in London. But I have not done this, and have today, had my interview with Arch-Bishop Feehan to ask his permission for your Order to enter this Diocese and his approval of my enterprise in bringing your Sisters out. His Lordship was very glad to give his endorsement and approbation, saying "we cannot have too many of such Orders, who honestly and humbly give themselves to serving God and ministering to the suffering." I read him the letter you sent me from Simeoni, and told him of your work in Rome & Florence and in Sydney. He asked what means you had for support & I answered "none but contributions & such pay as those nursed choose to give." The field is great here

CHICAGO

and I have no question whatever as to the success of the venture in time.

Now what I wish to say is this. I will undertake bringing such Sisters from England to Chicago as you consider wise and proper to send. I would rent a house for their comfortable maintenance for such time as they need and until they have been long enough established in Chicago to decide which is the most suitable quarter for a permanent establishment. In my own opinion its location should be not far from the Jesuit Church & house, or near the Benedictine Fathers, both of which Orders are in the midst of large populations of not poor, but very medium class people. I shall furnish the house simply, supply articles needed for the room set apart as a Chapel, supply fuel and

2.

Letter from Charles Mair to Mother Mary Potter (1892)

2. Page 2 of Charles Mair's letter

San Antonio de Areco
December 26th 1898

My Dear Revd Mother

Please let me know can the Sisters come now. The Hospital being almost ready (which in a month will be completed) I hope if it be possible that they come soon.

The way of your answer shall remit the necessary funds for their journey.

When in Rome a year ago I thought long before this the good Sisters would be in San Antonio de Areco but unforseen obstacles prevented me from doing so.

Now that every thing here is in order I hope there will be no more difficulties in their path

Awaiting your answer Please remember me most kindly to all the good kind Srs whom I had the honor of knowing while in Rome, and you

4.

[Page 5 — top left]

CHARLES A. MAIR,
ROYAL INS. BUILDING.

CHICAGO ....

food until the Sisters get
on their feet and find their
reward from those they serve.

In other words I wish to
act as their protector in giving
them shelter & food till they are
able to do without such aid
and to bring them out.

I shall await your answer
to this with interest and you
must write me fully of any
ideas you have different to or
contrary to the matters set out
above.

I have been exceedingly
well since returning and hope
equally good health has been your
lot and that of your sisters.

I am Rev. Mother,
Yours very sincerely,
Chas A. Mair.

5.

5. Page 3 of Charles Mair's letter

[Page 6 — bottom left]

Rev Mother all kind
of fond wishes
from your most
obediently
Margaret Morgan

6.

[Page 7 — top right]

Story of the Chicago Foundation
Opened 31st May - 1893 -

The first Convent of the "Little Company"
in America was donated in loving
memory of his wife - whom the
Sisters had nursed during her
illness in Rome - by Charles A. Mair
who brought them over from Europe
and provided for all their wants
until they were fully started in
their new home.

On the 24th of April 1893 - with the
Blessing and approbation of our
Holy Father Leo XIII - on their mission
and with the fervent prayers and
blessing of our dear Mother General
and all the Community - the three
M. M. Veronica, M. M. Patrick, & Sr. Philo—

7.

[Page 8 — bottom right]

appointed to open this our first
Convent in the New World - bade
farewell to dear old Rome & all
the loved ones there. Dear M. M.
Philip & M. M. Cecilia accompanied
them to Genoa, where they arrived
the morning of the 25th
good Mrs White received them &
and on the morning of the 26th
Feast of "Our Lady of good Counsel"
After Mass - Holy Communion and
Benediction of the most Holy Sacrament
we went on board the S.S. Kaiser W—
bound for New York. As we steamed
out of the harbour, the little band
stood on deck looking with tearful
eyes at dear M. M. Philip & Cecilia
they stood on shore waving their
handkerchiefs till they became
lost in the distance. & then we
felt quite alone!
But our dear Lord was good to—
in giving us the happiness of

8.

Mother M. Stanislaus Madigan, Mother M. Dorothea Dwight,
Sister M. Fidelis Ward, Sister Mary Anne Kohler (1938)
Operating Room Sister (1939)
Newspaper article about the Little Company of Mary
(Buenos Aires) (1938)
Sisters in surgery (1951)
New convent — Evergreen Park (1951)
A relaxing moment (1956)

THE BLUE NUNS

A Little-Known Religious Order

AFTER the usual monthly meeting of the ladies of the Catholic Club, held yesterday afternoon in the library of the Merced Church, Mrs. Nona Greene, the president, accompanied by many of the members, including Mrs. R. M. Konan, wife of the British consul-general, paid a visit to the Little Company of Mary, a religious order of trained hospital nurses who are busy turning a beautiful, large, family mansion into a modern, practical nursing home at Avenida Alvear 3576.

The order of the Little Company of Mary is English and was founded in England by Mother Mary Potter in 1877, although its headquarters are in Rome. Its religious have charge of 25 private hospitals in all parts of the world; a large one in Chicago, one in Australia, Sidney, and the Calvary Hospital in Rome, being amongst the best known. Its members possess the highest nursing certificates and are popularly known as the "Blue Nuns" because of the colour of their veils.

The ladies were received at the inviting and spacious entrance of the edifice, by the Mother Superior and shown all over the building by her and three other nuns who are supervising the work of reorganisation. The Mother Superior, who has been eight years in this country, was previously at San Antonio de Areco, where a hospital run by this order was established by Mrs. Clara Morgan.

It is hoped to open the new nursing home in about three months' time. The building was formerly the property of the Goldaracena family, and is only about eight years old. Many structural changes will have to be made, such as the building of an operating theatre on the top floor, the addition of many bathrooms on the floor where the previous residents had their reception rooms, a corridor the length of the rooms on this floor and the division of two of the rooms into smaller ones.

Enthusiasm shone on the bright faces of the nuns as they explained all their plans for the conversion of the building and all their hopes for the future. Down a few steps at the entrance, is a large room which it is proposed to turn into a chapel, and down a few more steps at one side, are two smaller, low chambers, one of which may be suitable for the sacristy.

The roomy drawing-room, with its marble table, and mantelpiece, will be divided into two single rooms, and a ward will open off it onto a glassed-in enclosure which looks onto the lovely garden at the back of the premises where a beautiful" loggia" adjoins a fine fives court. Enormous marble shelves and sinks are built in the vast pantry, which will probably be re-arranged for maternity cases.

The bedrooms and bathrooms on the next floor will require little alterations. They are equipped with numerous luxurious bathrooms, with marble fittings, and built in cupboards, and the principal bedroom is a magnificent apartment with rounded-off corners. A lovely view out over Avenida Alvear can be seen from the balcony of these bedrooms, and specially charming was that from the balcony of the room used by the young lady of the family.

A splendid laundry occupies the top floor, and should be of great practical use to the new nursing-home, as will also be the extensive kitchen and servants' quarters which were the last parts of the mansion to be visited by the admiring members of the Catholic Club. A new commodious kitchen range is in pro-

of being installed in the -tiled kitchen, and a chute all refuse down from each to the incinerator below in the basement is the fur- for the central heating.

The nursing-home is to have about twenty-five beds, and later the sisters hope to start an efficient training school for nurses.

4.

5.

1. Sister & Newborn (1964)
2. Religious Profession (1964)
3. Celebrating Christmas in Syracuse (1956)
4. Final resting place of Venerable
   Mary Potter — St. Barnabas
   Cathedral — Nottingham (1997)
5. Original By-Laws of the
   Little Company of Mary
6. Hospital — San Antonio de Areco
7. Sister M. Michael Murray with
   nurses in pediatrics

The Little Company of Mary
Incorporated

— By-Laws of the Society —

Article 1.
— Name and Object —

Section 1. This Society shall be known as The Little Company of Mary; its principal office and location shall be in Chicago, Cook County, Illinois.

Sec 2. The object and purpose of this society is the establishing and conducting of a house or houses for the practice and promotion of Christian charity and especially of nursing and caring for the sick and indigent and of providing and training nurses for such purpose in the State of Illinois, and particularly in the city of Chicago in said

5.

6.

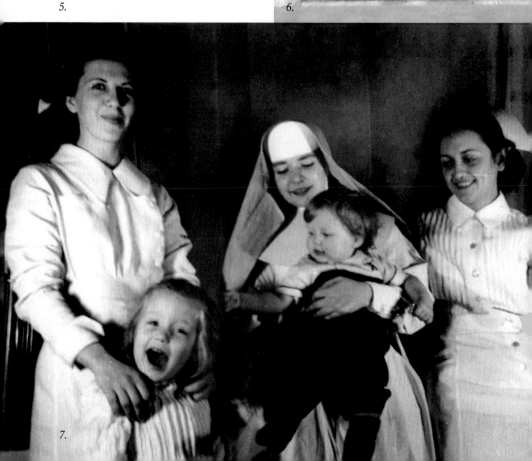

7.

CHAPTER SIX

PROMISES TO KEEP

Letter dated December 26, 1898, from Margaret Morgan to Mother Mary Potter requesting that the LCM Sisters come to Argentina.

San Antonio de Areco, one of the oldest settlements in Argentina, lies almost six thousand miles southwest of Chicago in the heart of the humid pampas—a fertile, grassy plain known for cattle raising and sheep ranching. In 1913, four sisters from the Little Company of Mary's Chicago Foundation arrived there to begin working in a tiny rural hospital amid the area's Irish-Argentine people. How they happened to be in such a distant place is tied to events that occurred in 1893, twenty years earlier. But the Spanish-Irish connection—an integral part of the story—dates back to the beginning of the nineteenth century.

At that time in Ireland, many of the harsh Penal Laws imposed on Catholics by English Protestants after the Reformation were still in effect. These laws, which severely restricted education, landholding, marriage, inheritance, and even the practice of the Catholic faith, led thousands of Irish to leave their homeland for countries that offered greater opportunity and freedom.

Between 1845 and 1849, a pernicious blight destroyed Ireland's potato crop. One million people starved during the Great Famine, and emigration intensified. Escaping from the Emerald Isle became not so much a bid to improve one's life but rather a desperate attempt to avoid dying. Almost one hundred thousand predominantly Catholic Irish immigrated to London. Like America, Argentina was thought of as a land of possibility, so it subsequently became the destination of the largest Irish migration to a non-English-speaking land during the nineteenth century. [1]

Historian Patrick McKenna offers two reasons why nearly forty-five thousand Irish [2] uprooted themselves from the "old sod" to live in a remote place where the language and culture were so different from their Celtic traditions. The people of Ireland and Spain had a long-standing connection because of trade that flourished between the Irish port of Galway and the Spanish port of Cadiz, which eventually led to a transfer of population. The two countries also shared a strong Catholic identity dating back to the Middle Ages. A few centuries later, thousands of Irish fled to Catholic Europe and many settled in Spain during the religious persecution that occurred after the Reformation. [3]

This preexisting bond contributed to the willingness of many Irish to relocate to a country whose culture resembled that of Spain. In addition, the promise that nineteenth-century Argentina offered for employment as well as for land ownership tempted ambitious individuals who were willing to endure the arduous voyage required to reach a country located near the bottom of the world.

The first Irish immigrants settled in the nation's capital, but by the 1820s, when the government started to import European sheep, there was a growing Irish involvement in the wool industry and a subsequent migration to the Argentine countryside near San Antonio de Areco,[4] which was considered to be one of the most fertile areas of the country.[5] Within a short time, a number of Irish immigrants became quite successful in their new livelihood, not simply because "the native *gauchos* preferred cattle and had no interest in sheep,"[6] but primarily because they were "hard workers, inured to privation, [and] readily accepted the heavy seasonal labors of lambing...."[7]

One such immigrant was a young Irishman named William Mooney, who started out as a merchant in Buenos Aires[8] but quickly took up sheep farming and soon became a wealthy landowner of *estanchías* or "estates" (ranches). His daughter Margaret fell in love with Edward Morgan, whose father owned a nearby *estancía* after emigrating from Ireland via the United States. The Morgans had similarly prospered in their adopted land and in neighboring Uruguay.

Margaret Mooney and Edward Morgan, the children of two of Argentina's most successful immigrant landowners married in 1861 and were blessed with eleven children—eight boys and three girls—five of whom died in infancy or childhood.[9] After their second daughter, Catherine, died in 1878, Mrs. Morgan became even closer to her sole-surviving daughter, Mary Clare. In 1893, the two of them (accompanied by at least two sons) embarked on an adventure to the World's Columbian Exposition in Chicago.[10]

The Morgans left Buenos Aires that spring on a somewhat circuitous journey of more than twelve thousand miles that would first take them to England and then to America. Why they did not sail directly to New York is not recorded, although at that time ships traveled between Buenos Aires and Liverpool much more frequently than between Buenos Aires and New York. This itinerary would have also put them very close to Ireland, giving them the opportunity to visit relatives, something most Irish expatriates living in Argentina could not do. The vast majority of emigrants knew that once they left Ireland, they would never return to their homeland.[11]

When the Morgans boarded their ship in England, two of their fellow passengers were members of the Little Company of Mary—Sister M. Evangelist Tuohy and Sister M. Laurence Delaney. The sisters were also en route to Chicago to join the new foundation, which had begun several months earlier. Their assignment from England to the United States would bolster the community's number in America from three to five sisters. During their transatlantic crossing, Sister Evangelist and Sister Laurence became acquainted with the two Irish-Argentine women with whom they had much in common—the same faith, Irish heritage, and final destination: Chicago.

The shipboard encounter between the Morgan women and the sisters did not end when their ship docked in New York. Their chance meeting would have a significant and lasting effect on both the Morgan family and the Little Company of Mary.

The long-awaited dream of visiting the Columbian Exposition turned into a nightmare when Mary Clare suddenly became seriously ill. A priest contacted the Little Company of Mary on Mrs. Morgan's behalf to ask for their help in caring for her daughter.[12] Mother Veronica and Sister Laurence responded immediately to the Morgans' temporary residence at 6238 Drexel Avenue.[13] Despite their efforts, the young woman's condition worsened, and several days later, Mary Clare Morgan died of a cerebral hemorrhage.[14] The date was August 1, 1893, exactly one month after her twenty-eighth birthday.[15] The young Irish-Argentine woman was buried the following day in Chicago's Mount Olivet Cemetery—a temporary resting place until her remains were returned to Argentina on November 8, 1897.[16]

The loss of her third and last daughter was particularly devastating to Margaret Morgan. Her faith sustained her, however, and she was deeply touched by the sisters' devoted care of Mary Clare as well as by the kindness that they extended to her family following her daughter's death. Before leaving Chicago, Mrs. Morgan and her sons visited the sisters. She told them that she would never forget all that they had done,[17] and promised that she would build a hospital near her home in memory of her daughter, which the Little Company of Mary would own and run.

There is no record of an actual meeting between Margaret Morgan and the founder of the Little Company of Mary in 1893, although it is quite possible that the grieving mother visited Rome before returning to South America. She did visit Rome in 1897.[18] By then, Mother [Mary

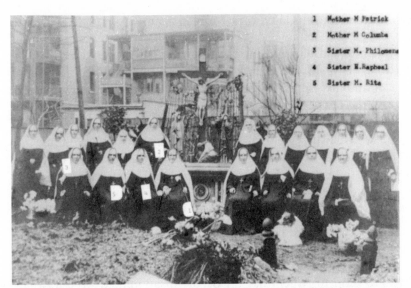

1   Mother M Patrick
2   Mother M Columba
3   Sister M. Philomena
4   Sister M.Rapheal
5   Sister M. Rita

LCM Sisters in Chicago (1913) just before five sisters (named on list) left for Argentina.

Potter] knew of Mrs. Morgan's plans of building a hospital in San Antonio de Areco and assured her that she would send the sisters necessary to run the facility.

When Margaret Morgan arrived back in San Antonio de Areco, she began working toward her goal, but the project took much longer than she had imagined. Part of the delay was due to politics. At that time, virtually all hospitals in Argentina were state-owned and operated. Consequently, civil authorities objected to Mrs. Morgan's plan to open a private institution. She also encountered opposition from contractors regarding the way in which she wanted the hospital built. All this resistance cost precious time.

Margaret Morgan's steadfast will finally prevailed. At the end of 1898, the hospital, named after her daughter, was almost finished. It was a small facility consisting of two ten-bed wards—one for men, one for women; a few private rooms; a small chapel that included a marble statue of Mary Clare Morgan; and a convent, which could accommodate nine sisters.

The day after Christmas, Mrs. Morgan wrote to the founder of the Little Company, "Please let me know. Can the Sisters come now, the hospital being about ready? Within a month it will be complete...."[19]

Five years had elapsed since Mrs. Morgan had initially shared her plans with Mother. During that time, sisters had been sent to other foundations as the need arose, so there were no sisters available for South

America. Six months later, Mrs. Morgan again wrote:

> I went to consult a most Catholic Lawyer [and] he told me that you
> would have to come or have some one here to represent your
> Community to make the transfer of the hospital to the Little
> Company of Mary legal. Now Rev. Mother, this is what I promise ...
> the title deed of the hospital is to be made to the Little Company of
> Mary while they remain in the Argentine Republic. Should the
> Sisters leave, (which I hope not), then the hospital will be placed
> under the care of the Curia "Ecclesiastical." I promise to pay all
> expenses for the hospital for ... one year. The first Sisters of the
> L.C.M. that will come ... we will pay their passage and present them
> with four hundred pounds.... [20]

Unfortunately, the situation had not changed. Mother still had no
sisters to send to Argentina.[21] A deeply disappointed Mrs. Morgan was
forced to look elsewhere for suitable nurses. She discovered that the
Sisters of Charity of St. Vincent de Paul could spare a few members of
their congregation. The community staffed Maria Clara Morgan Hospital
for twelve years, but in 1912, their Superior decided to remove them from
San Antonio de Areco and send them to a large hospital in the province
of Cordova.[22]

When this happened, Mrs. Morgan sent another letter to Rome:

> I enclose our Bishop's invitation for the Nuns of the Little Company
> of Mary to take charge of the Hospital that was built and intended
> for the Little Company of Mary as one of these sisters minded my
> daughter in her last illness in Chicago.... I hope there will be no dif-
> ficulty that you will send four sisters to take charge of this Hospital
> that was really built for them.... [23]

Margaret Morgan never relinquished the hope of bringing members
of the Little Company of Mary to the hospital that memorialized her
daughter, and ultimately, she was not disappointed. During the final
months of her life, Mother approved the creation of a new foundation in
Argentina—her community's first venture to South America and the fifth
continent to benefit from her sisters' healing presence.

In September 1912, Margaret Morgan replied to Mother Patrick in
Chicago, "Your very welcome letter has just arrived. I am pleased to hear
that there are hopes to have the Little Company of Mary in, and proprietors

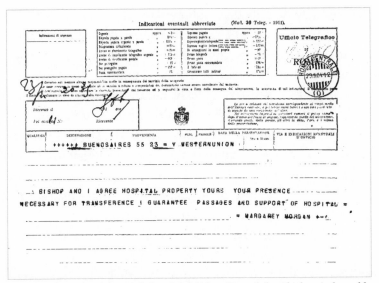

Telegram from Mrs. Morgan informing Mother General that the hospital would belong to the Little Company of Mary.

of, Maria Clara Morgan Hospital."[24] She also inquired about Sister Laurence, who had taken care of her daughter, and expressed her hope that Mother Patrick might be transferred to San Antonio. The week before Christmas, Margaret Morgan acknowledged receipt of Mother's cable from Rome, informing her "the Nuns going from Chicago," and replied, "[I] will send immediately the money for … their journey here. I am troubling you Rev. Mother as a letter reaches Rome in twenty days; it takes over a month to get to Chicago."[25]

On May 13, 1913, one month after Mary Potter's death, four members of the Little Company of Mary, accompanied by Mother M. Patrick Tuohy, Superior of the Chicago Foundation, arrived in Buenos Aires. Heading the group was Mother M. Columba Kealy, who had been appointed Superior; Sister M. Philomena Haslem, one of the original three sisters to come to the United States; Sister M. Raphael McCarthy, and Sister M. Rita Carroll. The group was warmly welcomed by the Morgan family as well as by Father Richard Gearty, who served as the chaplain to the Irish settlers, and by a group of Sisters of Mercy who ran a nearby school.

The following day, the sisters of the Little Company arrived at their new home, seventy miles northwest of Buenos Aires. It was not quite what they had expected. Conditions within the Maria Clara Morgan

Hospital could be described as rudimentary at best, since it had neither running water nor electricity. Items that normally would be considered essential for nursing care were nonexistent or unavailable. In addition, during the time that the hospital had been empty, it had become filthy and bug-infested. The sisters quickly began cleaning and painting in order to get the facility in suitable condition to accept patients.

Mother Patrick remained in San Antonio de Areco for six months, working to secure an agreement from the government that would recognize the Little Company of Mary as a civil entity—a necessary legal protection for the community because of Argentine law. After ensuring that this concession had been granted, she returned to Chicago.

When the four sisters began their nursing service at the Maria Clara Morgan Hospital, the facility belonged to the local diocese, since Mrs. Morgan had donated it to the bishop years earlier. The deed given to His Excellency, Juan Nepomuceno Terrero y Escalada, stipulated that the hospital had to retain its original name and that it could not be used for any purpose other than a hospital. Now that members of the Little Company of Mary were involved, Mrs. Morgan wanted to place the property in their hands. The prelate did not object to her request, but the high tax that this transaction would have incurred made the transfer prohibitive. Eventually the bishop ceded the hospital to the Little Company of Mary, with a clause stating that it would revert to the diocese if the sisters ever left.[26]

Life was a constant challenge for the first sisters who served in San Antonio de Areco. Much of their struggle was financial because the hospital fees did not even cover their expenses. After their first year, the members of the Little Company received no additional economic support from Mrs. Morgan, so they often had to depend on the kindness of their neighbors to provide food for their patients and themselves. The physical stamina of the pioneer sisters was continuously tested, since they had to pump water by hand for all of their needs, including the hospital linens, and prepare meals for their patients in conditions of enervating heat and humidity.

Their greatest difficulty, however, appears to have been emotional deprivation. The sisters found themselves in a secluded rural area of Argentina—thousands of miles away from the comforts of Chicago—having to adapt to an entirely different climate, culture, and standard of living. With the exception of their Irish-Argentine neighbors, they were "foreigners" living in a country whose language they neither spoke nor understood.

Adding to the community's sense of isolation was San Antonio de Areco's physical remoteness from other foundations. The sisters' only means of communication was written correspondence, and since it took a month's time for a letter to arrive from the United States,[27] the small group was often bereft of emotional support. Regarding this hardship, one of the original members of San Antonio de Areco wrote, "Privations can be put up with, but loneliness is a great handicap."[28] Despite all of this, the little group persevered.

At the end of December 1913, the sisters sent a letter to Rome that provides a glimpse into their lives in Argentina:

> Everything is such a tremendous hustle and bustle here in South America, [but] I thought I would seize the opportunity now presented to tell you how we are down here and how we spent our first Christmas....

> We were preparing for the past few weeks, house-cleaning, etc.... On Tuesday evening, in the middle of cleaning the chapel, a man was brought in, badly injured at the railway station. The four of us, and our Chaplain, Father Antonio, were all around him praying.... He was an Italian and had not been to his [Easter] duty for so long a time that he could not remember when; but was quite conscious and able to make his confession and was anointed....

> S. M. Raphael had the altars as pretty as could be, and our little crib is a dream ... not very large but neat and complete as possible.... We had everything ready and all finished in good time for Midnight Mass, which was a *Missa cantata*, no less. Then we went to the refectory and had our breakfast, as much like we used to have in Chicago as we could. You may be sure we were rather lonely, only four so far away from the other Houses, but everyone kept up fine and tried to be as bright and cheery as possible....

> It is not customary here as in the United States to give Christmas presents, so it seemed quiet and strange, no parcels to examine as in Chicago. There we always went to the Community [room] after breakfast and spent 2 or 3 hours opening and enjoying the many and varied presents sent by numerous friends and well-wishers.... But we received a goose from Mrs. Morgan and a young pig from her sister, Miss Mooney.... [N]ot one of us received any letters from relatives, but there was ... a little personal note with pictures for each from dear M. M. Patrick, written before she reached New York, and

mailed so that we would have them in time for Christmas....

We went to bed at 2 a.m. and got up at 5:45 a.m. as we expected Mrs. Morgan in to Mass early ... [and] she came at 7 a.m. After Mass Father Antonio walked down to the Crib and took out the dear little Infant Jesus and stood on the altar steps and presented Him to all present to kiss.... This is a custom in this country, where there is such a mixture of faith and devotion with ... non-observance of the laws of the Church.

[W]e spent Christmas Day very quietly.... We had a very nice dinner, roast goose, roast pig, potatoes and beans out of our own garden, rice soup, plum pudding made by S. M. Raphael, fruit and nuts, and a delicious cup of tea. We sat out in the garden after dinner.... Dear S. M. Columba read some letters for us.... We always enjoy dear S. M. Hilda's, they are so full of news, and thanks to dear M. M. Philip for her Christmas letter ... and the nice book of pictures she sent us.

The day was ... hot in the sun, but delightfully cool with a nice breeze in the shade. The garden is looking lovely, and on Christmas Day we ate the first ripe figs. There are also peach, nectarines, custard-apple and orange trees ... all are loaded, so very soon we shall have plenty of fresh, ripe fruit. The grape vines are well laden ... I wonder if it would be possible to ship a case to you....

We had a quiet day on Friday, and in the afternoon S. M. Columba told us all to take a siesta, the first time we have been able to do it since we came here. It is the custom of the country to take a siesta every afternoon.

All the Sisters join in very fond love to each dear Mother and Sisters, and wishing you all the joy of the coming New Year. How glad we shall be when 1913 is ended....[29]

Five years into their mission, the sisters suffered the loss of Mother M. Columba, the Superior who had provided leadership and example to the small community. She became seriously ill and died suddenly in November 1918. In early February 1919, Sister M. Rita Carroll received a letter from the Motherhouse in Rome notifying her that she was to be in charge of the community:

First of all ... what a comfort in this sad time of trial and sorrow the knowledge of your loyalty and having cared for our dear Mother Columba has been to all of us. You have acted as our dear Lady would have wished ... and she will reward and help you now in your loneliness and sorrow.... Now dear Mother wishes me to tell you that for the present ... you must take charge of the little community in San Antonio. You have worked with our loved Mother Columba and know so well what she wished and planned and will do your best to carry out everything she desired....

You will be glad to know that dear Mother Patrick is sending you two Sisters from Chicago and they may arrive, perhaps, before this reaches you. As yet we do not know who they are, as we have only had a cable to say that they are leaving for Buenos Aires on the 18th of the month. But whomever Mother Patrick may have chosen, they are sure to be ones whom she can trust to help and comfort you all in your loneliness....

And now she wants you, dear Sister, to take up the work and the responsibility, for the time being, that our dear one had carried so bravely, and she begs you to do your best to encourage and to help the other Sisters.... Keep close to our Lady's Sweet Maternal Heart and she will give you the light and grace to fulfill God's Will....[30]

As the years passed, the sisters learned to speak Spanish—hesitantly at first, and then more comfortably—allowing them to extend their nursing care outside the confines of the hospital and into the homes of families who did not speak English.[31]

In 1924, Mother M. Alocoque D'Arcy was appointed to represent the South American community at the General Chapter in Rome. The following year, Sister M. Joseph Sullivan from the Chicago Foundation was named as the new Superior. Thirteen years would go by, however, before a canonical visit to San Antonio de Areco took place—attesting to its inaccessibility. On May 27, 1926, Mother M. Hilda Potter, the Superior General of the congregation, along with Mother M. Gonzaga Maddigan, visited the sisters in Argentina for the first time in thirteen years.

During her visitation, Mother Hilda planned to announce that the sisters would leave the Maria Clara Morgan Hospital. Several reasons factored into her decision—the size of the hospital, the small number of patients, the few sisters available, and even the almost total lack of local vocations to the community. Even though the population of the surrounding area was virtually one hundred percent Catholic, only one young woman from the area had joined the Little Company.

Mother Hilda met with Francisco Alberti, the Bishop of La Plata, only to have him deny her request to have the sisters leave the diocese. Instead, His Excellency proposed that the community expand their nursing to include maternity cases as well as those with infectious diseases. He assured the Superior General that a new building would be provided for patients needing to be quarantined. She accepted his offer, and in 1927 the people of San Antonio de Areco generously donated the money required to construct a pavilion, which opened later that year, for patients with yellow fever, typhoid, cholera, and similar endemic diseases. In 1929, Sister M. Fintan Kealy (sister of the late Mother Columba), became the community's fourth Superior, and the facility grew to include fifty beds and ten sisters.[32]

The work of the sisters in South America eventually expanded—first, with a small private hospital in Buenos Aires, then with a larger city hospital, and finally to the people in the nearby *villas,* the temporary migrant shantytowns. In 1956, the members of the Little Company of Mary left the remote Argentine countryside to work solely within the nation's capital.

But the promise made by a grief-stricken Irish-Argentine mother to build a hospital for the nursing sisters who had provided comfort and compassion during her daughter's final hours had been kept. And the commitment of the founder of the Little Company of Mary to send some of her own daughters to South America was likewise fulfilled.

For forty-three years, the promises made good by two loving mothers resulted in a mission of hope and healing in a remote section of Argentina by a small group of nursing sisters—mostly Irish-born or of Irish-American heritage—who soon became known by their Spanish name: *Pequeña Compañía de María.*[33]

Statue of Mary Clare Morgan, originally situated within the hospital chapel at San Antonio de Areco, today can be found in the courtyard.

The inscription, "Blessed is he who considers the needy and the poor" (Psalm 40) is followed by the words, "She flew to a better life from Chicago— August 1, 1893—Pray for her.

CHAPTER SEVEN

FIELD OF DREAMS

An empty prairie field became the unlikely site for the first LCM hospital in America.

Two members of the Little Company of Mary en route from Rome to Chicago reached New York on the morning of the June 6, 1925. One of them, Mother M. Xavier Roarty, had just been appointed to a three-year term as Superior of the still-fledgling American foundation. The other, Sister M. Padua O'Neill, was assigned to perform whatever duties the community required.

Summer would not officially begin for another two weeks, but the sisters' first day in America was unbearably hot. They had been invited to stay at the Convent of the Good Shepherd for several days by the Superior, Sister Rosalita. As they made their way to 90th Street and East River Drive, they encountered the shrieks and laughter of children who ran through streams of water and jumped into the huge puddles created by hoses manned by members of the New York Fire Department, which provided some relief from the sweltering heat.[1] For Mother Xavier and Sister Padua, their first impression of America was that it was a place of constant rush and noise.[2]

During their brief stay in New York City, the sisters attended a Requiem Mass at St. Patrick's Cathedral for Monsignor Charles O'Hern, whom they had known in Rome, where he was rector of the American College. The forty-three-year-old former native of Chicago had died several weeks earlier of pneumonia while visiting his family.[3] Afterwards, the sisters were presented to Patrick Joseph Cardinal Hayes, head of the Archdiocese of New York.[4] Several days later on their journey westward, they also met with the bishop of Rochester. Such meetings would prove crucial to the expansion of the Little Company of Mary because the congregation was still fairly new to the United States and, unlike larger and older communities of religious, was not well known outside of Chicago.

By the time the Little Company of Mary Sisters came to the United States, the first Catholic sisters, Ursulines from France, had already been working in the country for 166 years. These pioneering women religious, who arrived in 1727, settled in New Orleans and quickly established an academy for young women in that city. Eighty-two years later, twenty-nine-year-old Elizabeth Bayley Seton, a widow with five children and a convert to Catholicism, founded the Sisters of Charity, the first American religious community for women and the one which initiated the country's first parochial school system in Baltimore.[5] Throughout the 1800s, dozens of European religious congregations sent sisters to America.

In 1827, seven Sisters of Charity became the first nursing sisters in America when they started working at the Baltimore Infirmary in Maryland.[6] The following year, the Daughters of Charity founded the first Catholic hospital in Saint Louis,[7] and "Between 1828 and 1860, these Sisters ... opened eighteen hospitals in ten different states and the District of Columbia; ... more than half of the twenty-eight Catholic hospitals established before the Civil War."[8]

In 1847, seven Irish Sisters of Mercy established the first Catholic school in a backwater, iron-making town called Pittsburgh where Catholics numbered twelve thousand.[9] John Fialka, author of *Sisters: Catholic Nuns and the Making of America* explains:

> House calls were the beginning and the end of medical treatment west of the Alleghenies in those days. It was Bishop O'Connor's long-standing dream to build Pittsburgh's first hospital, and he and the Mercies collaborated to turn a building the sisters had used as a convent and an academy into a hospital capable of handling 150 patients. [10]

Four years later, they established Mercy Hospital in Chicago, where some of the first members of Little Company of Mary in the United States would later receive their training.

Exactly what duties the earliest nursing sisters provided is not recorded, but it is likely that their responsibilities included dispensing medication, treating wounds, changing dressings, bathing patients, changing bed linens, serving food, and providing spiritual support. [11]

As the Civil War raged between 1861 and 1865, numerous sisters distinguished themselves by caring for both Union and Confederate soldiers. According to historian Sister Mary Denis Maher, the religious who engaged in those nursing activities " ... probably represented one-fifth of all the sisters in the United States at the outbreak of the war."[12] Twelve different congregations offered their services, with the Daughters of Charity of Emmitsburg, Maryland, by far contributing the most sisters—two hundred thirty-two—during the course of the conflict, in thirty different locations. [13]

Their heroic efforts saved countless lives and provided physical relief and spiritual assistance under horrific circumstances. In addition, Maher singles out several major contributions that arose from their dedicated service:

First, they brought a tradition and history of commitment to nursing derived from centuries of European sisters being involved in care of the sick. Second, they earned the recognition on both sides of the Atlantic, from Nightingale and others who desired to initiate reforms for the betterment of the sick ... with their two-fold combination of nursing skills and religious commitment.... Third, the communities running the Catholic hospitals ... showed a willingness to consider service to other hospitals when the need arose. Fourth and foremost, the written regulations of their community life served as a training manual for how patients should be treated.... [14]

An unexpected consequence of the sisters' nursing service at this time was a change in attitude toward Catholics. Fialka contends that the Civil War marked a major change in the perception of many Americans:

It was a new era for Catholics in the U.S. While bigotry certainly still lingered on in the nation's many social nooks and crannies, the searing experience of the Civil War had demystified Catholics for the average American. Soldiers on both sides had fought alongside Catholics and found they carried their share of the battle. As for the sisters, they were heroes to hundreds of thousands of young men who had never met a Catholic. But they had seen nuns working under fire and in the blood, gore, pain, and chaos of military hospitals. [15]

When the first members of the Little Company of Mary arrived in America in 1893, the Civil War had been over for twenty-eight years. Seven years later, at the turn of the century, the number of Catholic sisters in the United States had grown to 46,000. By 1920, that number had almost doubled, as "approximately 90,000 women, representing 300 separate religious communities were working in American education, health care, or social service institutions." [16]

The situation that the pioneering sisters encountered in Chicago was appreciably different from what the first sisters experienced in Nottingham in 1877 or in Rome in 1882, where the Little Company of Mary was able to provide nursing services that had not previously existed. Numerous nursing congregations preceded the blue-veiled sisters to Chicago, some predating the "newcomers" by as many as sixty-five years. In addition, during the late 1920s, when the Little Company of Mary was still planning to build its first hospital, several Catholic hospitals run by nursing sisters had been operating in Chicago for more than fifty years. Thus, Mary Potter's daughters found themselves at another disadvantage— they were neither as large as many of the religious communities in the Chicago area, nor had they the chance to establish a widespread reputation through decades of hospital service.

Mother Xavier would have been aware of this as she headed westward to Chicago. She was about to begin her tenure as Superior, during which she would lay the groundwork for a new phase in the history of the Chicago Foundation. The previous three decades in America had been a time of financial difficulty for the growing community of the Little Company of Mary. Although Charles Mair had covered the initial expenses of the sisters' journey to America's heartland and had provided them with their first home, the community members had been responsible for the expenses of their everyday lives for more than thirty years.

The sisters earned part of their living through the nursing cases that they took on, but in the early years, this sometimes did not provide enough income. The apostolate of the Little Company of Mary required that the sisters assist all who sought their help. Years before, their founder had written, "If the sick are in a position in which they can pay, the Sisters will receive remuneration. They will always nurse the poor gratis."[17] At times, they did receive payment for their services, but frequently the sisters were given food or another form of recompense, and there were occasions when they received almost nothing. Like the earliest members of the community in Hyson Green, the sisters had to resort to begging for their sustenance, even to the point of going to the car barns on payday to seek contributions from the trolley operators.[18] As the Little Company of Mary became better known throughout the area, pastors of nearby Catholic churches occasionally invited them to seek contributions from church members.

Halfway through their third decade in Chicago, the number of sisters had increased more than seven-fold from their original membership of three. In addition to their growth, the foundation itself was slowly becoming more self-supporting, and in 1925 the sisters became the beneficiary of a generous and unexpected bequest from the estate of the late Mr. Mair's second wife.

This gift meant that the sisters could seriously consider building their own hospital. It could not have come at a better time. Although home nursing was both practical and appropriate in the 1800s and through the early years of the twentieth century, medicine was quickly becoming more sophisticated. Hospitals allowed for new procedures and treatments, which were not possible in homes. Two crucial technological diagnostic procedures—x-rays and blood tests—had become commonplace by the 1920s, and both had to be performed within a hospital setting.[19] In addition, an overwhelming sociological change was taking place as more people became willing to go to hospitals. "In 1900, less than five percent of women gave birth in hospitals. By 1921, thirty to fifty percent of women gave birth in [U.S.] hospitals."[20]

America was in the midst of these changes when Mother Xavier and Sister Padua left the convent in Rochester while it was still dark to catch the early train for Chicago. It was June 13, 1925, the feast of St. Anthony, and after a long and hot fifteen-hour journey, the two were met by Mother M. Stanislaus Madigan, Mother M. Christopher Collins, and Sister M. Rosarii Hassett, who escorted them to their new home. A new phase in the apostolate of the Little Company of Mary was about to begin.

Six days after her arrival in Chicago, Mother Xavier and Sister Padua went to the Chancery office of the Archdiocese of Chicago to meet with Monsignor Sheil. He surprised them by arranging an audience with His Eminence, George Cardinal Mundelein, who had been named the first cardinal west of the Allegheny only the year before.[21] Within the next two years, the prelate would give his approval and support for the Little Company of Mary to build its own hospital. For the time being, however, he simply "received the newcomers to Chicago most graciously." [22]

As head of the American mission, Mother Xavier wasted no time. She immediately began to gather information, a prerequisite before any consideration of building. In the next months, she and Sister Padua visited numerous hospitals in the Midwest, including the renowned Mayo Institute in Rochester, Minnesota; Waukegan Hospital; and Mercy, Chicago's oldest Catholic hospital.

Although much had changed during the thirty-two years that had elapsed since the first sisters came to America, the pace of work had not. In spite of their increased numbers, the assignments that awaited them also grew. One of Mother Xavier's first tasks that summer was making sure that her hardworking sisters had a well-deserved break from their seemingly endless duties. Like those who preceded her, the new Superior understood the importance of a change of scenery and time away from hectic nursing routines. On July 21, she and Mother Stanislaus made a day trip to Wisconsin by train, where they found a suitable cottage in Lake Delavan which would provide the community with a quiet, lakeside retreat. During the next five weeks, the sisters took turns covering all the nursing cases in Chicago and spending two tranquil weeks in Wisconsin.[23] When summer ended, the sisters returned to their normal work schedule and three of them began nurse's training at St. Elizabeth's Hospital.

Shortly after the new year began, the Little Company of Mary discovered a new source of support for its future hospital. On January 8, five women who were familiar with the community suggested the formation of an Auxiliary, which would help collect funds for this venture. Several weeks later, they held their first meeting and eighty-one members enrolled. [24]

While the sisters continued searching for a suitable hospital site throughout the spring of 1926, Auxiliary membership increased and donations started to come in through various means, including "mite" banks, which were distributed to the members and returned filled with cash and coins; by money raised at card parties; by donations from friends and benefactors; and from bequests to the Little Company of Mary.

That summer, a particularly momentous event took place in Chicago. The Twenty-eighth International Eucharistic Congress, a devotional gathering honoring Christ in the Blessed Sacrament, was held in the Windy City from June 20 to June 24. Forty-nine cardinals attended the Congress, and almost one million Catholics joined them. Since this biannual celebration, first held in France in 1881, had never before come to the United States. "The announcement that [Cardinal] Mundelein had secured Chicago's selection ... signaled the importance of the United States to world Catholicism."[25]

On July 26, Mother M. Hilda Potter, Mother General of the Little Company, arrived in Chicago along with Mother M. Gonzaga Maddigan after visiting the Little Company's house in San Antonio de Areco.[26] This was a momentous occasion for the sisters because Mother Hilda was the first Mother General to visit the community in the United States. Her presence was especially meaningful because she was the niece of Mary Potter, the beloved founder of the Little Company. During Mother Hilda's two-month stay, she met with each of the sisters; inspected potential hospital sites in River Forest, La Grange, and Beverly with Mother Xavier and

Mother Stanislaus; attended an Auxiliary meeting at which she addressed the members; and participated in the entrance ceremony of Margaret O'Halloran by giving her the postulant's cap before returning to Rome in October.[27]

By autumn, the sisters had chosen a site for their future hospital in River Forest and had received permission from the archdiocese to purchase the land. There was one problem, however. The property was zoned for residential usage. On September 25, 1926, John H. McGeary, representing the Little Company of Mary, filed a petition for rezoning with the Village Clerk of River Forest that stated:

> I am acting as agent for the several owners of the block of property bounded by Division and Berkshire Streets, William and Monroe Avenues in River Forest. The respective purchasers anticipate the erection of a sanitarium or general hospital with a nurses' home in connection. I do not find any specific ruling in the zoning ordinance for buildings of this character.... The building will be set back far enough from the lot lines and will not be of the ordinary box type of hospital design. Trees and shrubbery will be planted and the ground beautified.... It is contemplated to [be] a five-story building.[28]

At a November 1 public hearing, numerous River Forest property owners objected to the request. As a result, the Village Committee later determined that the building of a hospital in an "A Use District" (i.e., residential area) "would be a violation of the Zoning Ordinance of the Village and would also depreciate the value of property in such districts."[29] The Zoning Commission's desire to keep another tax-free institution out of the village may have also influenced their decision.[30] For its relatively small number of residents (about sixty-five thousand in 1925),[31] the village already had an inordinate number of church-affiliated institutions, including St. Thomas Aquinas Priory, Rosary College, and Concordia University. The committee's decision meant that the Little Company of Mary would have to look elsewhere for a hospital site.

On November 2, the Feast of All Souls, the members of the Chicago Foundation learned of the death of Mother M. Patrick in London. The community's pioneering member and former Superior who had been transferred back to Europe in 1921 had died suddenly of pneumonia after being ill for only four days. Bishop Hoban celebrated a solemn

Requiem Mass for the repose of her soul in the community chapel the following week, and in his homily recalled Mother Patrick's work and virtues and particularly her special devotion to the poor. [32]

The community renewed its search for a possible hospital site when spring began. The community's second location choice was far different from the comfortable suburb of River Forest with its tree-lined streets and large, sprawling homes. Evergreen Park was an undeveloped area of prairie, forest, and swampland located about fourteen miles southwest of downtown Chicago. It had once been home to a number of tribes of Native Americans, but when the last tribe of Potawatomi was forced to relocate west of the Mississippi in the 1830s, emigrants from Germany and Holland named Graefens, Haas, Leppins, and Seipps took their place on the land.[33] They called their settlement Evergreen Park because of the numerous pine trees in the park at 97th and Homan. In the late 1920s, the population of the village numbered about fifteen hundred, although much of the area was still farmland,[34] a place where hardworking farmers toiled the earth's rich black soil to produce crops of wheat and cabbages, potatoes and onions.

Several factors contributed to the community's choice of Evergreen Park. The cost of the land was certainly a primary consideration. The Triezenberg family offered ten acres of farmland for $60,000—a price that was more reasonable and cost-effective than a similarly sized parcel of land located within the city of Chicago. A more important factor that likely affected the sisters' decision, however, was a concern that Mary Potter had expressed in a letter dated March 4, 1894:

> If the Hospital project in course of years came to anything, it might be useful, but I should not encourage it at present, especially if other sisters in Chicago have a Hospital. If they are doing their duty, why should strange sisters come in over them. I would always avoid even seeming to do this. [35]

Although Mother had gone to the Lord fourteen years earlier, her daughters remembered her wishes concerning the Little Company and her insistence that their apostolate neither interfere with nor adversely affect the work of other congregations. When the first three members of the Little Company arrived in Chicago, Catholic sisters were already working in five hospitals in the city, and in 1929, as the Little Company began building its own hospital, eight different religious communities were nursing in thirteen of Chicago's general hospitals:

> St. Anne's Hospital—29 Poor Handmaids of Jesus Christ; St. Anthony's Hospital—43 Franciscan Sisters of the Sacred Heart; St. Bernard's Hotel Dieu Hospital—23 Religious Hospitallers of St. Joseph; Columbus Hospital—Missionary Sisters of the Sacred Heart of Jesus; Mother Cabrini Memorial Hospital—25 Missionary Sisters of the Sacred Heart of Jesus; Misericordia Hospital and Home for Infants—4 Sisters of Mercy; St. Elizabeth's Hospital—40 Poor Handmaids of Jesus Christ; St. Joseph's Hospital—21 Daughters of Charity of St. Vincent de Paul; St. Mary of Nazareth Hospital—60 Sisters of the Holy Family of Nazareth; Municipal Isolation Hospital—4 Poor Handmaids of Jesus Christ; John B. Murphy Hospital—5 Sisters of Mercy; Mercy Hospital—52 Sisters of Mercy; Sheridan Park Hospital.[36]

Religious also staffed two maternity hospitals (Lewis Memorial, run by the Sisters of Charity of Providence, and St. Vincent's Infant Asylum and Maternity Hospital, conducted by the Daughters of Charity of St. Vincent de Paul).

In addition to honoring Mary Potter's concerns, technology played a role in the choice of a hospital site. American society was becoming increasingly mobile as automobiles were being made faster and cheaper. Midway through the 1920s, the ten millionth Model T rolled off the assembly line, and the price of a new car fell to $398. The fact that more and more Americans owned cars contributed to the Little Company of Mary's decision to consider a rural location outside of Chicago.

It has been said that God in His wisdom and providence sometimes takes us to places where we otherwise would not have gone. This seems to be especially true regarding the Little Company of Mary's selection of Evergreen Park. Following the rejection of their petition in River Forest, the community was guided to pick a location in the middle of nowhere. By distancing themselves from any other Catholic hospital, the sisters both honored their founder's desire of not stepping on the toes of other congregations of nursing sisters, and they also put themselves in the advantageous position of being able to offer hospital services where none had previously existed.

The logbook entry for April 27 indicates that the sisters moved very quickly on their final decision:

Today, the business of purchasing the property (ten acres) at 95th and California Avenue was completed. Mother M. Xavier and Mother M. Stanislaus went to Messrs. Kennally and Megan's office and there the check was handed over by them to the owner's representatives. A cash transaction.... Thank God for all! May God bless the project of the hospital. [37]

On April 30, Mothers Xavier and Stanislaus received the approval of Bishop Hoban and Cardinal Mundelein regarding the choice of Joseph McCarthy as the architect for their hospital. Later that spring, several members of the Little Company of Mary met with a member of the Examining Board from Springfield who advised them of the minimum requirements for the hospital. They also visited numerous hospitals—St. Luke's, West Suburban, Oak Park, as well as hospitals in Maywood and Elmwood, and looked at the plans for the new St. Anne's Hospital, which was under construction.

As the fall of 1927 began, several changes took place within the Chicago Foundation, which along with the rest of the Little Company of Mary had celebrated the congregation's fiftieth anniversary. Mother Xavier left Chicago for a new assignment in Italy, and Sister Padua was transferred to Nottingham. On the final day of September 1927, Mother M. de Pazzi announced that Mother M. Stanislaus Madigan had been elected Superior of the Chicago house. American-born Mother M. Dorothea Dwight was named as her assistant. As a recent graduate of Mercy Hospital's Training School, she brought with her the knowledge of efficient hospital management gained from her own firsthand experience in Chicago's oldest Catholic hospital. Mother M. Callista, a native of Ireland who had arrived in August was appointed Mistress of Novices.[38] This trio would oversee the upcoming hospital construction and the establishment of the community's first novitiate within the United States.

During the spring of 1928, Mothers Stanislaus and Dorothea met with Cardinal Mundelein. Over the years, the first American-born archbishop and native New Yorker had earned a reputation for being "both a builder and a prudent executive."[39] On April 17, after hearing of their plans, he gave his permission for the Little Company of Mary to begin construction of a hospital at 95th Street and California Avenue. [40]

Late in the summer, one of the sisters wrote, "The picture or painting of our new Hospital came, which caused great excitement. After everyone had taken a good look at it, it was taken up to the chapel and Mother M. Stanislaus said [a] Litany and prayers for its success."[41] Two weeks later, the Cardinal was shown a drawing of the proposed hospital and was "very pleased with it."[42]

The *New World*, one of Chicago's Catholic newspapers, ran a feature story on September 9, 1928, with the headline, "Little Company Builds Hospital in Evergreen Park." The article reported:

> Work to begin at once on Chicago's newest hospital to be built at 95th Street and California Avenue, Evergreen Park, by the Little Company of Mary, long known as nursing sisters at Indiana Avenue and 41st Street. Joe W. McCarthy is the architect.
>
> The sisters plan to build one unit of the hospital ... with the power plant and laundry separate. Later, a second unit will be added with a convent and chapel at the center....
>
> Property was bought about a year ago; with this cost and that of building, the sisters face an expenditure of almost a million dollars. They are now launching a drive for funds. Their first appeal to the public, although they have been nursing the sick of Chicago for thirty-five years.
>
> While the Little Company will continue to nurse the sick in their homes, as formerly, the sisters have long felt the need of their own hospital for cases that cannot be treated adequately at home and for the training of novices in the nursing profession. The project has the approval of His Eminence, Cardinal Mundelein.... [43]

As the sisters were busy preparing for their new hospital, that fall, for the first time in the nation's history, a Catholic was making a serious bid for the presidency of the United States. Alfred E. Smith, the Democrat governor of New York, was resoundingly defeated by Herbert Hoover, and the prejudice that surrounded the election "rekindled anti-Catholic hostilities."[44] Catholics again realized that they were not considered full citizens. More than a decade later, Cardinal Mundelein advised James A. Farley, the Catholic chairman of the Democratic Party, against running for the presidency because the prelate did not believe a Catholic could possibly win.[45] Another quarter century would elapse before he would be proven wrong.

The year 1929 began full of hope for the Sisters of the Little Company of Mary. On a frigid day, February 6, they took the first step toward fulfilling their dream of building their own hospital by breaking ground on a windswept field far removed from the buildings and population of Chicago. On that blustery but joyous afternoon, they had no inkling of the faith that would be required of them in the coming months when their money would run out, or later when the country would reel from the effects of "Black Monday," when the American stock market crashed, the consequences of which direly affected millions of Americans and threatened the success of the sisters' endeavor.

The logbook entry for February 6, 1929 describes that eventful day:

> … Mother M. Stanislaus, Mother M. Dorothea, with some professed Sisters went to 95th and California to be present at the ceremony of breaking ground for the new Hospital. There were six priests present and quite a few of the Auxiliary Members … [as well as] the architect and contractor … Father Hurley had not yet arrived to bless the ground, so Father Croke from St. Cecilia's blessed it instead and dug up the first shovel full. Mother M. Stanislaus dug the second…. The photographers were busy all this time. We must have made a picture in the snow, which was gently falling all the time and had been ever since early morning.…

> After a few minutes, Father Hurley appeared on the scene and was persuaded to bless the ground again, which he did…. The big steam shovel, which had been close by … began and made a swoop down into the earth and brought up a large quantity of dirt and flung it to one side…. It was interesting to watch, but it was too cold to remain standing for long.… [46]

And so it began. Two months later, on a more temperate mid-April morning, Bishop Bernard J. Sheil blessed the cornerstone during a formal dedication ceremony. Priests from the nearby parishes assisted him while the Sisters of the Little Company of Mary and members of other religious congregations, along with hundreds of interested residents from surrounding communities, looked on.

*Sisters arriving for the laying of the cornerstone of their future
hospital in Evergreen Park in April 1929.*

Throughout the spring, as concrete was being poured and steel
girders were rising, fundraising for the hospital continued. A benefit
concert held at Orchestra Hall on Easter Monday kicked off a three
hundred thousand dollar building drive. In addition to card parties,
raffles, dances, a carnival, and other Auxiliary-sponsored events, the
community sought financial contributions from South Works, which
later became U.S. Steel; and other major South Side corporations, some
of which contributed substantially.

Despite all of these efforts, the future of the hospital was threatened
when money ran out during the first week of June, causing all work to
come to a sudden standstill. On June 12, Mothers Stanislaus and Dorothea
again visited Cardinal Mundelein, who had come to the Archdiocese of
Chicago "with designs to make the local Church a financially solvent
institution."[47] The prelate had a reputation for his administrative talents
and money management[48] as well as his savvy in financial matters, which
included setting up the central banking system for the entire archdiocese.[49]
He counseled them to take out a loan. The sisters quickly notified the
Motherhouse of his advice. On June 17, the American community
received permission from Rome to borrow the required amount.[50] Work

resumed during the third week of July after seven weeks of inactivity.

Construction continued throughout the autumn. Fortunately, the building was near completion on October 28, 1929, one of the bleakest days in American economic history. Given the financial hardship that occurred during the ensuing Great Depression, it would have been very unlikely that the hospital could have been built for a number of years, had it not been almost finished before the stock market crashed and money tightened.

On January 19, 1930, less than a year after the groundbreaking ceremony, the first American hospital owned by the Little Company of Mary opened its doors. What was once a barren field had been transformed into a healing oasis, a magnificent 150-bed facility solidly built of buff-colored brick rising four stories and topped with a Cross—the sign of their faith and the symbol of Calvary to which the community was devoted. The hospital itself formed the shape of a Cross, with a rotunda at the center of each floor and with various wings housing different departments: operating rooms and scrub rooms, the emergency and outpatient departments, the pharmacy and x-ray departments, the kitchen and dining facilities, delivery rooms and nursery, a temporary chapel, sleeping quarters for hospital personnel, and separate wings for the sisters and novices.

The hospital's remote location, which many originally thought foolish, was later seen as a wise choice. The foresight and ability of the sisters to recognize the possibilities of the improbable is strangely reminiscent of the classic American movie, *Field of Dreams*, which tells the story of a young farmer in Iowa who is inspired to build a baseball field in the midst of his cornfields. Disregarding common sense and the ridicule of those who think him crazy, he responds to a voice that tells him, "If you build it, they [players and fans] will come."

The decision of the Little Company of Mary to choose a remote field in Evergreen Park ran counter to both reason and the judgment of those who tried to dissuade the community from building in the middle of nowhere. The choice of a location paralleled that of the community's founder, who was similarly criticized by people who thought that by choosing Santo Stefano Rotondo as the site for Calvary Hospital she was sending the community "out into the outskirts of Rome to a deserted place where no one would ever come...."[51]

Just as the faith of the farmer and Mary Potter was rewarded, so too was the belief of the members of the Little Company of Mary. The once muddy field turned into a place where hopes and dreams became reality—where families experienced the miracle of birth, where health was restored to the young and the old, where the comfort of faith and compassion was offered to those on their final journey back to God.

The Little Company of Mary Hospital in Evergreen Park, Illinois, was but the first of several hospitals that the sisters would build and operate in what eventually became the American Province. In subsequent decades, it would expand to meet the needs of the growing community of Evergreen Park and to incorporate the latest advances in medicine, surgery, and diagnostic technology. Despite changes, additions, and renovations to the facility, which occurred as the century progressed, the underlying focus of the Little Company of Mary remained constant. Then, and today, the sisters continue to mirror the spirit of Calvary as they attend to the physical and spiritual health of all in their care, and in so doing fulfill another dream—one that Mary Potter had for all her daughters.

CHAPTER EIGHT

LIGHT AMID
THE DARKNESS

Through the worst of the Great Depression, the newly opened LCM Hospital in Evergreen Park offered a place of hope and healing.

The initial joy that the sisters experienced following the opening of their own hospital in Evergreen Park in January 1930 was tempered by the difficulties that the Little Company of Mary, along with millions of others, would face over the course of the next few years, the most difficult financial time ever experienced in the history of the United States, which became known as the Great Depression.

As the Chicago Foundation finalized plans for its first hospital during the late 1920s, America was experiencing an economic boom, with unemployment at an almost record-low three percent in 1929, a number that almost tripled in 1930 after the collapse of the stock market. By 1933, more than thirteen million workers—one of every four—were out of work, and for the next two years, the percentage would remain over twenty percent.[1] Even those fortunate enough to hang onto their jobs saw their income fall by an average of forty percent.[2]

Statistics, however, cannot begin to capture the misery that the Depression wreaked on individuals, families, and businesses. Only a few years earlier, the Statue of Liberty had welcomed millions of immigrants with the bright promise of endless possibility and with engraved words on its base that read: "Give me your tired, your poor/Your huddled masses yearning to breathe free...."[3] Now millions of Americans were tired and poor and huddled against the cold. Hunger reached epidemic proportions and feelings of despair ran rampant.

The faith that sustained the community was sorely tested during these years, not only by the suffering of those whom they encountered but also by the circumstances in which they found themselves. Several days after the hospital opened, only two patients had been admitted. The sisters strategically placed them across the hall from one another so neither would be looking into an empty room.[4] Lights were turned on in vacant rooms so that from the outside the hospital would not appear empty. As the weeks passed, the number of patients steadily increased, so this subterfuge was no longer necessary, but the sisters soon found themselves facing another problem.

Because of the Depression, many patients were unable to fully pay for their hospitalization. The community had experienced financial difficulties in their early years in Chicago, but it was one thing to have a few sisters not be fully compensated for home nursing and quite another to have a large percentage of patients unable to pay their bills while having to meet a payroll and being responsible for operating a hospital.

Generosity has always been one of the hallmarks of the Little Company of Mary, and Mary Potter had insisted that the sisters provide nursing care to the poor. Her daughters in Evergreen Park soon found themselves facing the growing challenge of keeping their new facility running when many patients could only pay a fraction of their care. Despite their financial hardship, they provided for the poor and hungry who "... would line up every day for something to eat—their clothes so worn and thin. They would stand close to the radiator waiting for their soup and sandwiches...."[5]

Their dire economic situation was hardly indicative of the prudent manner in which the community had managed its financial resources since arriving in America. In previous years the Chicago Foundation had scrimped and saved to pay off existing loans as quickly as possible. The sisters had even remortgaged their property, which allowed them to send substantial contributions to the Motherhouse "to aid in purchasing property in Fiesole...."[6] Now, however, the sisters were struggling just to pay their bills and were hard-pressed to scrape together even the interest they owed on their loans.

In spite of these financial challenges, the sisters continued to focus on the better days that lay ahead. Mother Stanislaus realized the importance of having a nurses' training school of their own, as this would mean that members of the community would not have to go elsewhere for their education. In addition, secular nurses trained under their auspices would receive the benefit of Little Company of Mary values—something that had been a vital concern to the congregation's founder when she established St. Gregory's nursing school at Calvary Hospital in Rome twenty years earlier. Mother Stanislaus consequently initiated plans for a school of nursing that opened the following year and soon became affiliated with DePaul University.[7]

One of the most encouraging developments was the ever-increasing number of young women who entered the Little Company of Mary throughout the 1930s. The foundation logbook indicates the arrival and capping of numerous postulants, as well as the new religious names of novices receiving their white veils, the temporary profession of blue novices, and ceremonies of final profession.

The community was growing so quickly that a new novitiate was needed for those in the process of religious formation. During a visit to Chicago in June 1932, Mother Hilda met with Cardinal Mundelein and received his initial approval to move the novitiate from 4130 South Indiana Avenue to the hospital in Evergreen Park.[8] After the Cardinal's assistant Monsignor Murray visited the hospital and determined that the new living arrangements fulfilled the requirements of Canon Law, the novices, in the company of Mother General, headed to their new home. On the first day of summer 1932, the last remaining sisters left the cottage, which had been their first convent and a place of residence for almost forty years.[9]

Halfway through the decade, the sisters' reputation for hard work and nursing excellence had even reached the West Coast. Early in February 1935, John Joseph Cantwell, the Limerick-born bishop of Los Angeles, wrote to the Little Company of Mary, asking them to take over a hospital in Pomona and inviting the Superior "to see this Hospital before deciding anything." [10]

On March 3, Mother Stanislaus and Sister M. Callista, the Mistress of Novices, headed to California. The two concurred that the facility was "up-to-date and everything [was] satisfactory."[11] They returned to the Midwest two weeks later hopeful that the apostolate of the Little Company of Mary would soon be expanding westward.

Nine months elapsed before the community learned that their dream of running a hospital on the West Coast would not be realized—at least not at that time. On December 21, 1935, Dr. Swindt, head of the Pomona Community Hospital, notified Mother Stanislaus that "the majority [of committee members] was not in favour of having Catholic Sisters take over [the] hospital."[12] The Chief of Staff openly expressed his unhappiness with the committee's decision.

Unlike thousands of others who headed to California in the mid-1930s, farming families fleeing from the two-year drought that literally turned their parched land into a dust bowl, and countless individuals who believed that California offered the chance for a fresh start, the Little Company of Mary Sisters remained in the Midwest.

During the summer of 1936, Bishop Cantwell once again contacted the Little Company of Mary regarding the possibility of coming into his diocese —this time to run a facility located in Santa Monica. The prelate expressed his hope that they could take over this hospital "as soon as possible." [13]

In mid-July, three members of the Australian Province of the Little Company of Mary en route to Chicago via the Pacific route visited the Santa Monica hospital. Heading the group was Mother M. Boniface O'Connor, the Australian Provincial. Their initial reaction must have been encouraging because three months later, John J. Cantwell, who had recently become Archbishop-elect of Los Angeles, wrote to Mother General, "For a few years now it has been my ambition to find some place in this great diocese for your great community. Perhaps one of the blessings of the new Archbishop will be to have you with us." [14]

Mother Stanislaus was in Rome that autumn for the General Chapter, so she did not visit the hospital until the following year. During the interim, the Santa Monica project had been steadily moving forward, and on May 7, 1937, Dr. Louis E. Mahoney, one of the committee members, wrote to the Chicago Superior:

> No doubt you are wondering about the progress made towards the new hospital project in Santa Monica.... [W]e called a meeting of interested physicians at the Wilshire Hospital and ... invited all of the [staff] members ... plus such other doctors as we knew were heart and soul in favor of the new hospital.... [A] great deal of favorable sentiment has been generated in the community....
>
> An escrow is being established ... and there are already sufficient funds to make the ten percent payment on the adjoining lots.... The property is being placed in the name of your order, and the bank fund is entitled "Little Company of Mary Hospital Fund."
>
> Certain opposition has developed as would be expected from the owners ... but this is transitory and will not affect the success of our undertaking to any appreciable degree. [15]

A week after hearing from Dr. Mahoney, Mother Stanislaus informed Mother M. Ambrose O'Donnell, the new Mother General, of her concerns:

> ... We are glad that you are in England for we know that when you are through over there you will turn your steps towards your children in the U.S.A. We need you Mother dear as there are many problems to be discussed, both for here and for California.
>
> We have not taken any legal steps towards taking over this Hospital ... but they [finance committee members] have done it themselves under

the advice of Archbishop Cantwell and Msgr. Conneally.... *Maybe some day we will be able to work with them and not have to borrow*, it will no doubt be a grand opening for our Sisters.... [italics mine] [16]

Mother Stanislaus had pinpointed the problem. The Chicago Foundation could not afford to borrow more money since it was already heavily burdened by the debt incurred to build the new hospital in Evergreen Park—a situation that was exacerbated by the Depression.

Five years earlier, the community had asked its creditors "to extend the respective maturity dates of all said bonds five years ... and ... to reduce the interest rate ... from six percent (6%) to four percent (4%) per annum."[17] This request was granted, and the Little Company of Mary was given until March 1, 1940, to meet its obligations. Their financial struggle becomes readily understandable in light of the fact that as late as January 1935, " ... twelve percent of [Little Company of Mary Hospital's] services [were] rendered at no cost to patients and ... forty-three percent of the Hospital's patients paid only nominal charges."[18]

In order to take over the facility in California, the Little Company of Mary would have had to secure a substantial loan. Although the economy " ... had made a steady, if undramatic, recovery, particularly after 1934,"[19] the United States experienced a recession between the end of 1937 and the middle of 1938. While it paled in comparison to what had happened in 1929, it had a tremendous emotional impact on the country, particularly on investors and lenders. Given the indebtedness of the Chicago Foundation and the financial instability the country was still experiencing, it appears very unlikely that the community could have secured the loans necessary to take over the hospital in California.

The Santa Monica situation was not resolved for almost a year. Mother Ambrose arrived in Chicago in April 1938 and quickly headed to California with Mother Stanislaus several days later. After a two-week stay, they returned to the Midwest.[20] Despite their apparent optimism, it soon became evident that there was simply no way of getting around the impossible situation of having to borrow in order for the project to continue.

For the second time in three years, the hopes of both the sisters and the prelate from Los Angeles would not be realized. The members of the Little Company of Mary could not know then that their presence on the

West Coast would figure into God's plans for them—but not for another twenty years. For the present and near future, the sisters focused their efforts on their hospital in Evergreen Park, on expanding their work in Argentina, and on taking care of the needs of their growing community.

More than five years had passed since the sisters had moved into the hospital, and during that time the increasing number of patients necessitated the use of additional hospital rooms occupied by the sisters. To allow for more patients, the novices temporarily moved into a portable building. Seven months later, construction of the new convent was completed, and the sisters moved into their new home on the feast of the Epiphany—January 6, 1938.

After visiting the United States, Mother Ambrose left for San Antonio de Areco. While in South America, she authorized an expansion of the community that would include a thirty-bed hospital in Buenos Aires, a decision likely influenced by the fact that a member of the Argentine community had been named as the beneficiary of a sizable inheritance, which provided credit for the loans needed for this expansion.[21]

The new facility would be quite different from the Maria Clara Morgan Hospital, whose rather primitive conditions were atypical of hospitals run by members of the Little Company of Mary. The sisters themselves would oversee the plans for their hospital in Buenos Aires, so it would unquestionably meet their demanding standards. Because the Argentine government mandated that the community, now officially known as the *Pequeña Compania de María*, "be considered as an organization for the making of a profit in order to comply with the law,"[22] the new hospital would be a private facility ensuring that the congregation could earn enough money to fulfill the country's legal requirements.

Mother Ambrose decided that instead of building, the community should find a suitable property that could be converted into a hospital. The sisters enlisted the firm of F. B. O'Grady to assist them in their search. In a memorandum to the Superior General, the firm's owner described a spacious thirty-room residence on Avenida Alvear, which he thought might be of interest:

> Marble and the best of material was [*sic*] used. It has two automobile entrances, and room for two or three autos in the front garage, which could easily be utilized for other purposes. There are two or

three offices on the first floor, or rooms with toilets and closets. The kitchen is on the first floor and it is three times the size of the one we saw the other day....

Then there are three or four rooms for living purposes. In the rear there is a nice park ... [and] patio spaces ... so as to provide light and air. On the second floor there is a beautiful hall with a colored artistic glass skylight, a magnificent dining room, and four or five other rooms....

The top floor has seven bedrooms at least. There is a very large kitchenette, almost big enough for an operating room, and I believe four bath rooms [sic].... [T]he rear of the house is about as attractive as the front. Plenty of sun and air. On the roof there [are] big whitetiled [sic] washing and ironing rooms, a big water tank, and the roof is of the best red flat tile.[23]

The nine-year-old house compared favorably with several other sites, and the community moved quickly to purchase the property. Three weeks later, they signed a contract and began the necessary remodeling. The project, which took almost ten months to complete, was funded by private donations, bank loans, and generous loan support from both the Irish and Australian Provinces, the latter donating one thousand pounds sterling to the endeavor. When the work was finished, the sisters sent out the following announcement:

Those who appreciate good nursing will welcome the inauguration of a modern 35-bed hospital to be opened during July 1939, at Avenida Alvear 3576, overlooking the Palermo Gardens.

Buenos Aires has first class medical talent but the need for thoroughly trained nurses has not yet been fully supplied. English-speaking nurses are respected throughout the world. Since the day of Florence Nightingale, such women have attained very high standards in the profession. This new hospital will be owned and operated by Nursing Sisters of the Little Company of Mary, several of whom have come from abroad where their hospitals have proven successful. Here their new institution promises to offer excellent service....[24]

The advance promotional material indicated that in addition to featuring an excellent location and environment, the new facility offered, "The last

In 1939, the LCM opened a small sanatorio (hospital) on Avenida Alvear, Buenos Aires.

word in operating rooms, x-ray machines, [a] silent nurse call system, together with improved hospital-type beds, etc. . . . . Moreover, patients can take advantage of this good nursing in a model place, attended by a reputable surgeon or physician of their own choice." [25]

Notwithstanding its modern equipment, the hospital's greatest asset was its competent staff comprised of registered nurses, a pharmacist, and a bacteriologist, and the care they could provide. The reputation of both the Little Company of Mary Sisters and their hospitals in Europe, Australia, and the United States turned out to be their greatest advantage.

In the months before the hospital opened, O'Grady had advised the Superior General to:

> ... tell them [the people of Buenos Aires] that the Sisters are from Chicago, that you have a 200-bed modern hospital there, that Mother Fintan had 17 years experience there, [and] they become much interested. Understand that the Cardinal told the Sisters yesterday that a Doctor friend of his was recently in the States and that he told him that the Sisters have most marvelous organizations and hospitals there, while here they are almost in the back-yard stage. [26]

The "back-yard stage" might have described the facility that had been provided for the sisters in San Antonio de Areco, but their new hospital, situated on a wide street in a lovely area of Buenos Aires near the Italian embassy, was completely first-rate.

Forty years earlier, the Maria Clara Morgan Hospital had encountered opposition by those who believed that hospitals should be owned and run by the state. The hospital on Avenida Alvear also experienced some resistance, but for different reasons. Not only were physicians in Buenos Aires unaccustomed to the idea of women religious owning and running their own facilities, but since many doctors either operated or were shareholders of private *sanatorios*, they were also unwilling to send their patients to a private hospital.

In addition, the Little Company of Mary encountered a widely held prejudice that they had been forewarned of the previous year when they had been cautioned to " ... remember that local hospitals and local Sisters here [in Argentina] have a reputation of being poor grade."[27] To overcome this stereotype, the community was urged to contact area doctors who had traveled to the United States because:

> ... [they] must know about how Catholic hospitals are run up there and that Nursing Sisters are deserving of respect as competent nurses and of consideration because [those things] are practically unknown in this city [Buenos Aires]....[28]

On July 29, 1939, Santiago Luis Copello, Cardinal Archbishop of Buenos Aires, blessed the new hospital. The first months of operation were arduous, as a letter from Sister M. Rita Carroll to the Superior in Chicago makes clear:

> ... the work will be a success, but only, Mother Dear, if you send some help at once. If you could only look in and see the poor Sisters doubling up, trying to do day and night duty ... living under impossible circumstances while the work was going on and all the expenses with practically no income.... Would it be possible ... to borrow five or six hundred pounds more...? I have not the slightest doubt that the place will rapidly pay for itself.... Mr. O'Grady has been wonderful all through and has succeeded in getting us six months' credit ... but that is only to help us operate; that is, for food, wages, etc....

S. M. Christopher is working like two people and she really ought not to have to work so ... after her hard years in Chicago as well as here, but she is generous and self-sacrificing, and is working ... as if she were only commencing life. Mother M. Xavier has gone on the nursing staff, but that is not right either, as she has so many things to see to, so PLEASE, dearest Mother, take pity on the Sisters in the new house and send them some help as soon as you possibly can.... The great thing that everyone speaks of is that the Sisters are to do the nursing and if we get in seculars, at least during the first year, the place will be a failure, that is my honest opinion.... [N]urses may be got to help after a year, but just now it would kill all, I am sure.... I know you want the house to be a success just as much as we do, and the two principal factors at the present moment are Sisters and a little more money as soon as we can get both.

[T]hings today are very different from years ago, and those who told us it was so easy to start a Private Hospital in B.A. were very much mistaken—there are very strict rules and heavy taxes, which have made a hole in our money.... [29]

Six additional sisters were sent to Argentina during the next fifteen months—four from Chicago, one from Sydney, one from South Africa.[30] Within a short time, the reputation of the facility and of the nursing skills of Mother M. Fintan Kealy and her staff spread throughout the Argentine capital, dispelling the initial negativity.

Within fifteen years, there was such a demand for the sisters' services, especially for maternity and surgical care, that the Little Company of Mary opened a much larger hospital. The state-mandated profit, which the sisters derived from their work, as well as from the sale of the private hospital some years later, provided a portion of the funds necessary to make the construction of the larger facility a reality.

For the members of the Chicago Foundation, the 1930s had been a time of struggle and achievement, of pain and promise. The decade began and ended with the opening of two new hospitals—one southwest of Chicago, the other in the northern section of Buenos Aires. This was a time of growth in both the number of patients cared for and the number of sisters who cared for them. In nine years' time, Little Company of Mary Hospital went from being nearly empty in its early weeks to recording "the biggest number of patients since it was opened"[31] in January of 1939, following an outbreak of influenza. The sisters' first hospital in the United States had become a successful healing institution begging for additional space to accommodate a rising number of patients as the population in and around Evergreen Park steadily increased.

During the hospital's earliest days, the sisters made sure the empty rooms were lit to provide an illusion of occupancy. Before the end of the decade, lights illuminated every hospital room, and they were no illusion. More important, however, was the symbolic light that the members of the Little Company provided to those who needed their help during some of the darkest days of the Great Depression.

Even as they found themselves in daunting circumstances, Mother Potter's daughters remained true to one of their founder's principles—providing nursing care to those who could not afford it. Although the sisters could hardly extend themselves further financially, they never turned away patients who could only pay part of their hospitalization costs. Throughout those challenging times, the community learned how to walk the fine line between generosity and what was required to successfully run a solvent medical institution.

As the sisters provided a ray of hope to others, the congregation was transformed in ways that would allow its work to shine even more brightly in the future. The Little Company of Mary Sisters became better known throughout the Chicago area as a result of building and operating their own hospital. Consequently, the number of young women who entered the community continued to increase. Between 1922 and 1928, six postulants entered the Little Company. That number almost doubled from 1929 to 1931.[32] The steady growth in membership, which occurred throughout this otherwise bleak period, had several positive consequences.

Only a decade or two earlier, the vast majority of sisters who comprised the Chicago Foundation were born in Ireland. Now, as more American women joined the Chicago community, it was becoming increasingly self-sufficient—no longer having to depend on members from Europe or Australia to accomplish its mission. The growing number of native-born sisters also meant that in the not-too-distant future the apostolate of the Little Company of Mary in the United States could expand from America's heartland—east to Massachusetts and west to California, as well as to several other places in between.

CHAPTER NINE

A TIME OF
UNIMAGINABLE DEVASTATION

Two Little Company of Mary Sisters praying in San Pierre.

By the time the members of the Little Company of Mary celebrated the tenth anniversary of their hospital in Evergreen Park on January 19, 1940, the great hardship that they and others shared during much of the 1930s had lessened considerably, but two menacing ideologies—Nazism and Communism—were gathering strength and would soon affect the lives of millions of people and shatter any semblance of peace throughout the world.

Pius XI had addressed these matters in two encyclicals issued in March 1937. In his first letter addressed to the bishops of Germany, the pontiff warned, "Whoever exalts race, or the people, or the State ... and divinizes them to an idolatrous level, distorts and perverts an order of the world planned and created by God...."[1] The Holy Father's second letter, released only five days later, condemned atheistic Communism as a social system in which "There is no recognition of any right of the individual...."[2] The Pontiff denounced Communism because it "... strips man of his liberty, [and] robs human personality of all its dignity...."[3]

Pius XI's admonitions against the evil inherent in both forms of totalitarianism could not stop their spread throughout Europe and the Soviet Union. In the final year of the turbulent thirties, the pope who had worked and prayed so hard for the preservation of peace died, and with him, his dream for an end to aggression and warfare. Seven months later, on September 1, 1939, Germany invaded Poland—the ominous first step in a conflict that eventually reached global proportions. Within the next ten years, the dual evils of Nazism and Communism would engulf much of continental Europe and the Soviet Union.

As the 1940s began, the sisters in Evergreen Park were mindful of what their fellow sisters on the other side of the Atlantic were facing. Like most Americans, however, they were isolated from the events that were taking place in Europe. The year began auspiciously with the arrival of a new postulant on January 1.[4] Several months later, the community received heartening news when an elderly gentleman named John Tierney who lived in San Pierre, Indiana, wrote to the Little Company of his interest in donating his property to them. At the time, "owing to sickness of many of the Sisters,"[5] no one was able to visit him, but several months later, in early July, Mother M. Dunstan Kelleher and Mother M. Stanislaus Madigan headed to northwestern Indiana to meet their potential benefactor.

John Tierney was instrumental in bringing the sisters to a remote area of northwestern Indiana.

Mr. Tierney's relationship with the Little Company of Mary dated back to 1918 when America, along with much of the world, had been in the grip of an outbreak of an influenza, described as "the most devastating epidemic in recorded world history."[6] In just two years, one-fifth of the world's population was infected, and an estimated 675,000 Americans died, most between twenty and forty years of age.... [7] "More people died of influenza in a single year than in four years of the Black Death (bubonic plague) from 1347 to 1351."[8]

At that time, Tierney had sought help for his cousin, who was close to death from the flu. The Superior sent Sister M. Rosarii Hassett to care for Mr. Tierney's relative, who eventually recovered. More than two decades later, John Tierney "recalled that his cousin had been tenderly cared for" by a member of the Little Company and was considering leaving his property to the congregation. Several days after meeting with Mother Dunstan, he called to inform her of his decision to bequeath his home and Indiana acreage to the community.

Sister M. Solace Hannigan, who provided most of the nursing care during the final nine months of John Tierney's life, kept a detailed account of those days:

While vacationing [at the sisters' cottage at Bass Lake], Mother Dunstan told each group [of sisters] to visit Mr. Tierney and try to persuade him to come to the hospital for care; he would not listen to anyone. Being apprised of the man's condition, and thinking to bring a bit of cheer into his [life], on a beautiful May morning [along] with Sister M. Virginia, [I] walked the distance to the farm of the sick man. In response to our door knock, [a] kindly and mentally alert old man appeared ... and invited us to sit on the porch.... It was obvious that the old gentleman was keenly conscious of [the] condition of his face—the whole right side was [destroyed by] cancer. Some years ago while repairing a fence, a nail ... struck Mr. Tierney in the left eye. Lacking confidence in doctors, he attempted to care for the injury himself. The malignant condition of his face was the result. He was a scholarly man and had mastered to fluency ... French, Latin, German, and Greek. When he retired from teaching, with his sister Matilda, he settled down to a life of ease.

When he learned that I, like they [his parents], was Irish born, he asked me what part of Ireland I came from and I said from County Mayo. "How lovely," he said. "There's where my mother came from." [I told him], " Mr. Tierney, we want you to come into the hospital with us where you can get much needed treatment," but he replied, "Sister, I want to live and die in San Pierre. How about you coming here to take care of me?"

We returned to Bass Lake and I called Mother Stanislaus and told her of Mr. Tierney's request. [The following day the sisters returned.] There was so much debris on the floor, I picked up my habit [and] followed him through the dining room and kitchen to the stairway leading to the attic. Both sides of the stairs were packed with books and at the top of the stairs ... was a double bed made out of the trunks of trees. The mattress was stuffed with cornhusks. Anytime you touched the mattress, mice hopped out.

Although it was midday, the house was almost dark inside. The smoke from the old stove had made all the windows opaque and the window shades that had been drawn for years crumpled at the touch of the hand. Sister and I surveyed the second floor for a place to hang our habits. There was none. We placed a newspaper on a chair to lay our habits on, and we changed [in]to overalls. Taking my hammer and a screwdriver, I removed a window. Sunshine stream[ed] into that room for the first time in many years....

We throw out the window the years' accumulation of useless objects. From the ceiling were suspended hornets' nests as large as grapefruit. Valiantly, Sister Virginia remove[d] the nests while hornets fill[ed] the room with buzzing.... After long scrubbing, we have the second floor in fairly presentable condition.... Sister and I now turn our attention to the first floor.... We remove[d] the entire contents of the room to the outdoors.... That evening we have a carefully watched bonfire. The room we cleaned throughout. It now looks livable.

We've come to the end of the day's cleaning. I announce to Sister Virginia that I am going to give Mr. Tierney a bath. Taking a pail of water and soap, I start for his room. I told the old gentleman that I am going to bathe him. He utters not a word. In my long years of nursing, I've never seen a more neglected person. His clothing, I put in the incinerator. His poor body looked as though he had slept in a coal bin. Now, he is bathed and dressed in new underwear and a new suit....

[T]he house is now ready for much needed repairs and decorating. We have built a bathroom, and wallboarded the dining room, put linoleum on the kitchen and dining room floors ... installed electricity, and a kerosene stove ... [and] the house is comfortably habitable.

Sister Virginia ... love[d] to work in the garden. She wore high, knee-length rubber boots raking leaves and when she'd finish, she'd look around and all the leaves would have blown back. But she persevered [so] the outside no longer looked deserted. Sister Virginia was a bookkeeper in Evergreen [Park] and had to go back from time to time so that I had long stretches of time alone. She would come for a few days when she could. It is very lonesome here now, away from everyone. But God gives us the necessary grace to endure....

For reasons we never tried to ascertain, Mr. Tierney had remained away from his religious duties over 40 years. Good Fr. John ... brought him back to the faith.... The change wrought ... has been one of from sinner to great saintliness. Truly I can say [that] I've never heard the old gentleman utter one uncharitable word....

Summer is ... waning and the foliage ... has on colors of beautiful tint.... All being comfortable with my patient, I walk daily to the Catechist Chapel to hear Mass.... [W]hen I returned, I'd get Mr. Tierney up, dress him and walk him to the kitchen and sit him in the rocking chair. Every morning I dressed the wounds on his face....

I fed him, as he was practically blind, although he could walk around the cottage.

[T]he late autumnal rains have made the adjacent harvest fields all green.... Soon winter is upon us, and the countryside is heavily blanketed with snow. I shovel the snow around the house and make a path to the mailbox and the milk box.... The patient is almost tearfully appreciative for the care that is given him.... Mr. Tierney is growing old and feeble; but his mental alertness is remarkable.

One evening a violent storm blew up—thunder and lightening [sic], high winds and gales. I thought it would blow the cottage away. The temperature dropped to 30 or 40 degrees in the cottage ... [even though] I kept feeding the stove with wood. I moved Mr. Tierney's bed into the kitchen to keep him warm for the night.... [Mother] Dunstan sent him a radio, which he'd never had before. He followed the news of World War II. As he was a scholar, he knew every corridor of World War II, and he was just glued to that radio.

It is now Christmas time of 1940 and I'm still alone in San Pierre with the dear patient.... On Christmas Eve, the Catechist brought the children from San Pierre to the farm to sing ... carols for us. Mr. Tierney and I went to Midnight Mass.... I had arranged colored light bulbs in the front windows, and a well-lit Christmas tree. Later I learned that a number of San Pierre residents had come past the house ... to see the tree and lights, as it was the first time in the memory of any of them that a light had been seen in the Tierney home.

... real cold weather is with us and the cold snow-laden winds from the north swirl the snow drifts about the house into fantastic shapes.... The loneliness of the place has deepened now that the somber days of mid-winter are with us; the loneliness is accentuated by the brevity of daylight.... Each breaking dawn gives way to skies heavily gray that betoken more snow and the stillness of it all is a bit eerie.

The long winter is now past, and nature's perrenial [sic] promise of the Resurrection to come is again with us.... Sister Virginia has ... returned to the farm. She has purchased two thoroughbred colts from Fr. John's brother. I have come into possession of a beautiful cat; the only domestic animal on these three hundred and eighty-eight acres....

[I]n the fine spring days we are finishing repairs on the house ... and we've started to put the long neglected farm into shape.... I make my first investment in livestock for the cowless and hogless farm. I buy a pig.... During the early spring we raised 500 white leghorn chicks in the Tierney garage. Mother M. Stanislaus was here at the farm the day the chicks arrived. She blessed each chick.... So many difficulties have we encountered here, and happily overcome....

On July 4, 1941, the dear old man passed away peacefully. He was waked two nights at the cottage at his own request. We had a Solemn High Mass at All Saints ... [and his] remains ... were laid to rest with his father, mother, and sister in St. Joseph's Cemetery at Sandusky, [Ohio].

Through the generosity of Mr. Tierney, the San Pierre Church of All Saints was rebuilt.... He took keen delight in visits of the Nuns to his home and always implored them to prolong their visit. It was his wish that at his demise all of his belongings revert to the Little Company of Mary as a memorial to his late sister, Matilda.... Mr. Tierney was prompted by a twofold desire—that of assisting the Sisters in a most worthy cause and at the same time utilizing a substantial portion of his worldly belongings toward the betterment of the community in which he made his home for ... sixty-five years....[9]

Earlier in the year it had been decided that the novitiate should be relocated from Chicago to San Pierre. On November 24, the sisters broke ground for the new building.[10] Several days later, Samuel Alphonsus Stritch, who had become Chicago's archbishop following the death of Cardinal Mundelein, visited the Little Company of Mary Hospital, convent, and novitiate for the first time.

Throughout this time, the thoughts and prayers of all of the sisters in the United States turned increasingly to the safety and welfare of their fellow sisters in England. On September 7, 1940, almost 350 German bombers dropped their ordnances on London, and the ensuing fires guided subsequent aircraft in a raid that lasted until 4:30 the next morning. Ernie Pyle, the famous American war correspondent, described the conflagration as "a night when London was ringed and stabbed with fire."[11] Thus began "a period of intense bombing of London and other [English] cities,"[12] known as the Blitz, which continued until the following May.

The Tierney farmland, first the site of a novitiate, then of a convalescent facility.

The bombing affected several of the houses of the Little Company in England. The sisters at the Provincial House, novitiate, and nursing home in Hillingdon Court, Uxbridge, found themselves in the direct line of fire because they were "near an airfield and Royal Air Force chaplains are billetted in it."[13] According to one sister, "[O]n October 29, 1940, ... seven bombs [made] a direct hit ... devastating the grounds. A hole is blown in the wall of the house. Windows are shattered and debris is mountains high. But not one person is injured and the *Deo Gratias* [Thanks be to God] is profound."[14] The sisters working in London's East End, "[took] charge of a First Aid post ... to deal with air raid casualties."[15]

Even the members of the Little Company of Mary in Nottingham were not out of harm's way. "On the evening of November 14, 1940, some 515 German bombers crossed the English coast, heading inland toward the country's industrial Midlands."[16] Their target was Coventry, England, located eighty-seven kilometers (fifty-four miles) southwest of Nottingham. That night, virtually every street in Coventry's central district was on fire.

Three weeks later, on Sunday morning December 7, 1941, the U.S. Naval Base at Pearl Harbor, Honolulu, suffered a surprise air attack by Japanese aircraft, which caused the deaths of more than twenty-four

Capping Ceremony in Evergreen Park (February 1942).
Nurses pictured with Sister M. Paul Hurtubise, L.C.M.

hundred Americans. The next day, the Congress of the United States declared war.

The logbook contains only a few direct references to the war, but the sisters in Evergreen Park felt the impact most acutely in the loss of many of their doctors who were serving in the Armed Forces. The sudden depletion of staff physicians had another repercussion, as one sister reported: "The hospital is becoming so crowded that all outside doctors [have] refused to bring patients to the hospital...."[17]

Mother Dunstan chronicled some of the events that were taking place in Evergreen Park as well as her fellow sisters' reactions to them:

> [T]he war in Europe is making terrible destruction, but even though we listen faithfully for news each day, it really doesn't seem to bring home to us the awful feeling of what might happen—only when some of our staff men from the hospital got into uniform and left us, did [it] seem real. Even with this, we seem to exist in a dream of future events until December 8, [sic] 1941, the attack on Pearl Harbor really stunned us: then the whole world seemed to change, and the atmosphere in the hospital changed too.

As the weeks and months passed by, each day brought with it new sorrow. The Doctors became restless; also the nurses. The Doctors were drafted; their homes were sold; and their families separated or else the family accompanied them wherever they were stationed. The Nuns had brothers gone or going to war and this was [a] sorrow to their families and to them.

The hospital became [under]staffed in Doctors and nurses. There were no internes [*sic*], no orderlies: the help situation became a nightmare as all available help was employed in factories and receiving high salaries.... There were black-out drills in the hospital, fire drills, casualty drills performed in Ryan Woods: army cots were sent out from the Red Cross with army blankets to be prepared for anything....

Sixty-five of our Doctors were gone to war, scattered in all the countries one could name—Australia, Africa, China, Mary Ann Island [*sic*], Hawaii, England, North Ireland, Germany, France, Italy, and many others as well as different parts of the United States.... The Doctors Room was no longer crowded—the loud happy laugh of the Doctors had died away ... only a few of the older men and men disqualified for service met, now to enjoy a cup of coffee and a sandwich, and even when they met their hearts were not in it....

The hospital ... was crowded with patients because anyone who was sick now would have to come to the hospital as the Doctors were unable to make all the home calls. The rotonda [*sic*] and the halls of the hospital seemed to take on an air of quietness and loneliness.

Each day ... brought news to us of some family loss of their dear son "killed in action." We Sisters tried to keep in touch with all the Doctors' wives and families in order to give them hope for better days.... [We] poor, dear Nuns did not forget to pray.... [E]ach night a Sister was appointed to make an hour night-watch for all soldiers, sailors and marines. [18]

The sisters in the United States lost touch with the members of the Little Company in Europe for most of the war. Throughout all of 1942, the only reference to the sisters in Italy is a terse logbook entry stating, "Heard directly from Dear [Mother] General. All are well but food supply is strictly rationed." [19]

It was most unlikely that the American community was even aware of the hardships that their sisters in Malta were experiencing because the

Mother M. Stanislaus Madigan and Mother M. Dunstan Kelleher with three LCMH doctors serving in the U.S. Armed Forces. (L to R, Dr. Clifford Sullivan, Dr. George Fitzgerald, and Dr. Theodore Gasteyer.)

sisters had no direct communication with England or Rome at this time. According to historian James Holland, the island:

> ... held the key to dominance in the Mediterranean and North Africa ... [and was] the ideal place from which to attack shipping lines supplying Italian and German forces in North Africa. To save Egypt, the Suez Canal, and the Middle East oil fields from Nazi control, it was essential that the island be held at all costs. [20]

Sister Philippina Becket, who was serving in Malta, kept a journal detailing the suffering, privations, and near starvation that those on the island endured between 1940 and 1943. "It is indescribable," she wrote. "Night and day the bombs and big guns.... Nearly the whole of Malta is in ruins."[21] In March and April 1942, "more bombs fell on Malta than on London during the entire Blitz."[22]

That summer, the sisters' work in Evergreen Park was also affected by a change in government policy recorded in the community's logbook: "Medical schools beginning July 1st [*sic*] will be under Army Regulations."[23] For the duration of the war, the members of the Little Company of Mary would have to keep the hospital running without the assistance of interns.

When autumn began, the Catholic Church's opposition to the Nazis intensified. More than six years had elapsed since Pius XI had admonished the German bishops about the dangers of a fascist state, and his warning had predated any knowledge of Hitler's plan to eliminate all Jews. Now, as the systematic extinction of the Jewish people became known, members of the hierarchy vociferously condemned the genocide. On October 16, 1943, his successor, Pius XII, intervened to impede the deportation of Jews in Rome. In addition, he ordered the opening of cloistered convents to provide sanctuary to Jewish refugees.[24]

Despite rationing, occasional blackouts, and the large number of women who undertook jobs that had been done solely by men prior to the war, much of life in the United States continued as it had before the war began. In early 1944, the novitiate in San Pierre was nearing completion. At the end of March, the first of several shipments of furniture was sent to Indiana, and Sister M. Teresa Oleniczak and Sister M. Genevieve Canty took up residence in what had been Mr. Tierney's cottage in order to make final preparations for the transition.[25] A logbook entry for April 26 notes:

> Moving day—the long looked forward to day has finally arrived. The van arrived bright and early. What a time getting everything packed.... The next thing—our last dinner together—then the final farewell. How little did we realize how hard it would be to say goodbye.... After dinner M. M. Callista O'Donoghue, Sr. M. Genevieve and the Novices after bidding farewell to the Evergreen Park Sisters climbed into the station wagon and headed for San Pierre....[26]

As the novices were settling into their new home amid the peaceful tranquility of rural Indiana and learning to farm and plant a garden, the Allied forces were making final preparations for the invasion of Europe. On June 6, 1944, in the largest military action ever undertaken,[27] 156,000 men landed the beaches of Normandy, France. That event, known as "D-Day," marked the beginning of the end of World War II, as American, British, Canadian, and Australian servicemen slowly forged their way toward Germany.

Three weeks after D-Day, the official dedication and blessing of the building took place on June 29, the feast of Saints Peter and Paul—a most appropriate day, as the novitiate was located in a town called San Pierre. "In spite of the gas rationing and tire shortage, about seventy priests and about a thousand people were present...."[28] at the ceremony in which John Francis Noll, bishop of Ft. Wayne officiated.

On December 25, 1944, the logbook for the sisters in America's heartland includes the following entry: "A white Christmas, the ground covered with snow and more falling. All spent a rather quiet Christmas."[29] While the members of the Little Company celebrated the birth of the Prince of Peace, five thousand miles away in Belgium's dense Ardennes forest on the German/Belgian border, 655,000 members of the Allied forces engaged in the largest battle of World War II, which resulted in eighty-one thousand American casualties, including nineteen thousand deaths on "the coldest, snowiest Christmas in memory." [30]

Another half year would pass before the fighting ended in Europe. Meanwhile, the war in the Pacific dragged on for another two months. On August 14, 1945, Japan surrendered unconditionally, and the most devastating war in world history ended. Its carnage extended from the holocaust of the concentration camps and the deaths of more than twelve million Russians at the hands of Stalin to the almost total obliteration of Hiroshima and Nagasaki.

Throughout late 1945 and into early 1946, millions of American servicemen slowly returned to the United States. The world was once again at relative peace, but the lives of those who had taken part in the conflict were forever changed. One sister in Evergreen Park observed:

> ... our boys are back but somehow different—they were only boys
> going away: they have come back, men of experience ... of other
> countries, ... of life seen in all its horrible cruelty ... knowledge of
> how other people live.... If I had only kept the letters written to me
> by some of these good men ... we might realize to the full extent the
> price of war and its aftermath.[31]

Throughout the first half of the 1940s, the members of the Little Company of Mary in the United States continued their healing mission by providing nursing care on the home front and asking God's blessing on the brave men and women who were willing to lay down their lives to ensure the freedom of others. Perhaps most important, given their special apostolate of prayer for the souls of the dying, the sisters in America asked God's mercy for all who were close to death, even those who were responsible for causing such utter destruction.

CHAPTER TEN

A SMALL BUT
SPLENDID BAND

Novices gardening in San Pierre during the early 1940s.

Five weeks before the war in Europe ended, during a month when more than ten thousand Americans died in the European Theater of Operations as the Allied forces made their final push into the heart of Nazi Germany,[1] the sisters in Evergreen Park received a long-awaited letter from the Motherhouse in Santo Stefano Rotondo. Mother M. Hilda Potter's correspondence, dated Easter 1945, conveyed belated Paschal blessings to her daughters in America and informed them of a momentous occurrence that had taken place two-and-a-half years earlier:

> It is a great pleasure to be able to write to you again after all these years of silence....
>
> There is so much to tell after these sad and difficult years, but I am sure what you would most like to know would be the happy event which took place, in the midst of the war years, the Introduction of the Cause of the Beatification and Canonization of Our loved Mother Foundress....
>
> On the 30th of December 1942, in the presence of [Monsignor] Traglia, Vice[regent] of Rome, representing the Cardinal Vicar, the Informative Process of the "Cause of the Beatification and Canonization of the Servant of God, Mother Mary Potter" was formally opened....
>
> On January 22, 1943, the first meeting of the Tribunal took place.... Mother Catherine was called first ... [and her] evidence lasted for three meetings and after she had finished, Father Benedict Williamson was called and then the other Sisters and secular witnesses.... The weekly meetings went on from January to July 1943, then they were suspended, partly on account of the summer weather and ... afterwards on account of the conditions of Rome.... [A]ll the documents necessary were sent to England and Ireland, so that the supplementary Tribunal could be set up there to get evidence ... [from] the Sisters in those houses and ... [others] who knew Mother. But it was a long time before this could be done on account of the difficulty in getting the necessary documents over, during the War. [O]nly after the liberation of Rome, [was] ... the Cause ... commenced in Westminster.
>
> The Process, so far as I know, is going favourably.... But the great thing needed now are [sic] *miracles* ... in order to carry the Cause on

to the next stage, that of the Apostolic Process.... [Y]ou can all help very much by encouraging devotion to Mother and confidence in her intercession, asking her to obtain cures or other great favours, if it be pleasing to Our Lord, in order to hasten her Beatification....[2]

Shortly after receiving this joyful news from Rome, the sisters (along with the rest of the world), were stunned by the news of the sudden death of President Franklin Delano Roosevelt from a cerebral hemorrhage. Eighteen days later, Adolf Hitler committed suicide, and on May 7, 1945, Germany surrendered. The war in Europe was over. Exactly one hundred days later, the war in the Pacific came to an end.[3]

As wartime transitioned into peacetime and the soldiers returned home, the Little Company of Mary was planning to expand its apostolate in both the United States and South America. During December 1945, in anticipation of building a new hospital, the community in Buenos Aires formed the *Asociación María Potter*, which gave the Little Company of Mary a legal status that the government of Argentina would recognize.[4] Sister M. Fintan Kealy was named president; Sister M. Regina Powell, secretary; and the seven other sisters in Buenos Aires were listed as members. That month the community also sent one thousand pounds sterling to the Irish Province, which "cancel[ed] half the debt contracted with the Australian Province in 1939."[5] The following April, Reverend Mother General authorized the purchase of property in the city by a friend of the Little Company who would hold it until the sisters' financial situation improved.[6]

While the Buenos Aires community was repaying past loans and securing a site for its new hospital, the community in Evergreen Park was feeling the squeeze that was typical of the postwar years. One sister wrote, "1946 finds us with such crowded conditions that the hospital administration has become a nightmare."[7] The minutes of a Council Meeting on July 6, 1946, contain the following:

Permission has been obtained from Cardinal Stritch and the Roman Council to borrow one million and a quarter [dollars] for the hospital. All the final papers [are in order] regarding the completion of the building, and we have received permission to start work whenever we can obtain the material to do so.[8]

The planned addition of several more floors to the Little Company of Mary Hospital in Evergreen Park would add 150 more beds to the facility, enabling the sisters to care for more patients. The following spring, the cardinal gave his final approval to the project. [9]

A community member described the temporary havoc caused by the expansion:

> The scaffolding was erected in June 1947, and the noise of ... building really began. You have never experienced ... noise until someone removes a temporary roof ... especially if you are a sick patient. I often wonder what the poor people suffered in the underground during the black-out [sic] and bombing[s] ... of course we had no fear of anything dropping on us here! But the noise was nothing compared to what happened when ... workers forgot to fix the covering on the temporary roof and the rain poured down in torrents on [the] 4th floor and especially in the Operating Room—even coming through the light fixtures....
>
> In the midst of all the noise and bustle, we are brought to the full realization that the building is costing us a great deal more than was ever anticipated. We will only be able to put up two floors ... another visit to the Chancery Office, another delay in waiting and finally permission given to borrow more money and at least complete three floors.... [10]

At the same time that the sisters in Evergreen Park were enlarging their hospital, the community in San Antonio de Areco was facing a very different situation. During her canonical visit there in May 1948, Mother M. Bernard Martin (who had been elected Mother General the previous spring) announced her intention to withdraw the members of the Little Company from the Maria Clara Morgan Hospital. Her decision was based primarily on two factors. First, she felt that the hospital did not measure up to the standards required to provide an acceptable level of patient care. In spite of some minor improvements, the facility was still substandard compared to the other hospitals run by the community worldwide. In addition, she had some serious concerns about the welfare of the sisters serving there. [11]

Mother Bernard's resolve to recall the sisters from the remote Argentine outpost came twenty-two years after Mother Hilda had

The residents of San Antonio de Areco contributed to expand Sanatorio Maria Clara Morgan to forty-five beds.

proposed a similar plan, which would have resulted in the sisters leaving in 1926. This did not occur, however, because the bishop had insisted that the members of the Little Company remain in his diocese. Two decades later, it would not be the local prelate who was able to change Mother's mind, but the people of San Antonio de Areco themselves. They pledged to renovate the existing structure and add a new building if the sisters stayed. Mother General eventually acquiesced to their pleas, and the local residents fulfilled their commitment within two years, remodeling and slightly enlarging the Maria Clara Morgan Hospital so that it had a patient capacity of forty-five.

Seventy-five miles south, in Buenos Aires, the sisters were ready to expand the work they had begun when they opened their first *sanatorio* in 1939. The community now planned to build a facility that would replace that small private hospital. On August 22, 1948, the foundation stone was laid for the new Little Company of Mary Hospital in the Argentine capital and blessed by His Eminence, Luis Santiago Cardinal Copello.

Several months later, as members of the South American community watched the support structures for their future hospital being firmly anchored in the ground of Buenos Aires, their sisters in North America gazed skyward as their hospital rose higher and higher above Evergreen Park.

The hospital expansion in Illinois would ultimately include five additional stories, more than doubling the facility's space and providing extra beds during the boom of the fifties when the United States experienced the largest growth in its history—an addition of almost thirty million people.[12] More than eighty percent of the total population growth occurred in the suburbs,[13] so areas like Evergreen Park grew substantially.

After two years, the building project was not yet completed, but one sister documented some of the tangible benefits:

> And now in the evening of March 17, 1949, ... patients are being admitted to the new 5th floor.... Some weeks later, [the] sixth floor is opened for the tonsil season.... Six weeks later [the] 7th floor ... so we have plenty of space at last....[14]

Along with the external transformation that was taking place at the hospital, a significant change had also taken place within the Evergreen Park community. Mother M. Genevieve Canty was appointed as Superior—also responsible for San Pierre—while Mother M. Stanislaus was named to supervise the construction of a new hospital to be built in southern Indiana.[15]

The early fifties were defined by amazing technological innovations and society-altering developments. Thanks to the GI Bill, which paid for veterans' tuition, college enrollment reached record levels. The first commercial computer was marketed in 1951,[16] and by the end of 1952, almost nineteen million homes had television.[17] The following year, James Watson and Francis Crick unraveled the mystery of DNA, the genetic blueprint of life, and innovations were occurring in medicine and nursing that would have seemed inconceivable a decade earlier. One of the sisters in Evergreen Park chronicled some of those changes:

> The new scientific methods now adopted have changed the entire course of the hospital. Surgical cases are dismissed ... in six or seven days; they are up and about now after an operation on the second day. Mothers and babies go home on the fifth day instead of on the tenth. The pneumonia jacket and the camphorated oil rub are now almost like medical history and the new sulfa drugs ... [and] penicillin take care of everything, not to mention cortisone and ACTH.... Eye Banks, Blood Banks, Kidney Banks, Bone Banks.... [W]ho would miss living in the golden age of 1950 ... with all its advancements....[18]

Surprisingly, this list did not include a remarkable, history-making event that had taken place in Evergreen Park on June 17, 1950, when a team of surgeons lead by Dr. Richard Lawler performed the world's first successful human organ (kidney) transplant at Little Company of Mary Hospital. [19]

During this "golden age," postwar America found itself in the midst of a construction boom as millions of servicemen returned home, married, and needed housing for their new families. "The GI Bill allowed veterans to buy a home with no money down and even guaranteed the loans so lenders were not at risk."[20] As a result, "Nationwide, housing starts soared ... to a high of 12 per 1,000 in 1950, a number not equaled since." [21]

The Little Company of Mary in Evergreen Park found itself part of this building expansion. For decades, the sisters had experienced growing pains as its members put up with less-than-optimal living conditions— overcrowding, temporary residences, barrack-style housing, and even seeing the community split up when the novitiate was moved to San Pierre in 1944. Now it was time to remedy this situation.

In August 1950, ground was broken for a new convent that would not only comfortably accommodate the increasing number of sisters in the foundation, but would also provide enough space for a novitiate.

That summer was filled with hopeful promise for the community. For some Americans, however, it turned out to be "… a dark time, [as] America was reluctantly being drawn into a world it had never made…,"[22] a place called Korea. One sister reflected:

> [N]ow again we see the war clouds gathering—the war in Korea has broken out—more preparations are being made for the approach of the enemy—Russia.…
>
> Nurses from the last Reserves are being called back to duty. Our young Doctors are again going into uniform and called to foreign parts. The residency in our departments [is] cancelled for the term of the war.… The world is once more full of unrest, the communist[s] seem to have sway.… [23]

During World War II, almost all steel production had been directed toward the war effort, but the ongoing conflict did not include rationing of building materials, so construction of the sisters' new home continued on schedule. The work was completed eighteen months later, and on

March 14, 1952, the sisters moved into the Convent of the Maternal Heart, a fitting five-story brick residence conveniently situated just steps from their hospital.

That same year, the Little Company of Mary reached out to a second rural Indiana community—the town of Jasper. Nestled within the rolling hills of southern Indiana, 212 miles southwest of San Pierre, Jasper was the largest of a handful of towns in sparsely populated Dubois County, whose entire population numbered less than twenty-four thousand during the early 1950s. [24]

The area's first settlers had arrived from Kentucky and Tennessee around 1801, bringing with them English ancestry and Protestant beliefs.[25] At the beginning of the nineteenth century, Dubois County had virtually no Catholic families in spite of the fact that "Catholicism reached the boundaries of . . . [what is now] present-day Indiana long before any other of the European faiths."[26] Although Catholic priests had accompanied French explorers throughout the Midwest as early as the 1670s,[27] and a Jesuit mission appears to have existed in nearby Vincennes in 1710,[28] it was not until 1836 that Catholic immigrants from Germany began settling in Evansville and in Jasper.[29]

Two years later, "Father Joseph Kundek of the Archdiocese of Agram, Croatia, came to the Diocese of Vincennes after hearing of the need for German-speaking missionaries."[30] That September, he was sent to Jasper to establish a mission parish for five Catholic families living there. As Dubois County's first resident Catholic priest, he attempted to "encourage Catholic immigration to Indiana [as well as] to establish Catholic colonies where Catholics could practice their religion freely and be protected from the nativism which was already intense in many parts of the country." [31]

Father Kundek's efforts to recruit German immigrants to Jasper and neighboring Ferdinand, which he founded, were so successful that by the 1860s, "southeastern and central Dubois County [were] populated predominantly by German Catholics."[32] Even today—almost a century and a half later—more than fifty percent of Jasper's residents can trace their roots back to Germany.[33] In the early fifties, some were still involved in the woodworking skills of their forefathers, and virtually all retained their ancestors' values, particularly the German work ethic.[34] That trait, evident in so many of Jasper's citizens, became even more apparent after the town was chosen to be the site of a much-needed hospital.

Once the decision was made, a group of local businessmen formed the Dubois County Hospital Association, which determined early on that a congregation of Catholic nursing sisters should operate and administer the facility. Jasper resident Sister Alma Cecile Keeley, a member of the Sisters of Providence, recommended the Little Company of Mary based on her personal knowledge of the community.[35] When Bishop Henry Joseph Grimmelsman of Evansville heard of the reputation that the blue-veiled sisters had earned during their almost sixty years of nursing service in Chicago and their two decades of operational and administrative experience in Evergreen Park, he sent Monsignor Leonard Wernsing to make his case to Mother M. Stanislaus, who listened with interest. After meeting with members of the hospital association, considerable discussion, reflection, and prayer, and with the approval of the Motherhouse, the sisters accepted the invitation to run Jasper's future hospital.

The people of Jasper and their neighbors had started raising money in December 1945 in order to make Memorial Hospital a reality[36] in an area where medical facilities were few and far between. To qualify for federal funding, they needed to come up with a half-million dollars. Individuals and civic groups contributed. The townspeople held bake sales and fund-raising street dances. Virtually the entire community became involved—the Knights of Columbus and the Masons, the American Legion and the Kiwanis Club. From the youngest residents who hosted a two-day "kids' carnival" to the generous Jasper Manufacturing Association, which guaranteed the balance of funds needed—more than $29,000[37]—the people of Dubois County responded wholeheartedly, exceeding their $500,000 goal by $15,000. The federal government provided an additional $360,000, and the Little Company of Mary contributed $225,000[38] to cover the remaining cost of the hospital.

On February 12, 1948, Mother Stanislaus and two other sisters visited Jasper to take charge of the hospital project.[39] They returned numerous times in the ensuing months to confer with members of the hospital association, visit the future building site, and work out the endless details. Two years later, on a wintry day in February, Mother Dunstan and Mother Stanislaus looked on as Monsignor Wernsing blessed the cornerstone. The building of the hospital was about to begin in earnest.

LCM Sisters at their first convent in Jasper, Indiana, a ranch-style home located on MacArthur Street.

For more than a year, the Sisters of Providence graciously opened their doors to members of the Little Company.[40] Their records indicate that beginning in mid-June 1950, "Mother Stanislaus, Sister Catherine, and, off and on, two others [unnamed LCM members] stayed at St. Joseph Convent as they supervised the construction of the hospital and made necessary purchases."[41]

A contingent left Evergreen Park for their new assignment three weeks before the hospital's scheduled opening, which was set for June 15, 1951. The initial group of sisters in Jasper numbered only ten, including Mother Stanislaus, who would be both the Superior of the congregation and in charge of the hospital. The fledgling community quickly settled into a ranch-style house on MacArthur Street that was to serve as their convent.

During their first days in southern Indiana, the sisters tried to get used to "weather [that] was beastly hot,"[42] and to "endless rains,"[43] which turned the surrounding area into a sea of mud. While preparing to open their new facility, the community relied on their new friends to chauffeur them to and from the hospital during the relentless summer downpours. One sister admitted, "Most of us have lost [our] pride and will ride in almost any kind of vehicle,"[44] which included a Coca-Cola truck, a massive piece of street-paving machinery, and even an outlandishly outdated covered wagon. [45]

The sisters soon encountered something that surprised them even more than the brutal heat and humidity of their first Hoosier summer—the concerted effort of Jasper residents. One of the pioneering sisters observed, "One can but stand back in astonishment and admiration at the co-operative spirit of the people of this community. My, how they work!" [46]

On July 8, 1951, Bishop Grimmelsman officiated at the dedication of Memorial Hospital—the result of the combined efforts of the people of Jasper and their neighbors. That same day, a local newspaper caption, "Honors Memory of County's Heroic Dead," [47] announced the opening of the hospital, which was dedicated "to those men and women ... who have served our country in times of war...." [48]

Numerous surgeries kept the sisters "quite busy" [49] for the first few weeks, but on August 16, 1951, the Little Company took time from their hectic schedules to repay a small part of the hospitality that they had received during the previous two years. When the Sisters of Providence returned to Jasper after spending several months at their Motherhouse in Saint-Mary-of-the-Woods, "they were greeted with a welcome sign from the Little Company Sisters and an invitation to dinner...." [50] In the following years this "Welcome Home" meal became a late-summer tradition for the two communities of religious who called Jasper home.

Shortly after it opened, the new hospital experienced an initial rush of admissions, but that autumn and throughout much of the winter there was a troubling lack of patients. In September, a community member noted, "Only a few surgical cases now." [51] The following month showed no improvement. "Business is bad ... (O.B. floor)," wrote one sister. "No mothers—3 babies." Another memo indicated, "Patient census very low—no new admissions," [52] and an entry from early December revealed two concerns:

> ... malicious gossip floating about. [G]ood Father Fichter [admonishes], "Let the Sisters remember they are pioneering." Mother M. Catherine [Barrett] made a statement of our financial status. If our patient census is 40 or above we are in the black, but if below 40, we are in the red. Father Fichter [says] these trials we are having now will bring upon us a great blessing, if we bear with them. [53]

During even the most difficult days, the sisters maintained their trust

The loving nursing care provided by the LCM Sisters at Calvary Convalescent Home meant an ever-increasing number of patients.

in God and continued to provide excellent nursing care to the sick and offer spiritual assistance to all. At the end of their first year in Jasper, they had overseen the treatment of 1,337 patients and had joyfully recorded the birth of 385 babies.[54] Several years later, a member of the Little Company reflected, "Things seem entirely changed since three years ago when we were praying hard for patients. Now the patients are placed in the hall, and even glad of a hospital bed."[55] Father Fichter's counsel had been correct.

In mid-June 1952, the novitiate was transferred from San Pierre to Evergreen Park,[56] where the fourth floor of the new convent was designated as the new novitiate. This allowed the white-veiled novices to be part of the larger community while fulfilling the canonical regulation that required them to maintain a degree of separation from the professed sisters. The novices' former residence was turned into a convalescent home after their exodus. In doing this, the sisters fulfilled the wish of John Tierney, who had requested that the Little Company of Mary build a nursing home for the aged and the infirm "so that San Pierre could be proud."[57]

In early September 1952, the sisters welcomed the first of fifty-seven patients whom they cared for during Calvary Convalescent Home's initial year of operation. Seven months later, Mother M. Patricia Dooley was appointed to be San Pierre's first Superior,[58] and by its first anniversary, the facility had run out of space. "[W]e needed more room for patients," wrote one sister. "The solarium on the second floor was painted and seven [additional] beds were bought...."[59] As the years went on, more and more Indiana residents sought care from the Little Company of Mary, and the facility continued to grow.

Americans were becoming increasingly prosperous, educated, and mobile during the early years of the fifties. Historian David Halberstam characterizes these years as "a good time to be young and get on with family...."[60] The sisters involved in maternity nursing in Evergreen Park witnessed firsthand the accuracy of his observation. Thanks to the baby boom which took place at this time, the Catholic population in the United States grew by an incredible forty-four percent....[61] The war's end had an unexpected bonus for the community. Halfway through the decade, Little Company of Mary Hospital achieved the distinction of being "second only to Cook County Hospital in the number of babies delivered in the Chicago area,"[62] which resulted in its fondly being referred to as "The Baby Hospital." [63]

For most Americans, this was a decade of unprecedented progress and economic optimism, yet it was also a time of escalating tension. The Communist Soviet Union had detonated its first atomic bomb in 1949, and as the Soviets continued to increase their military might and expansion throughout Eastern Europe, the Cold War heated up. One 1953 cover of the *Bulletin of the Atomic Scientists* featured a clock with its hands showing two minutes to midnight, fueling fear that "Doomsday" was approaching. The imminent threat of nuclear war seemed even more credible when the U.S. Government published a pamphlet entitled *You Can Survive,* containing information on how to build a backyard bomb shelter.[64]

The Catholic Church responded to the threats of atheism and the possibility of all-out war with a renewed emphasis on devotion to the Blessed Virgin Mary. Pius XII promulgated *Munificentissimus Deus* ("The most bountiful God"),[65] which asserted as dogma the belief that the Mother of God was assumed into heaven body and soul. He also declared 1953–1954 a "Marian Year" in celebration of the 100th anniversary of the proclamation of the Immaculate Conception, and published *Ad Caeli*

Reginam ("To the Queen of Heaven"),[66] which formally established the feast of the Queenship of Mary.[67]

Since faith was viewed as a powerful antidote for atheistic Communism, the United States experienced a revitalized interest in religion, which even touched the highest office in the land. In spite of the separation of church and state, Dwight D. Eisenhower authorized the addition of the words "under God" to the Pledge of Allegiance. "In this way," the President explained, "we are reaffirming the transcendence of religious faith in America's heritage and future...."[68]

The most recognizable Catholic clergyman in the United States in 1953 was Fulton J. Sheen, the auxiliary bishop of New York, whose television show *Life Is Worth Living* had a weekly audience of ten million viewers.[69] The bishop viewed the menace of the Soviet Union as an overriding concern as historian J. Ronald Oakley has pointed out. "[T]he subject he [Sheen] turned to again and again was [C]ommunism and its dangers to America and the rest of the Christian world...," states Oakley. He warned over and over ... that America must save the world from the hammer and sickle, just as she had once saved it from the swastika."[70]

At midyear, major hostilities ended in Korea. The peninsula was divided along the 38th parallel between the Communist north and non-Communist south,[71] and the conflict, which had been called "a war that no one wanted, in a desolate harsh land,"[72] dissolved into an uneasy truce.

Several months later, the new hospital in Buenos Aires was completed. On October 11, 1953, the Feast of the Maternal Heart, a Mass of Thanksgiving was celebrated in the hospital chapel, and two days later, patients were transferred from the original hospital on Avenida General San Martin (earlier named Avenida Alvear).[73] The official dedication, which took place in December, featured a front page article in *The Standard*, one of Buenos Aires' English-language periodicals. Under the headline, "Minister of Health Opens Little Company of Mary Hospital," the newspaper reported:

> In ... an impressive ceremony, attended by a very large gathering, the magnificent new hospital of the Little Company of Mary at San Martin de Tours 2952 was blessed yesterday morning by the Vicar-General of ... Buenos Aires, [Msgr.] Antonio Rocca representing the Cardinal Archbishop and opened by Dr. Ramon Carrillo, Minister of Health....

In 1953, the Little Company of Mary opened a new hospital in the center of Buenos Aires.

The official guests were welcomed by the Mother Superior, Sister M. Columba [Brady], and the Little Blue Sisters at the wide-pillared entrance to the new building....

The ceremony commenced with the singing of the Argentine National Anthem before Mass was said by [Msgr.] Carlos R. Copello at an altar raised on the lawns of the quadrangle and flanked with the Argentine and Papal flags, the golden hue and white of the latter being repeated in the gladioli on the altar....

Discussing the realization of the Sisters' dream of building a modern sanatorium in this city, Dr. Thomas [the hospital's technical director] paid tribute to the courage and enterprise of their small but splendid band, reminding his hearers that though the Order owned some fifty hospitals in different parts of the world, each of these is entirely independent....

Dr. Thomas desired to correct the impression that it was a luxury hospital, instead of one completely and ... modernly efficient which opened its doors ... to all that wished for its services for their physical and spiritual recovery, without distinction of race or creed....[74]

Unlike the remote location and relatively primitive conditions of Maria

Clara Morgan hospital, this new facility in a central district known as the Recoleta exemplified the highest medical and nursing standards. And in contrast to the Little Company's first *sanatorio* in the nation's capital, which had been a private facility, the new hospital would be accessible to all *porteños*, or residents, of Buenos Aires.

The scope of the mission of the Chicago Foundation continued to grow between 1945 and 1954, as did the places where its members served God by serving the needs of His people. Within five years, the sisters had significantly enlarged the Little Company of Mary Hospital in Evergreen Park (1949); established two facilities in Indiana: Memorial Hospital (1951) and Calvary Convalescent Home (1952); and opened a new hospital in the capital of Argentina (1953).

In both Jasper and San Pierre, as in Buenos Aires, the sisters initially numbered less than a dozen, but the ministry they accomplished was worthy of a much larger group. The words used by Dr. Thomas to commend the Little Company of Mary in Argentina could also have described the members who extended their gentle hands and loving hearts to the people of Indiana. Like their compeers in South America, these sisters also comprised a small but splendid band.

CHAPTER ELEVEN

CALLED TO
CRADLE AND CONSOLE

Sister M. Teresa Oleniczak, L.C.M., cares for children in the pediatrics department.

For both the Roman Catholic Church in the United States and the members of the Little Company of Mary who were working in three foundations in the American Midwest and in Argentina, the 1950s was truly a golden time. As a result of the postwar "baby boom," the Catholic Church in the United States was experiencing an explosion of growth, and unprecedented numbers of Catholics were answering God's call to serve His people through religious vocations. During this decade, eleven thousand new priests were ordained; seminary enrollment increased to almost forty thousand;[1] and the number of Catholic women religious in the United States reached an all-time high of more than one hundred eighty thousand sisters.[2]

Like many other religious communities, the membership of the Little Company of Mary grew substantially during these years. In the past, two or three young women usually entered the congregation as postulants at any one time, but now that number often doubled or tripled. The new convent, which had seemed so spacious when it had been built earlier in the decade, was quickly becoming filled to capacity.[3]

Nineteen fifty-five was a special year for the Little Company of Mary in America. On January 3, the sisters in the United States received word from Mother General that they had permission to form a new province of their own—the Province of the Immaculate Conception.[4] Mother M. Genevieve Canty was named as the first Provincial Superior and Mother M. Patricia Dooley, her assistant. Two months later, on the feast day of St. Patrick, the American Province became incorporated within the State of Illinois.[5] Not only had the U.S. community come of age, but within a year it would also expand eastward from America's heartland to include two new foundations—one in Massachusetts and one in New York.

That same year, Richard J. Cushing, the archbishop of Boston, invited the Little Company of Mary to work at Otis General in East Cambridge. Dr. James L. Lawlor, founder and medical director of that small, private hospital, had recently donated the facility to the archdiocese, and the prelate needed a congregation of Catholic sisters to run it and provide supervisory nursing. If the Little Company of Mary Sisters accepted this assignment, Cushing planned to turn Otis General over to them.

There are no records that explain why Archbishop Cushing chose the Little Company of Mary for this task. Although the community had a sterling reputation for both nursing and administrative skills, its closest

ARCHBISHOP'S HOUSE
2101 COMMONWEALTH AVENUE
BRIGHTON 35, MASS.

February 25, 1956

Dear Mother:

I thank you for your letter of February the 17th.

All goes well with your Sisters at the Otis General Hospital. We will have the Community incorporated in the near future and the name of the hospital will be changed to The Hospital of the Little Company of Mary. The Sisters first called it "Calvary Hospital" but I told them it should be called after the Community itself. They agreed.

Their future is bright in this Archdiocese. We will be of every possible service to them.

Begging God's choicest blessings upon you during this holy season of Lent, I am

Your devoted friend,

Archbishop of Boston

Mother Œenard
The Mother House
Little Company of Mary

The Archbishop of Boston saw a bright future for the LCM.

facility to Boston was in Indiana—almost a thousand miles from the Bay State. It also appears that the future cardinal was unaware of the "English Sisters" who ran Calvary Hospital because his time in Rome was limited to brief, occasional visits.[6]

However it was that Cushing heard of the Little Company of Mary, the community became one of approximately sixty religious congregations of men and women that he introduced into his archdiocese over three decades.[7] When the archbishop extended his invitation to the Little Company, various nursing communities, including the Daughters of Charity, the Daughters of Mary of the Immaculate Conception, and the Franciscan Missionaries of Mary, had been working within the Boston archdiocese for years,[8] and because they were already operating hospitals of their own, it is unlikely that any of them would have been interested in running Otis General, even temporarily.

To the members of the Little Company of Mary, the archbishop's invitation and his gift of Otis General seemed like the perfect opportunity to expand their apostolate to the East Coast. The offer was particularly appealing because it appeared that the archdiocese was willing to assist the community in building a new hospital of its own on the condition that the sisters serve at Otis General for a few years. That "understanding" would eventually prove to be incorrect.

*The deteriorating conditions at Otis General Hospital eventually
forced the LCM Sisters to leave East Cambridge, Massachusetts.*

The Little Company of Mary's newest apostolate took the sisters
to East Cambridge, an industrial section of the city that developed after
the completion of the Canal Bridge in 1809. Successive generations of
immigrants—English and German at first, then large numbers of Irish—
worked in the factories that quickly sprung up in the area. Municipal
records from the late 1800s show that the "majority of the city's Irish
lived in East Cambridge, laboring in unskilled jobs in the glass works and
furniture factories [where] they developed a close-knit community, centered
on and supported by the Catholic Church."[9] During the early twentieth
century, immigrants from southern Europe joined them. By the time the
sisters began their assignment, most people living in the neighborhoods
around the hospital were of Italian descent.

The hospital, located at the corner of Fourth and Otis Streets in East
Cambridge, was originally constructed as a three-story, single-family
residence in 1914,[10] and the red brick building was turned into a hospital
two years later as part of the Massachusetts College of Osteopathy.[11] The
structure was enlarged to four stories in 1922,[12] and during the 1940s,
became a private forty-bed medical hospital run by a group of local
doctors. When the members of the Little Company arrived, the facility
had a capacity of sixty-five beds.[13]

Sister M. Ignatius Dooley, Sister M. Virginia O'Brien, and Sister M.
Maura Tangney arrived in Boston on February 11, 1956, and stayed with

the Sisters of St. Joseph at Sacred Heart Convent for a few days.[14] On February 15, they began working at Otis General, the fifth foundation within the American Province. The sisters moved into two rooms on the third floor of the hospital, which served as their bedroom, living room, and chapel. The unsuitability of this arrangement led Mother Genevieve to find rooms for them in an adjacent building, and an entryway was cut to allow the sisters direct access into the hospital. Just how much of an improvement this was, is questionable. Their "very old, very rickety" apartment had tiny rooms, their bedroom ceilings sloped so drastically that it was impossible to stand completely upright, and the chapel contained only a single pew.[15] On March 8, the trio moved into their "new" residence,[16] which was a far cry from the comfortable accommodations of their four-year-old convent in Evergreen Park.

The following week, they met with Archbishop Cushing at his residence and recorded that the prelate "gave us great encouragement in our new work and used one of his favorite mottos as a guide to us: 'Make haste slowly.'"[17]

Because the hospital was so small, the sisters were often required to perform a variety of services. The admitting sister who answered the bell often also did the new patient's preliminary blood work and even ran it down to the lab. If simple x-rays were required, the sisters took them themselves and also occasionally operated the switchboard. Because the group worked almost nonstop seven days a week and nights, the assignment "seemed more like a mission"[18] to Sister Jean Stickney, one of the first sisters to serve in East Cambridge. Sister Maura, another of the pioneering members, recalled, "We were living very simply, helping the poor. We were very happy; we didn't know how miserable [things] were."[19]

The sisters slowly transformed the hospital from a secular facility to a Catholic institution. One sister documented that on April 10, "Crucifixes were hung in all the hospital rooms today. The hospital is beginning to take on a more religious atmosphere with the ... frequent reception of the Sacraments."[20]

During their first six months, the community, which now numbered six, worked at breakneck speed. The usual two-week summer vacation, which provided a brief respite from an otherwise hectic nursing schedule, was out of the question. The sisters simply had no replacements. Their sole getaway was the rooftop of their apartment. Mother Genevieve had assured them this was a lovely place to relax and walk around, but the views it afforded—of neighboring tenements, endless rows of clotheslines, and smoke from nearby factories—left something to be desired. Their neighborhood was only a few miles from the elite surroundings of America's oldest university, but Harvard's well-manicured campus seemed like another world.

In spite of the never-ending work, an aging hospital that was deteriorating daily, and cramped and dilapidated living conditions, the group maintained their spirit and their sense of humor. One oppressive day in August, they received a postcard from their fellow sisters in England who were spending their summer holiday at what appeared to be a charming spot along the English coast called Sutton-on-Sea. That evening, as they headed upstairs for a breath of fresh air atop their building, Sister Mary Jane Feil drolly remarked, "And here *we* are, going to Sittin'-on-Roof."[21]

A few days later, when the former board of trustees presented the sisters with their charter, Otis General officially became Little Company of Mary Hospital.[22] Before the month ended, a beautiful statue representing the Maternal Heart was added to the lobby, and within several weeks, Archbishop Cushing appointed the Franciscan friars from a nearby parish as hospital chaplains. Now the sisters could have Mass in their own convent chapel and patients had access to daily Communion.[23]

The hospital could not compete with Boston's large medical facilities, but it did fulfill two roles that religiously organized hospitals often assume.[24] First, it served a specific need within the community,[25] which for most residents of East Cambridge who were first- or second-generation working-class Americans was affordable, accessible medical treatment. The sisters kept the hospital running smoothly and efficiently and did everything they could to keep the cost down for their patients. Second, like a church, it provided a sense of identification for uprooted immigrants.[26] Despite the fact that the hospital was tiny and outdated, its newly established Church affiliation provided the Catholics of East Cambridge with the comforting presence of sisters—a powerful reminder of their shared faith, whether they happened to be of Irish, Italian, Portuguese, or Polish descent.

Two weeks after the foundation in Massachusetts was established, the Little Company of Mary began a somewhat different apostolate in upstate New York. The invitation to work at St. Mary's Hospital and Maternity Home came from Monsignor Joseph B. Toomey, who represented Walter A. Foery, bishop of the Diocese of Syracuse. For the previous fifty-five years, the Daughters of Charity of Emmitsburg, Maryland, had operated a home for unwed mothers and an orphanage in Syracuse, but during the mid-1950s the children's home was closed, and the archdiocese decided to expand St. Mary's into a general hospital.

In light of the archdiocese's new plans, the head of the Daughters of Charity informed Bishop Foery of her dilemma:

> It is true that our Sisters have been there [at St. Mary's] for more than half a century, but no one realizes more than Your Excellency the tremendous changes that have taken place during that time. It is also true that several of the Sisters have been there for over forty years, but this only means that replacements would soon be necessary. With the shortage [of qualified nursing sisters], there will be no one to send to take up these duties.[27]

The Daughters of Charity knew that they did not have the personnel to do what the bishop was asking of them. They also recognized that taking care of a small group of mothers and babies was one thing— administering a general hospital was quite another. This realization prompted the head of the community to reply to the bishop:

> Your letter of April 5 is so simple and direct that I am encouraged to respond in the same spirit.
>
> In appointing Sisters to staff Saint Mary's Infant Home and Maternity Hospital, we have always thought in terms of the children rather than of the patients. For the past years this was … natural and proper. From your letter it is apparent that the hospital has now become the principal part of the institution.…
>
> [Our present administrator] was sent there because of her experience in the work for children and unmarried mothers. Her hospital experience is quite negligible and we would not consider her highly qualified to administer the business of a modern and progressive hospital.
>
> The difficulty is that we have no one for the duty nor have we enough Sisters with hospital experience for the proper staffing.…[28]

In a subsequent letter, she explained, "As we shall not have anyone properly qualified in the foreseeable future, we believe that it will be in the best interests of all concerned that the institution be given over to others who will meet the [necessary] requirements."[29] Bishop Foery accepted her decision reluctantly and expressed his "deep and lasting gratitude for the magnificent service ... given [by the Daughters of Charity] over these many years at the Hospital and at the Home."[30]

In late autumn of 1955, he contacted the Little Company of Mary and asked the sisters to consider taking over the administration of St. Mary's "for a period of five years, after which time the title of the property [would be] turned over to the community."[31] The Little Company responded with interest. Several months later, two members of the community traveled to Syracuse to evaluate the situation firsthand. Following their visit, the sister in charge of St. Mary's wrote to her Superior:

> Wednesday at noon, Monsignor called and said he was bringing two Sisters from "The Little Company of Mary" from Chicago.... They arrived around 1:45. I took them through.... I do not know if they will take it or not. They only do hospital work and would not think of taking babies, unmarried mothers, etc.... I did not ask them any questions. They were very nice and businesslike. Monsignor told them in the office, he does not know which way to turn....[32]

At the end of January 1956, the prelate sent the following message to the Provincial Superior of the Daughters of Charity:

> I expected to have official assurance that another Community would take up the work at St. Mary's.... This has now come to us from Mother M. Genevieve of the Convent of the Maternal Heart of the Little Company of Mary at Evergreen Park, Ill. Mother Genevieve will send Sisters to take over the work at St. Mary's on the first of March....[33]

The Daughter of Charity who had written that the sisters "would not think of taking babies [and] unmarried mothers" must not have known of the Little Company of Mary's history, for the blue-veiled sisters had operated a facility for unwed mothers in London for fifty-three years, beginning in 1898.[34] The Little Company of Mary did accept the assignment at St. Mary's, and this foundation introduced a new dimension to the community's healing mission as the sisters in the American Province for the first time found themselves in charge of a facility for unwed mothers.

Reverence for life has always been a Catholic value, and the Church has had a long history of care for unmarried pregnant women. The Syracuse diocese's involvement can be traced back to 1900, when Patrick Anthony Ludden, the city's first bishop, asked the Daughters of Charity to take over the work started eleven years earlier by Mrs. B. Toohill. The widow had rented a house on Hawley Avenue "[for] the sole purpose of giving a home to abandoned babies and a shelter to unmarried mothers."[35] Fifty-six years later, the Little Company of Mary assumed this ministry.

Late in February 1956, Mother Provincial (M. Genevieve) and Mother M. Teresa Oleniczak, the newly appointed Superior for Syracuse, accompanied the three sisters who were en route to Boston to begin working at Otis General. A few days later, the two Superiors left for upstate New York and were waiting to welcome the new foundation's first members (Assistant Superior Mother M. Lucy Colgan, Sister M. Hilda O'Halloran, Sister M. Paula Rooney, and Sister M. Angela Ludwig) when they arrived on February 27. The group met with Bishop Foery at the Chancery Office that morning, and one of the sisters later wrote, "all were made to feel that they had a Father and Protector in their new Bishop."[36] For the next several days, the sisters stayed at the Hotel Syracuse and traveled back and forth to the hospital as they familiarized themselves with the workings of the facility with the help of two Daughters of Charity who had remained at St. Mary's to help acclimate them.

On March 1, 1956, the sisters' first official act in their new foundation was attending 6 a.m. Mass at St. Mary's Maternity Hospital,[37] then they quickly got to work. One of the earliest changes they made was to "lighten up" the place. Mother M. Teresa's initial impression of St. Mary's had been one of overwhelming drabness where "everything was painted brown."[38]

The facility's appearance may have had such a negative effect on the new Superior because she had an innate appreciation of color and a special talent for watercolors.[39] Even sixty years after seeing the Little Company of Mary Sisters for the first time, she still remembered the indelible impression that their distinctive pale blue veil and bright red cincture made on her, as it contrasted with the stark black and white worn by most other religious.[40]

Not surprisingly, then, the dull, monochromatic color scheme of the hospital was one of the first things "to go." "We started renovating and painted [using] all light colors,"[41] recalls Sister Teresa. Although this change was essentially cosmetic in nature, it positively affected the mood of both patients and staff. In addition, the nurseries that had been described in a local newspaper article as, "a place where many young Syracusans have received their first loving care from members of the Little Company of Mary...."[42] were freshly painted pale pink and blue. The new Superior of the Little Company of Mary was also instrumental in bringing about a major change in the living conditions of the young residents of the maternity home who in past years had lived on one of the upper floors of an older building located at the back of the property. Now a small cottage on the grounds was remodeled to provide the mothers-to-be with more of a real home during their stay.[43]

The sisters who served at St. Mary's speak of their mission with great fondness. Helping mothers and babies is especially fitting for a community centered on the maternal love of Mary, and maternity nursing has long been part of the work done by members of the Little Company. St. Mary's, however, posed a challenge that was somewhat different from their other foundations. For the first time, the sisters were called upon to provide a compassionate environment to a number of young women whose emotional state did not include the joy that usually accompanies the birth of a child. None of the residents had the supportive love of a husband, all would be giving up their babies for adoption, and most of them were just teenagers.

In the 1950s, out-of-wedlock pregnancy still carried with it a social stigma. To safeguard the identities of the residents of St. Mary's Maternity Home, each mother-to-be was addressed by a fictitious first name during her stay.[44] The sisters supported these young women as they underwent the physical and psychological changes of pregnancy and childbirth, and helped ease the pain of loss as each new mother gave up her newborn so the baby could be placed with a loving family.

The members of the Little Company of Mary quickly learned that what most of the unwed expectant mothers needed, more than anything else, was compassion and unconditional love, which they offered unreservedly. Even forty-seven years later, the former Superior at St. Mary's has not forgotten a sixteen-year-old resident who said that for the first time in her life she felt that she was in a place where she was truly loved.[45]

As the Syracuse sisters were settling into their new apostolate and transforming the facility, they were given an opportunity to make the Little Company of Mary better known to the residents of New York. A local priest interested in fostering vocations suggested that members of various religious congregations introduce themselves and their work to the public in a novel way—through a series of fifteen-minute television presentations. The sisters chose two members to represent their community. One sister, who wore the black habit and blue veil, provided a brief history of Mother Mary Potter; the other, in nursing whites, spoke of the congregation's various foundations and activities.[46]

During their first months in Syracuse, the community encountered situations that were unfamiliar and demanding. Mother Provincial, who was well aware of how serving at St. Mary's differed from an assignment at one of the other more established foundations, wrote to them, "Beginnings are hard. First, to adjust to a small hospital and a small community of Sisters; second, to new doctors, different methods of doing things...."[47] The pioneering group adapted quickly and soon faced their greatest challenge—keeping the maternity hospital running smoothly during its two-year transition into a larger, general facility.

On May 15, 1958, the members of the Syracuse foundation rejoiced in the opening of its enlarged hospital, which included the addition of forty-one beds for medical patients who did not need surgery. St. Mary's Hospital now provided seventy-seven adult beds and thirty-four bassinets for infants, a medical staff of sixty active physicians with an additional sixty-nine on the consultative and courtesy staff, along with sixty-two nursing personnel to aid the staff of seven members of the Little Company of Mary.

The Joint Commission on Accreditation of Hospitals acknowledged this remarkable achievement the following year. In a letter of approval sent to the community, the national standard-setting board noted, "The commission wishes to commend you for maintaining standards deserving of accreditation for your constant effort to improve the quality of patient care."[48]

As the American Province was expanding its mission to Massachusetts and New York in early 1956, it was about to lose its second-oldest foundation —San Antonio de Areco, Argentina. Several years earlier, Mother M.

Bernard Martin had assured the local residents that the Little Company would remain as long as there was a need for the sisters, but at the beginning of 1956, she decided that the community should withdraw from the small, rural hospital where the sisters had worked since 1913.

Several factors contributed to Mother General's change of heart.[49] Her primary concern was the welfare of the sisters for whom she was responsible. Argentina was going through an unsettling time, and there was a possibility of a revolution. In a remote and isolated area like San Antonio, the small group of religious would have been particularly vulnerable. It also appears that the *sanatorio* was having difficulty finding supportive hospital personnel, and the shortage of lay staff had reached a critical juncture.

The unexpected departure of the Little Company of Mary took the residents of San Antonio by surprise. They had contributed to the renovation of the hospital three years earlier and thought that the sisters would serve at San Antonio indefinitely. No one, however, could have anticipated the anti-religious climate of the Peronist régime, which necessitated the sisters' withdrawal. In June 1956, two sisters along with four novices left for Rome. The following month, after arrangements were completed for the hospital to revert back to the diocese, the remaining eight sisters departed from San Antonio de Areco. Despite the uncertainty and potential danger of the time, all had asked to be transferred to Buenos Aires, a request which Mother General granted, thus ending the community's forty-three year history of nursing service in rural Argentina. At a later unspecified date, the *Congregación Hijas de San Camilo* (Sisters of Saint Camillus) "accepted the foundation, purchased the two lots bequeathed by [the Morgan family], and began their hospital apostolate to the people of ... San Antonio de Areco,"[50] which the Little Company of Mary had initiated more than four decades before. General nursing services continued for another forty-six years, but in 2003, "Hospital Morgan," as it was called, became a geriatric residence.[51]

In 1956, the congregation also extended its mission from the *sanatorio* to adjacent poor neighborhoods, known as *villas miserias* (misery villages), which had sprung up following a recent influx of immigrants from some of Argentina's northern provinces and from Bolivia and Paraguay. Thousands of poor, uneducated, unskilled, and often unhealthy migrant workers saw Buenos Aires as a place of opportunity and hope. Unfortunately, almost all of them soon discovered that their new situation in the nation's capital was far worse than what they had left behind. Now, "home" meant either a makeshift hut made of tin or cardboard, or a wooden crate along a riverbank or near the city's abandoned railway lines.[52]

The pastor of Saint Martin de Tours contacted the Little Company of Mary to see if the sisters could do anything to alleviate the desperate plight of the men and their families who were living in one of these shantytowns located near his church and within walking distance of their *sanatorio*. In response to his request, two members of the congregation—one a native-born Argentine—soon established a corporal and spiritual ministry to distribute food and clothing, provide simple medical treatment, and prepare both children and adults for the Sacraments.

At about the same time, the community in San Pierre was preparing to expand its service to a greater number of people in northern Indiana. On September 16, 1956, ground was broken and a two-year project began which would modify and enlarge Calvary Convalescent Home to include a general hospital that would address the acute nursing needs of those in the local area.[53] An article on the planned expansion in a local newspaper reported, "This is the story of Faith—the faith of the Sisters in the dedication of their work and of the communities that have made this request for a general hospital to help themselves in the American tradition."[54]

The hospital's grand opening took place on a snowy Sunday afternoon during the first week in December 1958. The community had hoped that the ceremony could be held on the feast of the Immaculate Conception, but since December 8 fell on a Monday, the dedication was set for the day before. The Holy Father imparted his Apostolic Blessing to the community, patients, medical and nursing staff, and all attending the ceremony,[55] and the Mayor of Chicago sent the following telegram:

YOUR VERY GRACIOUS INVITATION TO ATTEND THE DEDICATION ... IS GREATLY APPRECIATED AND I REGRET MY INABILITY TO BE PRESENT. IT IS IN THE FINE TRADITION OF THE SISTERS OF THE LITTLE COMPANY OF MARY WHO HAVE PERFORMED SO MANY GOOD WORKS IN OUR COMMUNITY OF CHICAGO THAT THIS NEW HUMANITARIAN FACILITY IS BEING MADE AVAILABLE.

TO THE GOOD SISTERS AND THE HOSPITAL STAFF MY VERY
BEST WISHES. RICHARD J. DALEY[56]

An excerpt from the journal of Sister M. Solace Hannigan, the
primary caretaker for John Tierney, whose generous gift of land helped
make both facilities possible, offers a glimpse of the sisters' work in
San Pierre at that time:

Little did I dream ... as I accompanied him [John Tierney] on his
last journey home, that I would return one day, to spend my own
last days in the loving home he provided. I have again been assigned
to San Pierre [but] it is a little harder to see and do things than it was
before. As I walk the corridors, I think how happy he would be to see
all that I am now seeing. [T]he hospital section is beautiful with its
modern medical and surgical facilities ... [b]ut I know his heart
would especially warm to the 75-bed convalescent section.

How he would love to see baby Mary Rita, who has a weak heart
and the sweetest smile this side of heaven ... or Aunt Ede, who will
celebrate her 100th birthday next May [yet] still walks and talks
faster than most of her resident friends. [H]e would thrill to the
pediatric section filled with darling toddlers afflicted with various
forms of brain damage. I shouldn't use the word "afflicted" because
I have never seen a happier or more loving group of children.

He would truly appreciate the tears that came to the eyes of the poor
old man who was admitted this morning in almost the same condition
as Mr. Tierney when I first saw him. It will not be long before he is
clean and dressed warmly, eating a good meal.... [And] he would
laugh if he could have heard Tom, age 94, recite Irish poetry all the
while he had major surgery performed under a local anesthetic,
or to have danced with all the Sox fans the night they stayed up
to see their team win the pennant on TV. How he would smile at the
gracious 80-year-old sales lady who is in her glory at the gift counter.

[T]here will always be many to thank God that one old man's need,
which grew into a dream ... has become a reality....[57]

As the community's work was expanding in upstate New York and in
northwestern Indiana, the foundation in East Cambridge was about to
close. The hope of having a hospital of their own in Boston remained just

that. Archbishop Cushing, who had recently received the red hat of the cardinalate, was responsible for building six hospitals throughout the archdiocese,[58] but he may have had to change his mind regarding providing assistance to the Little Company of Mary when he realized just how over-bedded the area was. Boston alone had seven Catholic hospitals—Carney, St. Elizabeth's, St. Margaret's, Sancta Maria, St. John's, St. Joseph's, and Bon Secour.[59] The number of unused beds in those facilities meant that the prelate would have been hard-pressed to justify the cost of constructing another hospital and expecting the people within his archdiocese to pay for it.

Very little of the late cardinal's correspondence still exists[60] because Cushing was afraid that his letters might be mishandled after his death. Consequently, he rarely made copies of his own correspondence and destroyed almost all letters written to him.[61] One of the cardinal's few surviving letters, however, is a response to an inquiry about the Little Company of Mary from Edward L. Heston, C.S.C., a consultor to the Sacred Congregation for Religious[62] who was charged with conducting apostolic visitations to the community's various European foundations.[63] Cardinal Cushing's reply includes an evaluation of the Little Company of Mary and may also reveal a glimpse of his intentions, or lack thereof, regarding future diocesan support for them:

I thank you for your letter of March 6th [1958] concerning the Little Company of Mary, commonly known as The Blue Nuns.

Please be advised that these Sisters came here only in recent years. They have a small Hospital of about fifty or sixty beds that was given to them as a gift through my intercession. There are only a few of the Sisters here and I have found them exemplary in every way. The Hospital is doing very well and insofar as this unit is concerned, the Sisters have no financial problem. In the future *they hope to build* [italics mine] a new Hospital in a more popular area of the Archdiocese. In a word, I have found the small group of the Little Company of Mary in the Archdiocese model religious, very capable nurses and totally dedicated to their work.[64]

At least for a while, the Archbishop had encouraged the sisters' hope of building a new hospital in Boston. "His Excellency, Archbishop

Cushing, presented a drawing of a 'Proposed Catholic Hospital' to us today," wrote one community member. "He told us to hang it in the hospital lobby for the medical staff and the hospital personnel to see."[65] By 1959, the prelate had changed his mind. When the community realized that Cardinal Cushing had no intention of providing any financial assistance for their future endeavors, the sisters had no choice but to leave. They could not build a new hospital in Boston entirely on their own, but they could not continue their work in the rundown hospital in East Cambridge.

During their final months in East Cambridge, the Massachusetts Public Health Department decreed that the hospital should no longer provide acute care,[66] so surgery was discontinued. A week or two before the sisters left, the hospital became a facility for the chronically ill and remained as such for another three decades. On October 20, 1959, after three years and eight months of service, the small group of sisters left the Boston area.[67] Otis Hospital closed its doors for good in 1989,[68] and six years later, the building was razed.[69]

In late 1959, as their service was coming to an end on the East Coast, the congregation was about to open a new foundation on America's West Coast. The upcoming decade would not only hold some surprises for Catholics in the United States, but for the Little Company of Mary, it would also mark the beginning of a new ministry as the community extended its presence to California.

The mid-to-late 1950s were unique for the Catholic Church in the United States, especially in light of some of the unexpected and far-reaching changes that affected so many religious communities during the late 1960s and beyond. Martin E. Marty, the only Protestant to ever serve as president of the American Catholic Historical Association, described the 1950s as "good times not only for religion in general but for Catholicism in particular...."[70] During these years:

The Church reached new heights of membership, institutional strength, and active participation in its devotional life. Around seventy percent of all Catholics attended Mass on Sundays ... [and on] Saturday afternoons, lines formed outside of confessional booths.... Devout Catholics prayed novenas ... [p]etitioners for divine favors lighted candles ... [m]illions wore scapulas and holy medals, ... blessed themselves in public before meals, fasted before receiving

Holy Communion, [and] proudly displayed ashes on their foreheads on Ash Wednesday ... and everyone observed silence as a mark of reverence for the Blessed Sacrament in the tabernacle....[71]

Church historian George Stewart points out that this was also an era when many Catholic sisterhoods in America "by objective measurable standard ... reached their zenith ... experiencing a great burst into bloom."[72] This was certainly true for the American Province of the Little Company of Mary. Despite the closing of two small foundations (San Antonio and East Cambridge), the community was flourishing. The Little Company of Mary had not only expanded to new locations—Jasper and San Pierre, East Cambridge and Syracuse, as well as to California by late 1959—but their apostolate had also broadened.

All members of the community continued to pray for the dying, and most sisters still provided nursing services to the acutely ill, but now some sisters staffed a place of refuge and compassion for unwed mothers while others provided physical care and support to the aged as they faced their final days. More than ever, Mary Potter's daughters in the United States were reaching out to all of God's people—particularly to the most vulnerable. For the members of the Little Company of Mary in America, as well as for the many who benefited from their ever-growing healing presence, this was a golden time, indeed.

CHAPTER TWELVE

SEASONS OF HOPE

Two postulants about to receive the LCM habit during a Ceremony of Reception and Profession in the early 1960s.

In January of 1960, less than six weeks after the sisters departed from the American Province's easternmost foundation in East Cambridge, the Little Company of Mary opened a new hospital more than three thousand miles away on the Pacific Coast. The congregation had been invited into the Archdiocese of Los Angeles on two earlier occasions during the 1930s, but had been unable to accept either offer—the first, because a small number of staff doctors opposed the presence of Catholic sisters in their hospital,[1] and the second, because the Great Depression had caused such financial hardship for the newly opened hospital in Evergreen Park that the community could not incur any additional debt at that time.[2]

Twenty years later, however, the Little Company of Mary was in a much different position—its major facilities were thriving, the community's financial situation was far more solid than it had been during the 1930s, and the congregation's membership in the United States was larger than ever before.

The initial plans for a hospital in California had begun four years earlier, in 1956. In January of that year, the congregation's Provincial Superior, Mother M. Genevieve Canty, received a letter from Monsignor Thomas J. O'Dwyer of the Catholic Archdiocese of Los Angeles in which he wrote:

> With the full approval of His Eminence [Cardinal McIntyre], I am writing you regarding the need for a modern community hospital within Los Angeles County. A few months ago a group of doctors ... aided me in sponsoring a survey by a recognized fund-raising agency ... I am enclosing herewith a brief summary.
>
> I am suggesting that you arrange to come to Los Angeles at the earliest possible date....[3]

What Monsignor O'Dwyer had in mind was a section in the southwest corner of Los Angeles County—a place known as South Bay. Like most of southern California, this area had experienced an explosion of growth throughout the 1950s as more and more Americans became aware of the possibilities that the Golden State had to offer. After World War II, the Catholic population alone increased dramatically—eighty-two parishes were added to the Archdiocese of Los Angeles between the late 1940s and the early 1960s.[4]

The Little Company of Mary responded quickly to the monsignor's offer. Five months later, James Francis McIntyre, the first archbishop of a western state to be elevated to the rank of cardinal,[5] wrote to Mother Genevieve offering the sisters a ten-acre site in Torrance on which they could build a hospital.[6] The community was able to accept its third invitation to head westward. After twenty-five years, the Little Company of Mary was finally going to realize its dream of expanding the healing presence of its sisters to the West Coast.

Within a year, Mother Genevieve and Mother General M. Bernard Martin were in California finalizing the plans for their future hospital.[7] Mother M. Lucy Colgan and Sister M. Magdalen Nolan were chosen to be the first two sisters to lay the groundwork for the community's newest foundation. On November 21, 1957, they boarded a plane for California, and according to Sister Magdalen, soon looked out onto mountains that were "magnificent and awe-inspiring" and saw the sparkling Pacific for the first time. Upon landing they also experienced some of California's less desirable features—"[a] very foggy Los Angeles … partly hidden from our view"[8] and a sandstorm that left "[e]verything … covered with a fine brown dust, which was most irritating to our eyes, nose[s], and throat[s]."[9]

Mother Lucy and Sister Magdalen stayed with the Sisters of Saint Joseph of Orange at Nativity convent as they prepared to settle into a five-room gray frame house at 803 Portola Avenue, which would serve as both their office and new residence. During their first few days, they attended to countless details as they worked quickly to get their new home in order—purchasing the items needed to set up housekeeping and even making curtains, which Sister Magdalen wryly described as being "practically the same length!"[10]

The following week, Mother Lucy and Sister Magdalen celebrated Thanksgiving on their own, since the sisters with whom they were staying went to their own Motherhouse for the day. Sister Magdalen later recounted their first holiday alone:

> At noon time the two of us sat down to a grand lunch—chicken sandwiches, coffee, and pumpkin pie [which some of the parish women provided.] We certainly have much to be thankful for—the Sisters' charity, a nice little house, and everyone so friendly and desirous of the new hospital.[11]

Advent began three days later. That Sunday afternoon, Monsignor O'Dwyer blessed their new residence, and several days later they met with Cardinal McIntyre for the first time to discuss their immediate plans.

Less than a month after their arrival, Mother Lucy and Sister Magdalen took the first tangible step toward realizing their community's dream of building a hospital on the West Coast. On December 19, 1957, the two sisters, along with Mother Provincial, joined Monsignor O'Dwyer, Torrance Mayor Albert Isen, the city councilmen, and a group of doctors for lunch at the Palms, then "proceeded to the hospital site at the corner of Torrance and Earl Streets"[12] for the groundbreaking ceremony.

Throughout their early months in California, Mother Lucy and Sister Magdalen were often the guests of a group of fellow religious who went out of their way to share their hospitality with them:

> The Sisters of St. Joseph picked us up ... and drove us out to their beach home in Long Beach. We had a very lovely day—sat out on the porch facing the ocean—later went for a walk on the beach ... [and] listened to Christmas carols. After supper we returned home ... it was a very wonderful outing.[13]

Several days later, the Little Company of Mary community of two celebrated their first Christmas in California. A logbook entry for Christmas Eve reveals that the Sisters of St. Joseph graciously invited them to participate in their celebration of the feast and to share their festivities:

> Tuesday, December 24, 1957—Our mail is beginning to pile up with the packages under the tree. Franks furniture store lent us a television set so we could see the Holy Father's life on Christmas Day. Finished filling the Sisters' [of St. Joseph] stockings [with thread, ribbons, and candy] and we wrapped a set of gold vases [that] Mother Provincial had bought for them.... Sisters came for us about 11:45 p.m. and we went to midnight Mass in the convent for it is not held in the parish churches here. Afterwards we had a lovely breakfast and shared in their Christmas tree. They presented us with a 2-piece casserole set—blue and white, plus a house blessing.[14]

A subsequent memorandum provides a glimpse of the isolation that at least one of the sisters felt being almost two thousand miles from her own community. "Listening to the carols and seeing the Infant in His crib made me overcome with loneliness for all in Evergreen Park—for a few moments," admitted Sister Magdalen. "Tried to call the Sisters ... several times, but all lines were busy." But she quickly added, "Our first Christmas here in the West will be long remembered. Everyone has been most kind and thoughtful."[15]

As the New Year started, the work of fundraising began in earnest. One of the community's first challenges was an initial lack of support from the owners of local industry who were concerned that the hospital would increase their tax liability.[16] It was soon decided that instead of depending on local taxation or bonds, the new hospital would rely on charitable donations and matching funds, which were available from the government since this section of Los Angeles County qualified as a federal "disaster area" because of its lack of hospital beds.

During their first months in California, the sisters encountered situations that were every bit as challenging to them as those experienced by the pioneering members of the Little Company of Mary when they first arrived in the United States. Instead of having to master the art of boarding a Chicago streetcar, the sisters needed to learn to drive because California epitomized America's new mobile society. Sister Magdalen, whose capable hospital administration had been lauded by a Chicago-area newspaper as "a feat few women in business would care to attempt,"[17] soon confided to the logbook, "Driving lesson again today! Went out in traffic and was petrified!"[18] Despite her initial terror, she persisted and passed her driver's test five weeks later.[19]

Mother Lucy and Sister Magdalen were now on their own, and they needed to relearn skills that most laypeople take for granted but which, as religious, they had not used in years. Even grocery shopping posed its own challenges as the sisters learned to navigate the huge supermarkets, which were nonexistent a decade earlier but had sprung up throughout the Los Angeles suburbs during the 1950s. Sister Magdalen described her initial ordeal, which occurred on the very day that she and Mother Lucy moved into their new home:

> Went shopping for food supplies at the A & P food store. Had much confusion in keeping the whereabouts of my cart. Kept putting purchases in others' carts and removing things, putting them back on the shelf. Never realized there were so many grades of eggs, etc. After all my difficulty, arrived home without the eggs and some of the meat and vegetables! I can imagine the surprise others must

[have] receive[d] when they arrived at the cashier.[20]

For the first six months, the two sisters worked with groups to raise funds, visited other hospitals in the area, and met with architects and contractors. By mid-October 1958, enough work had been done to schedule an open house in early December to "show the members of the [local] community what progress has been made and ... increase interest in contributions."[21] The day turned out to be "cold, gray, [and] blustery— an 'Open House' in every sense of the word"[22] [because] windows had not yet been installed in the structure.

Nine months later, the facility was sufficiently finished so that the sisters could move out of their house and occupy the fourth floor of the hospital's west wing. Mother M. Patricia Dooley was named as the new Superior, and by August, three more sisters were added. The members of the Little Company of Mary in Torrance now numbered a half-dozen, one of whom wrote, "Six sisters! Now we [are] a real community!"[23] Within a year's time, that number almost doubled to eleven.[24]

Throughout the fall, the group oversaw the final stages of the facility's completion. On December 12, 1959, Little Company of Mary Hospital in Torrance was dedicated. Two weeks later, the sisters celebrated their first Christmas in the hospital chapel, which one sister described as "beautiful with candles and poinsettias.... [A]t Midnight Mass, the Infant was welcomed with the same awesome hush as always and the small choir ... came forth jubilantly ... in the remainder of the building there wasn't a sound—merely emptiness."[25]

The silence ended nine days later when the first Catholic hospital in South Bay officially opened to patients. On January 3, 1960, the Sisters of the Little Company of Mary began providing their nursing skills and expertise to the people of southern California.

The early 1960s was a time of hopeful anticipation for many Americans. In 1960, fifty percent of the population was under the age of twenty-five, and "for the first time, a college education was within the grasp of the majority of young people"[26]—a new generation called baby boomers, who would soon make their influence felt on the country. Before the year's end, the nation would elect a new president, and already a young senator named John Kennedy, of Irish heritage and Catholic faith, had begun his campaign for his party's nomination.

Many Catholics in the United States and throughout the world experienced similar feelings of optimism as they looked ahead to the new Church Council (the first in ninety-two years), which was set to begin in 1962. The announcement of the Council by John XXIII was startling. The recently elected pontiff, a compromise candidate who was one month short of his seventy-seventh birthday when he was chosen on the eleventh papal ballot,[27] was thought to be an interim pope who would not accomplish anything exceptional during his pontificate.

John XXIII's simplicity, warmth, and wit quickly endeared him to the world. His jovial manner and rotund appearance contrasted enormously with the cool, intellectual manner and ascetic appearance of Pius XII. The new pope poked fun at himself with self-deprecating humor. Shortly after his election "after catching a glimpse of himself into a full-length mirror, he murmured with a chuckle, 'Lord, this man is going to be a disaster on television.'"[28]

He refused to be restricted by papal protocols, which made no sense to him, such as the custom of having to dine alone, which had been proscribed since the days of Pius V in the late sixteenth century.[29] After enduring several solitary meals, he announced, "I have gone all through the Old Testament and the Holy Gospel, and I can't find a single word in them that says the Pope must eat alone. So I am not going to do it anymore."[30]

Unlike Pius XII, who adhered to rigid schedules and had ventured beyond the Vatican only once in nineteen years,[31] John "sallied out of the Vatican—to orphanages, jails, schools, and churches—139 times."[32] He loved impromptu walks in the Vatican garden and beyond. To the consternation of Vatican security and to the delight of the people of Rome, who called him *"il Papa buono"*—"the good Pope"[33] (an appellation that no other pope had ever received[34]), he appeared on to the streets outside Vatican City, often with only one attendant. After being criticized for going out too much during the day, he responded, "Very well, from now on I'll go out at night."[35] And so he did. When he attended a performance of *Murder in the Cathedral,* a drama about the martyrdom of Thomas à Becket, he became the first pope in more than two hundred years to go to the theater.[36]

Less than three months after his election to the papacy, with hardly any consultation of the Roman Curia (the powerful administrative group of Vatican prelates), "John stunned his team of old cardinals by announcing formally that he was summoning the twenty-first ecumenical council in the history of the Church."[37] Some Curia members, who were opposed to any ecclesiastical changes, hoped to drag out the preparations, knowing that the Holy Father was an old man with serious health problems. However, when one cardinal told him, "We cannot possibly get ready for a council in 1963," John simply replied, "Fine, then we will have it in 1962."[38]

In 1960, the sisters in the American Province also experienced much of the optimism that was evident throughout America and in the Catholic Church. Their newest facility in California was doing well and had received an unexpected number of patients just days after opening its doors. The community had "assumed that [the] census would climb slowly"[39] during its first days of operation since Torrance already had two smaller hospitals, but an outbreak of pneumonia and viral infections caused the number of patients to rise quickly.[40] As the year went on, the daily census was frequently "erratic," but as one sister noted, "on the whole, there has been a steady increase, especially in maternity,"[41] even though a new district hospital opened in Torrance six months later.

Except for Torrance, all of the Little Company of Mary foundations were located in northern areas of the United States. Consequently, many of the sisters serving there underwent a period of adjustment to southern California. Some members thought of Torrance as a real "mission," since it was a mainly non-Catholic area and required air travel—for most sisters, their first-ever plane trip.[42] Those serving in Torrance soon discovered that autumn days could be hot, and that "winter" meant the rainy season. The ever-present palm tree was a constant reminder that they were no longer in Illinois, Indiana, or New York, and caused one sister to lament "the absence of large shade trees, which add beauty and stateliness to [even] the drabbest of streets in the Midwest and in the East."[43] Stenciled snowflakes on the hospital windows helped ease the lonesomeness for snow felt by a number of sisters. [44]

The West Coast provided the Little Company of Mary with some unique situations. Sister Jean Stickney recalls:

> In January 1960, I was missioned to our new ... hospital in Torrance....
> As the Nursing Supervisor, I took charge and decided to check the
> diet kitchen. Upon opening the refrigerator, I discovered a tray of

A quarter century after their first invitation to California, the Little Company of Mary Sisters realized their hope of serving on the West Coast.

decaying fruit. Out it went! Later that day, a patient rang and asked for her fresh figs. Much to my embarrassment, I had to apologize to the patient and explain that, because I was a native of New Hampshire, I had never seen a fresh fig. It was the first of my many cultural experiences of California.[45]

The difference between the lifestyle of southern California and that of America's heartland became readily apparent to Sister Kathleen McIntyre:

One day a female teenager came into the ER due to a surfboard accident. She and her six friends were dressed—barely—in bikinis with no shoes. I felt that they were not dressed properly for a Catholic hospital, so I had the injured girl and each of her friends put on patient gowns. The physician thought that all seven of them were patients because they were wearing hospital gowns.... I became known as the Sister who would cause very high laundry bills because I put gowns on everyone.[46]

As the new community became more settled on the West Coast, the sisters in Evergreen Park continued to oversee the expansion of their hospital, which was scheduled for completion in late spring. The addition raised the total number of beds to six hundred[47]—four times the number of patients that the community had originally been able to care for when the facility first opened thirty years earlier.

Along with the additions and renovations that affected patient care, of particular importance to the community was the creation of a beautiful new chapel—the spiritual heart of the facility. By early April, work on the chapel was almost done. An intricate ceiling mosaic depicted the Holy Spirit hovering overhead, and the altars had been erected and the scaffolding removed, but the marble statues still had not been delivered. One sister later recorded:

> When, finally, the crucifixion group did arrive, it was Holy Week, and quite appropriately, the marble Corpus [Body] of Christ was raised to its place on the Cross by the workmen between the hours of 12 and 3 p.m. It was an awesome experience and recalled most vividly ... what might have occurred on Calvary on the first Good Friday.[48]

On June 25, 1960, Albert Cardinal Meyer, archbishop of Chicago, officially dedicated the chapel in a ceremony attended by virtually the entire Evergreen Park community as well as by Mother General M. Dominic Foley, who had arrived from Rome for this special occasion.

Like their hospital in Evergreen Park, the hospital in Buenos Aires was doing very well, and the Little Company of Mary was considering the idea of expanding outside the city. The Generalate in Rome was concerned with the lack of local vocations because only a handful of Argentine women had entered the community during its forty-seven-year history in South America, despite the fact that the country was overwhelmingly Catholic. Hoping to change this, Mother General called Francis O'Grady, whose firm had been looking out for the Little Company of Mary's interests in Argentina for more than thirty years. He quickly responded:

> It does not seem that there are many vocations for teaching or for nursing congregations in or about this big city of Buenos Aires. [W]hether there are apt to be more vocations in a rural district like Tandil [331 km./200 mi. from Buenos Aires] ... is somewhat problematic, [but] such towns are sufficiently far from Buenos Aires to have their own independent life and community spirit....

Tandil is under [the auspices of] the Bishop of Azul, Monsignor Manuel Marenco ... [who] I am told ... plans on going to the States next month.... [T]ry to induce the Bishop to visit your large hospital in Evergreen Park ... [or] your smaller hospital in Indiana. Quite a few people feel that if there is to be a real moral and religious resurgence in this country ... it will come about, first and foremost, in the inland towns....[49]

No immediate action was taken, but the belief that the country's outlying areas somehow held the answer for increasing the number of Argentine women in the congregation persisted—at least for a while.

Vocations were scarce in South America, but not in the United States. On August 15, 1960, the feast of the Assumption, the American Province celebrated its largest ceremony of religious profession since the Little Company of Mary arrived in the country sixty-seven years earlier.[50] In the new hospital chapel, eleven members professed final vows; three sisters made triennial vows; and ten postulants received the habit of the congregation. Mother General arrived from Rome for the ceremony, and later that day announced that Mother M. Oliver Carter from the Australian Province would be the new American Provincial. She also appointed four new Superiors: Mother M. Genevieve Canty (Buenos Aires), Mother M. Ignatius Dooley (Evergreen Park), Mother M. Catherine Barrett (San Pierre), and Mother M. Eugene Trenner (Jasper).[51]

The decade could not have started off more promisingly for the American Province. The community had successfully opened a new hospital in a new area of the country; membership was at an all-time high; the sisters had just celebrated the largest ceremony of profession in the history of the American houses; the number of new vocations was steady; St. Mary's now offered medical services in addition to maternity care; and the expansion of Little Company of Mary Hospital in Evergreen Park was almost completed. A new mission was under consideration for Argentina, and although the foundation then was not part of the American Province, it was very closely affiliated with it. In addition, the sisters in Syracuse received notification that their hospital had received full approval and accreditation from the Joint Commission on Accreditation,[52] a remarkable accomplishment within a short period of time.

As the year wound down, America elected its first Catholic president. Kennedy's plurality was only .1 percent of the total vote,[53] but "the nation had proven that religious toleration was a genuinely achievable component of the American ideal."[54] John Cogley, former editor of *Commonweal*, a Catholic periodical, believes that the election of a Catholic to the highest office in the land "finally seemed to remove the stigma of second-class citizenship [for Catholics] once and for all."[55] On January 20, 1961, John Fitzgerald Kennedy took the oath of office and in his Inaugural Address set the tone for the country by proclaiming:

> In the long history of the world, only a few generations have been granted the role of defending freedom in its hour of maximum danger.... The energy, the faith, the devotion, which we bring to this endeavor, will light our country and all who serve it, and the glow from that fire can truly light the world.[56]

The United States embarked on a new course of action fueled by ambitious ideals and pragmatic objectives. Some aspirations, like setting the goal of putting a man on the Moon by the end of the decade, aimed high. Others were more down-to-earth, such as the creation of the Peace Corps in March 1961—an "initiative [that] inspired ... hope and understanding among Americans and the rest of the world."[57] Soon, five hundred young Americans began teaching school and assisting people in eight developing countries. The new administration was also concerned with enforcing laws that prohibited racial discrimination. Attorney General Robert Kennedy worked energetically to implement his brother's commitment "to achieving true equality of opportunity. The basic reason is because it is right."[58]

Later in the spring, the American Province of the Little Company of Mary received additional good news relating to its northernmost and southernmost foundations. During April 1961, the sisters in Buenos Aires learned that they were to become part of the six-year-old American Province. In a letter to the American community, Mother General M. Dominic Foley explained:

> As our sisters in Argentina are very isolated and do not have regular Visitation, we have decided to annex the house in Buenos Aires to the Immaculate Conception Province.
>
> This step will ... be a great support and consolation to the sisters in Buenos Aires and the sisters in the Immaculate Conception Province

will be glad to co-operate and welcome this house and bring the Little Company of Mary closer.

The Province will be unable to help financially and with sisters at present as it is so heavily committed, but the moral support of "belonging" and having regular visitation and being able to use the novitiate for Argentine vocations will be a great help to our dear Little Company in Argentina.... [59]

That same month, Bishop Foery wrote to Mother M. Teresa in Syracuse, "I am pleased ... [with] the progress which the hospital has made under the administration of the Sisters.... [It seems] to me ... that you are in good financial condition and that the future appears to be very promising."[60]

The hopeful expectancy that the community experienced at this time was similarly felt by many Americans toward their country and by many Catholics toward their Church as final preparations were being completed for the first Council in almost a century. *Time* Rome Bureau Chief Wilton Wynn, assigned to cover the Vatican, reported:

The optimism generated by Good Pope John fit the mood of the times perfectly. His reign coincided with the most promising era mankind has enjoyed since the end of World War II. Western Europe had recovered from the devastation of war and had embarked on an epoch of unparalleled prosperity.... In the Communist world, dictatorship was mitigated by ... de-Stalinization.... In the United States, spirits were soaring with the election of the youngest of American presidents, a leader who inspired dreams of new frontiers, of peace and prosperity without limit.... [61]

Unfortunately, ominous developments were also taking place in the world. Five hundred kilometers north of the Vatican, East Germany built the Berlin Wall, closing its borders to West Berlin and separating the Free World from the Communist East.[62] And few Americans paid much attention as the United States provided its first direct military support of helicopters and a ground crew[63] to a small, little-known country on the other side of the world called South Vietnam.

Early in 1962, Léon Joseph Cardinal Suenens, the Archbishop of Malines-Brussels, published *The Nun in the World*, which critically examined women's religious life in the twentieth century. "The more a religious has the qualities of her times, "he wrote, "the better will she realize her vocation."[64] The cardinal urged, "She should appear as a woman vowed to God in the Church and in the world of today." [65]

In August, Superiors from each American foundation, including Buenos Aires, gathered in Evergreen Park for the first of several six-week sessions of Spiritual Renovation that would be attended by numerous community members. As some sisters were beginning their spiritual renewal, all in the American Province heard or read John XXIII's words addressed to women religious throughout the world:

> Let all who dedicate themselves to the active life remember that it is not by prayer alone but also by works that we shall obtain a new orientation of society based on the Gospel.... And since in the fields of education, charity, and social work one cannot make use of persons not prepared to meet the exacting conditions of present regulations, busy yourself under obedience at studying and obtaining the diplomas necessary to overcome all obstacles. Thus, apart from your professional competence, your spirit of devotion, patience, and sacrifice will be better appreciated.[66]

That autumn, an unprecedented number of sisters in the American Province were involved in part-time or full-time educational studies, which ranged from hospital nursing programs and classes at junior colleges to four-year degree programs and university postgraduate work. In keeping with their founder's vision that her spiritual daughters possess exemplary nursing and administrative skills and credentials, the community had always emphasized the importance of education, but during the early 1960s, more members of the community than ever before pursued their education.[67]

Some sisters maintained full-time jobs while going to school, as a feature newspaper story reported. The article headlined, "They Burn 'Midnight Oil' Between Studies, Hospital Duties" focused on the campus life of two Little Company of Mary Sisters enrolled at Syracuse University, an unusual situation because at that time women religious normally attended Catholic educational institutions. The presence of Catholic sisters on the campus of a nonsectarian college, which had Methodist Episcopal roots, provided a groundbreaking opportunity for young people of all backgrounds and faiths to interact with them as peers. As one sister

The sisters' presence expanded in new directions during the 1960s, including secular college campuses where they interacted with students who were unfamiliar with "nuns."

explained, "Some of the students in my class confessed they'd never talked to a nun [before]. We are quite accustomed to [being asked] if our coifs ever blow off—and why we have to wear long dresses."[68]

The Second Vatican Council opened on October 11, 1962, and an eyewitness reporter described the scene:

> Cardinals, patriarchs, and bishops of the Roman Catholic Church—more than 2,500 strong—shuffled slowly through the cobblestoned square of St. Peter's toward the huge bronze doors of the world's largest basilica, singing Veni, Creator Spiritus ["Come, Holy Ghost"].

> Grandly, the procession moved across the square, the Pope's white and gold robes catching the shafts of sunlight, which had broken through dark clouds only moments before. Amid the pomp and majesty, the man himself seemed lost—swallowed up by the vastness of the ceremony. But once inside the basilica, he was again a bishop among bishops.[69]

John XXIII had earlier said, "We are going to shake off the dust that has collected on the throne of Saint Peter since the time of Constantine and let in some fresh air." As he convened the opening session, he proclaimed:

> The Council now beginning rises in the Church like daybreak,
> a forerunner of most splendid light. It is now only dawn....
> Today ... Providence is guiding us toward a new order of human
> relationships, which thanks to human effort and yet surpassing
> human hopes, will bring us to the realization of still higher and
> undreamed of expectations....[70]

During the next three years, among other achievements, the Church would embrace a spirit of ecumenism, modify the liturgy, publish a historic declaration on religious freedom, and mandate all active religious congregations of priests, brothers, and sisters to update their rules and constitutions.

Ten days after the Council opened, the U.S. discovered that the Soviet Union had installed missile bases in Cuba, ninety miles from the U.S. mainland. Instead of listening to advisors who advocated direct military intervention, the President announced an air and sea quarantine of that island, adding, "They must be removed ... or else." At the same time, Kennedy gave the Soviet premier a face-saving way to resolve the impasse, by promising not to invade Cuba, and John XXIII appealed to both sides, urging negotiation, not war. During the six-day standoff, "the world teetered on the brink of nuclear destruction."[71] On October 26, Khrushchev backed down and agreed to remove the missiles and dismantle the bases. The Cuban missile crisis, which historians later described as "the world's closest brush with World War III," had been defused.

Throughout October and November, the Council considered and made recommendations to issues including the liturgy, mass communications, the Eastern Rite churches, and the nature of Revelation. The first session ended on December 8, 1962, and would reconvene the following autumn.

Six months later, on June 3, 1963, only five days after the Vatican announced his illness, the pope who had once admitted, "I wish to live a long time. I love life,"[72] died of stomach cancer. The pontiff, whom many thought would not accomplish anything out of the ordinary, had accomplished the extraordinary. He had built a bridge between Catholics and non-Catholics, whom he referred to as "separated brethren,"[73] and initiated the process of *aggiornamento*—updating the Church. He began a healing dialogue with those of the Jewish faith by replacing the harsh words of the Good Friday liturgy, which for centuries had proclaimed, "Let us pray for the faithless Jews," with a new invocation, "Let us pray also for the Jews to whom God our Lord first spoke. May He keep them in fidelity to His covenant....."[74] He also created the first black cardinal in Church history[75]—Laurean Rugambwa, archbishop of Dar es Salaam, Tanzania.

In August 1963, in response to Rome's call for congregations to update their religious garb, the Generalate sent out pictures of a proposed new habit—the first of numerous changes that would soon affect the community. Cardinal Suenens had urged religious the previous year to relinquish their traditional habits:

> The world today has no patience with mere ornamentation, useless complications, gofferings [pleatings or crimpings] and other oddities, whether starched or floating in the wind, which belong to another age: anything contrived or lacking in simplicity is rejected, and anything unpractical or unhygienic, anything that gives the impression that the nun is not only apart from the world but also a complete stranger to its evolution.[76]

In her book, *The Habit*, Elizabeth Kuhns points out that all religious congregations maintained traditions about their respective habits:

> The ensemble was a rich, symbolic clothing prescribed in their various constitutions and revered by society. Each article had a specific meaning, relating the physical body to the spiritual realm. As a sister dressed, she meditated on the metaphorical messages of her clothing, regarding the habit as more of a devotional item than mere modest attire.[77]

Kuhns particularly singles out the clothing worn by the members of Mary Potter's congregation:

> The Little Company of Mary used the colors of their habit to relate these meanings, as stated in their constitution: The black will remind the Sisters of their abandonment of the vanities of the world; the red [of the wool cincture] will remind them of the Precious Blood, and the Wounds of Jesus, and the spirit of mortification; and the blue of the Immaculate Virgin, and of the purity of life which their vocation requires....[78]

The photos of the proposed new habit prompted one sister to write, "The [guimpe] has been completely changed and simplified in keeping with directives from the Sacred Congregation. We are all anxious for the big "Change Day."[79] Four months later, on the feast of the Immaculate Conception, for which the American province was named, the sisters laid aside some of the religious garb that had been worn since the congregation's inception and "stepped out officially in the modified habit."[80] Their new look featured a slightly shortened skirt and a simplified headdress, but kept the distinctive veil of the Little Company of Mary, whose color often resulted in their being known as "the Blue Nuns." The response to the sisters' new habit was overwhelming positive; however, it did require a little adjustment by some laypeople. On the first day that the sisters appeared in their new garb, one doctor very obviously kept his eyes downcast while in an elevator with one of the sisters. The community later found out that he had been mistakenly assumed that in her haste to attend to her nursing duties she had inadvertently forgotten to put on part of her traditional habit.

Significant changes had been taking place in the Catholic Church, and now the United States was about to experience a social transformation of its own. Civil rights was considered "the greatest domestic issue of the early 1960s,"[81] and in the summer of 1963 the president federalized the Alabama National Guard to prevent an outbreak of violence against the first two black students to register at the University of Alabama. Despite death threats and intervention from the state's segregationist governor, the confrontation ended peacefully. In a televised address the following evening, the president reminded the nation: "We are confronted primarily with a moral issue ... as old as the Scriptures and ... as clear as the American Constitution. The heart of the question is whether all Americans are to be afforded equal rights and equal opportunities...."[82] A week later, he proposed the most far-reaching civil rights bill in U.S. history.[83]

Five months later, on November 22, 1963, after only one thousand days in office and less than six months after eulogizing John XXIII as a man whose "wisdom, compassion and kindly strength have bequeathed humanity a new legacy of purpose and courage for the future,"[84] the president himself was dead—his life suddenly extinguished by an assassin's bullets.

Television viewing was a rare occurrence for most religious during the early 1960s, but one member in Evergreen Park noted that like most other Americans, she and her fellow sisters watched history unfold that final weekend in November 1963:

The television was closely attended for news ... As many as were free watched the ... funeral cortège from the Capitol to St. Matthew's Church for the Requiem Mass, and then the procession to Arlington Cemetery and the burial services there. It was a sorrowful, yet inspiring tribute....[85]

America and the world mourned the loss of two men named John who against all odds had been elected to their respective offices. One was an eighty-one-year-old pontiff whose openness and goodness kept him young at heart—a shepherd of souls "whose hope was to return to the Church of Pentecost, to a time when the Spirit of God flowed freely through the congregation, inspiring *all*";[86] the other, a youthful president whose idealism and aspirations inspired a generation of young men and women and revitalized the spirits of older Americans. The loss of John XXIII and John Kennedy cast a pall over the wondrous sense of possibility that had existed for a few brief seasons.

The early years of the 1960s were a time of promise and potential for the Little Company of Mary in the United States, and many of the community's dreams were realized. But unforeseeable cultural changes were about to occur that would inevitably affect the country and even touch the lives of the sisters in the American Province.

CHAPTER THIRTEEN

WINDS OF CHANGE

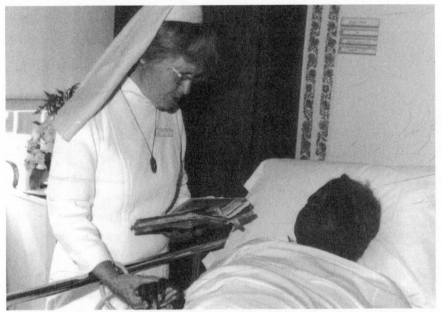

In her ministry of Pastoral Care, Sister Margaret Mary Doherty, L.C.M., prays with a patient.

Wh   hen Mary Potter founded the Little Company of Mary, she
                   told the members of her community, "We are not going to be
                   dead to the world. We are going to live in it."[1] Eighty-five years
later, across the expanse of the Atlantic, a series of dramatic and
far-reaching changes taught her daughters in the American Province just
how inextricably linked they truly were to the world around them.

In 1963, both the Roman Catholic Church and the United States
followed their respective, centuries-old traditions for the continuity of
leadership. Two weeks after John XXIII died, the College of Cardinals met
in a conclave and elected Giovanni Battista Cardinal Montini, who took
the name Paul VI. Only hours after John Kennedy was assassinated, Vice
President Lyndon Johnson was sworn into office. The transition went
smoothly for the Church and for the nation; the tempest would come
later on.

The Second Vatican Council resumed in September 1964. During the
next two years, Vatican II, as it was popularly called, brought the Church
back in touch with the rest of the world. The days of a priest "saying
Mass" quietly in Latin with his back to the congregation were almost
over. Before the year ended, the prayers would be in English (or whatever
the language of a particular parish), the priest would be facing the people,
and a "new liturgy" would involve the congregation more directly.

This was just the start of the many changes that American Catholics
soon encountered. Before long, even the terminology was different, and
the central form of Catholic worship, long referred to as "the Holy
Sacrifice of the Mass" would be called "the Celebration of the Eucharist."
Historian F. Michael Perko contends that "As the Mass and sacraments
became more understandable, they began more and more to be the center
of American Catholics' spirituality."[2] Long-cherished devotions, such as
novenas and the rosary, received less attention as the Church emphasized
the importance of reading the Bible and praying the psalms.

One of the Constitutions of Vatican II, entitled "The Church in the
Modern World," had declared, "Today the human race is passing through
a new stage in history. Profound and rapid changes are spreading by
degrees around the world.... Hence we can speak of a true cultural and
social transformation, one which has repercussions on [one's] religious
life as well."[3] During autumn of 1965, the Second Vatican Council
addressed the issue of religious communities and their relationship to the

After Vatican II, the traditional habit was modified several times. The sisters kept the distinctive pale blue veil of the LCM, although it was simplified and shortened.

present world. That October, the Council approved the "Decree on the Appropriate Renewal of Religious Life" (*Perfectae Caritatis*), which encouraged "adaptation to the changed conditions of our times," and also urged each congregation to look at its founder's unique vision, or charism, as part of its distinct mission.

Almost two years earlier, the Little Company of Mary had initially modified the community's habit, as Rome had requested, but in 1965, their clothing still looked very much like what the sisters had always worn. As the community complied with a new set of directives, far more sweeping changes ensued: the bandeau—the stiff material that had covered the forehead—was eliminated; the veil was significantly short-ened and designed to sit further back upon the head (allowing a sister's hair to be seen); and the skirt was raised from ankle length to just below the knees. These outward changes were a precursor of more substantial changes that would critically affect the community within the next few years.

When the Second Vatican Council ended in December 1965, the Catholic population of the United States was at an all-time high of 45.6 million—or almost twenty-five percent of all Americans. Priests numbered more than fifty-eight thousand; there were nearly forty-nine

Young LCM postulants and novices enjoy a songfest during recreation.

thousand seminarians; and more than two hundred nine thousand women were members of religious communities.[4] As historian George Stewart points out:

> These statistics demonstrate the awesome magnitude of the Church [in America]. In less than 200 years, it had grown from a tiny, fragile institution to the largest and most powerful religious denomination in the nation, and one of the strongest national Catholic churches in the world.... At each stage of American history, women religious played an increasingly vital role in the life of the Church, nurturing it with education, religious instruction, health care and charitable apostolates.[5]

Midway through the 1960s, there was no indication that this was about to change. "... Catholic optimism was loud and clear as plans were made for larger parishes ... for larger seminary and novitiate classes to come when the wartime babies reached maturity and for a contented, ever more educated and affluent laity...."[6] By the end of the decade, much of that optimism had dissolved.

On December 7, the day before the Second Vatican Council closed, Pope Paul VI promulgated the Declaration on Religious Freedom, a document drafted primarily by John Courtney Murray, an American theologian who "brought a particular American point of view to the Council deliberations."[7] Chester Gillis, Chair of the Department of Theology at Georgetown University explained, "Finally, fifty years after Leo XIII had condemned Americanism, the American church had an articulate defender of the American situation."[8] The issue in question was:

> ... the teaching of the Catholic Church on the proper relationship of church and state, particularly regarding freedom of worship. Deeply entrenched in Catholic tradition was the conviction that the state had the obligation to recognize the Catholic Church in its constitution, to give it preferential treatment in public affairs, and to suppress whatever or whoever opposed the Church or its teachings....[9]

This model had worked in Europe when most monarchs were Catholic, but it was an alien concept in America. During the 1950s, Murray theorized that the Catholic concept of "... making the government the servant of the Church was anachronistic. It had been outmoded by fresh insight coming out of the historical experience of modern democracy, particularly the kind of democracy found in the United States."[10] In July 1954, Murray was placed under censure by Rome—forbidden to speak or write about the subject. This restriction lasted until after the election of John XXIII in October 1958.

Even though the issue of religious freedom was high on the agenda[11] at the Second Vatican Council, the conservative Roman Curia made sure that Murray was not included. "[D]uring the first session of Vatican II," McClory points out, "a kind of impasse was reached on religious liberty with Cardinal Ottaviani [head of the Holy Office] and the Curia proposing the traditional model, and a growing coterie of bishops from America and Europe pressing for a more liberal interpretation."[12] Cardinal Spellman of New York used his influence to have Murray named as an official *peritus* (expert) to the Council so he could work on the wording of the final draft throughout 1964 and 1965.

The document "established the church's relationship to governments following the successful model of the United States...."[13] Among other things, it declared that "a person has the right to religious freedom; God has regard for the dignity of the person; and ... the right of all citizens ... to religious freedom should be recognized...."[14] Since an American was its author, and because " [it] was strongly supported by the United States bishops and their theologians in Rome, it quickly became known as the 'American' decree."[15] The final vote, before a full assembly of the Council, was a landslide: 2,308 in favor, 70 opposed. The year ended with feelings of exultation for the American representatives of the Catholic Church in Rome.

As changes in the Church left many American Catholics feeling hopeful and optimistic about the future of Catholicism, social and political concerns resulted in growing cynicism, protest, and dissension throughout the United States. Several factors contributed to this. America's involvement in Vietnam had escalated sharply. More than 540,000 U.S. troops were serving in Vietnam, and combat fatalities had reached more than thirty thousand by 1968.[16] The country was sharply divided between those who believed that a continued U.S. commitment was necessary to prevent Communism from over-running Southeast Asia and those who demanded that the United States pull out immediately. Such bitter divisiveness had not existed among Americans since the Civil War, and it would last long after the hostilities ended.

Conflict was heating up in some minority communities in major U.S. cities where frustration had been simmering over what was seen as a lack of tangible gains in civil rights. It now boiled over into incidents of violence in a number of inner cities, culminating in the six-day Watts Riot in a depressed black section of Los Angeles which left thirty-four dead and more than one thousand injured, and resulted in four thousand arrests and an estimated $200 million in property damage.[17] About the same time, supporters of "Women's Liberation" rallied together, insisting on the passage of the Equal Rights Amendment and advocating a pro-feminist, pro-choice agenda as they challenged and defied many values traditionally held by American women. All of these factors combined to bring about "the cultural revolution of the 1960s," which, according to historian John McWilliams, culminated in "the general rejection of authority and mainstream values."[18]

More than any other year of the decade, 1968 embodied just how far the country was from the optimism that it had experienced only five years before. Between April and June, two American leaders were assassinated: Dr. Martin Luther King, who headed the movement for the peaceful attainment of civil rights, and Senator Robert Kennedy, who had just declared his intention to seek the presidency that fall. Their violent deaths added to a growing sense of disillusionment and anger. During the following summer, when astronaut Neil Armstrong stepped out onto the rocky surface of the Moon, America fulfilled a goal set by President Kennedy eight years earlier—a brief moment of triumph for the United States beset by years of tumult.

In the summer of 1968, the Catholic Church in America experienced turmoil of its own. The precipitating event was the release of the encyclical *Humanae Vitae*. Early during the Second Vatican Council, some bishops, led by Léon Joseph Suenens, had asked for a reexamination of the Church's position on artificial contraception. One of the main issues was whether the use of the recently developed birth control pills could be considered a variation of the rhythm method, which the Church accepted as morally permissible. John XXIII appointed a commission of three theologians and three lay people to study the matter.

Paul VI enlarged the group to include thirteen, then seventy members. For more than two years, bishops and cardinals, physicians and biologists, theologians and sociologists, and even a married couple examined the issue. One American journalist remarked, "The fact that he [Paul VI] had not weighted the commission with traditionalists gave rise to new hopes that a change was in the making."[19] The commission concluded its work in 1966, but the pope decided to postpone announcing his decision for two years.

In July 1968, Paul VI released *Humanae Vitae*, which upheld the Church's traditional position. According to theologian Bernard Häring, "No papal teaching document has ever caused such an earthquake...."[20] The pontiff had rejected the papal commission's majority conclusion that married couples should be allowed more freedom of conscience in this matter,[21] and his decision appeared to be a rejection of the concept of collegiality established by the Second Vatican Council. Within days, dozens of theologians and canon lawyers throughout the United States and Europe signed statements of dissent. This open challenge to papal teaching authority left many lay Catholics in a state of confusion. At the same time, many religious congregations also experienced feelings of uncertainty as they were inundated with a series of postconciliar decrees regarding the renewal of religious life.

In the late 1960s, the Catholic Church in the United States witnessed an unprecedented exodus of priests and religious. For some members of the clergy, the defining issue was celibacy. In his 1967 encyclical (*Sacerdotalis Caelibatus*), Paul VI had acknowledged that celibacy was not divine law but a Church discipline that would remain in effect.[22] For others, the cause for concern was the actual changes that were taking place in religious life. As one sister involved in this process noted, "The decade of the 1960s was hardly the most stable time for the Church to ask institutions of religious to evaluate their lifestyle and government structure, particularly in the United States, where a massive cultural upheaval was underway."[23]

Ann Carey, who has studied what happened to American religious congregations at that time, concurs:

> [M]any sisters left religious life because the changes were so profound that the new model of religious life bore no resemblance to the life they had entered before renewal began. Others left because they felt reform wasn't happening fast enough and going far enough. And during the unstable time of renewal, fewer young women chose to commit themselves to a life that appeared to be transforming itself before their very eyes.[24]

Attrition hit almost all active (i.e., noncontemplative) congregations hard. Virtually all communities experienced an unprecedented loss of sisters—from novices and the temporarily professed to members who had made their final vows decades before. Between 1965 and 1970, the number of sisters decreased by nineteen thousand,[25] and during the next twenty years, the total sister-population of active apostolic communities had declined by almost forty-nine percent.[26]

The Little Company of Mary was no exception, as a logbook entry for 1972 indicates:

> With religious [life] changing as much as it has, many priests and religious have left their communities. We too have lost our share. For the past eight or nine months, we've had discussion groups and talks and self-studies made to reevaluate our goals and meaning of this life to us, now, at this day and age.[27]

In the American province, twenty-three sisters chose to leave the community between 1970 and 1972,[28] and more than twenty additional members departed between the mid-1960s and the mid-1980s.[29]

The Little Company of Mary could have recouped this loss if a sudden societal change had not taken place simultaneously. Prior to the mid-1960s, each decade of American history had seen an increase in the number of women religious.[30] In 1965, approximately eleven thousand young women were in religious formation as postulants, novices, and junior professed.[31] Starting in 1966, however, the number of vocations dropped off precipitously, so that by 1990, the total number of women in religious formation in the United States would be only twenty-two hundred.[32]

The dramatically diminished numbers of those entering religious life, combined with the large numbers of departing sisters, had a devastating impact on most active religious congregations. Between 1965 and 1975, the number of teaching sisters plummeted by almost fifty percent, from 104,000 to 56,000. By 1995, the number was less than 13,000[33] and in 2004, less than 8,000.[34] Consequently, young women lost the role model that teaching sisters had provided, resulting in even fewer new vocations. The effect was not as drastic for nursing sisters. In 1965, "over 13,000 sisters staffed some 808 hospitals that were owned and operated by religious orders."[35] By 2004, the number of hospitals had dropped to 583.[36] Stewart notes, "Even though few sister-operated hospitals closed, sister-nurses became a rare sight … another loss of 'witness' that had stimulated vocations in the past."[37]

Throughout the 1960s and 1970s, the community continued its nursing services, but reduced membership made the work more challenging. The congregation was aging: during its first sixty-six years in the United States (1893–1959), the Little Company of Mary recorded only nineteen deaths, but between 1960 and 1980, thirty-one sisters entered into eternal life.[38]

The mid-1970s was a transitional time as the community modified its rules to become more in tune with the twentieth century. Many rules governing religious life dated back to when each congregation first began but had become arcane in modern times, especially as sisters became more educated and responsible members of society. One community member pointed out the incongruity of a sister being able to make life-and-death decisions within the hospital, but having to ask permission for the most trivial of matters when she returned to the convent.

As the Little Company of Mary updated itself, change became a constant factor, touching almost every aspect of the sisters' lives. Prior to post-Vatican II reforms, for example, each sister had to request money for individual expenses; now the community experimented with the concept of personal budgets, allotting a monthly allowance for each member. Traditionally, as many sisters as possible had gathered together for prayer several times daily. Now, some devotions, such as recitation of the rosary or meditation could be done privately, at a time more convenient for each sister. Once "recreation" had meant that most sisters shared a communal hour of talk and relaxation, which one sister drolly described as "organized joy."[39] The sisters now had greater freedom in their use of leisure time. Community members were also given the option to return to their Baptismal names if they so desired,[40] and many opted to do so.

Until the late 1960s, all religious congregations had rules requiring their members to distance themselves from their previous lives "in the world." In the United States, a Little Company of Mary Sister was rarely permitted to return home—a week's visit was allowed about once every ten years[41]—and restrictions governed ordinary situations such as sharing a meal with relatives or staying overnight at a parent's home. After the Council and with the more liberal influence of a new Provincial, regulations were loosened, and the sisters were able to reestablish a more natural relationship with their own families.

Several major transformations also occurred in religious congregations at this time. One was the recognition of the importance of the individual. Within the Little Company of Mary, the sisters were encouraged to become involved in an area of the apostolate that was of particular interest to them. This differed vastly from the pre-Vatican II days when a Superior made all such decisions. In the past, religious were simply told what their assignments would be and were expected to obey without question.

The community also reevaluated its work ethic. Over the years, a "sister will do it" mentality had developed. No matter what, a Little Company of Mary member was always supposed to be "available." One sister related how, many years ago, she had stayed in the hospital all night because of an emergency which required her radiology skills, yet she was still "expected to work the next day."[42]

Religious had borne such incredible workloads for decades. Another member of the community explained, "Until John XXIII (i.e., the Second Vatican Council), 'work' was the big thing—the sisters worked seven days a week, often morning to night."[43]

As far back as 1891, Bishop Bagshawe had written to Mother [Mary Potter], "I would suggest [that you] revise the amount of devotional exercises. It appears to me that if the Rules be kept, the sisters are kept too hard at it from morning to night. It is to my mind too great a strain, especially when they come home too weary from nursing."[44] The founder of the Little Company of Mary had disagreed with his suggestion because she did not consider "the work of nursing to be the primary end of the Institute."[45] However, over the years, just from the hours put into their nursing duties, nursing *seemed* to be the sisters' principal task—even to the extent that sometimes the sisters had to "squeeze" their prayers into the remaining nonwork time, as illustrated in a letter from Mother Fintan Kealy to Mother General in 1939:

> I hope dear Mother [that] you are going to send us two or three Sisters very soon as they are badly needed and the help here is badly limited and it will be a great asset if we can do the nursing ourselves.... If you do not, I do not know how we can possibly get in our prayers and exercises.[46]

After Vatican II, work expectations were modified for the sisters' spiritual, emotional, and physical well-being.

From the mid-to-late 1970s, the Little Company of Mary also witnessed a change in the concept of community. Two groups of Evergreen Park sisters experimented with new living arrangements. In 1975, three members submitted a proposal for "Small Group Living," which was approved by the Superior General and her Council.[47] Instead of residing with thirty-one other sisters at the convent, they could now live together in a home at 8943 South Claremont in Chicago and even purchase a small, used car.

The "Claremont community," as they were called, lived by themselves for six years. More importantly, however, these sisters pioneered the way in which community would be lived in the future. Within the next decade, all community members in the American Province moved into individual homes comprised of just a few sisters. The traditional, large convents were used for other purposes or demolished to provide for the hospitals' expansions.

During the summer in which the nation celebrated its bicentennial anniversary, three members of the Little Company of Mary requested permission to join several members of the Sisters of the Holy Cross at Most Holy Redeemer parish for an experiment in intercommunity living.

In a letter to the Provincial Council, they explained:

> Our main purpose and focus is living together with these sisters in a
> truly religious atmosphere ... sharing and building community
> together and deepening our spiritual lives.... All of us view this
> experiment as a true and sincere effort to live together as religious
> women and share with each other whatever talents and gifts the
> Lord has given us.[48]

The trio received approval and the blessing of their Superior for
"building a community that is fully living out the spiritual heritage
of Mother Foundress with renewed vitality and strength."[49] This decision,
however, was not an easy one. One member of the newly formed
intercommunity group explained, "Our greatest pain and struggle has
been the thought of leaving the senior sisters. We have prayed over this
decision and cried over it. We have sought advice and still feel we are
called to do this, and we are willing to take the necessary risks."[50]

Sisters from the two congregations shared a time of mutual growth
and divided responsibilities as they participated in religious life together.
The experiment broadened the perspective of the members of the
Little Company of Mary by giving them an insight into the hardships of
diocesan teaching sisters—the challenges of dealing with parish councils
and of parents who failed to see any problem with children who were using
alcohol. Conversely, the nursing sisters helped educate those in the parish
as to what programs were available at Little Company of Mary Hospital.[51]

This endeavor, which they later described as "full of growth," lasted
for varying lengths of time for each of the sisters involved. "Living
intercommunity has helped us to have a more 'global vision' not only of
the entire Church but also of religious life," noted one sister. "We ... look
at the other sisters ... and are aware of their hopes and fears, joys and
sorrows, their struggles to serve the Lord in their varied apostolates."[52]
The Spirit of God, which had led the trio to embark on this joint venture
of communal living, eventually brought the sisters back to their LCM
community where two have remained and later guided one member of
the group to return to lay life.

The new openness to possibilities of intercommunity living allowed
for another opportunity for growth during the following decade when
Sister Adrian Davis lived with two Sisters of Mercy and a Dominican

Sister in northern Michigan as she developed expertise in the systems of hospital administration.[53]

Each of these changes marked a drastic shift from the way religious life had been lived prior to the Second Vatican Council. Soon, each sister would have even more choices—from what she would wear to the type of community in which she would live. For some sisters, this would even mean living by themselves.

The final years of the 1970s were trying times for the United States, the American Catholic Church, and most congregations of American religious. Although the Vietnam War had ended midway through the decade, the bitter feelings of both war supporters and anti-war demonstrators lingered. Thousands of Americans lost their homes when double-digit inflation caused interest rates to skyrocket to fifteen percent. Energy supplies dwindled, and during the summer of 1979, "sixty percent of the nation's gas stations had closed because of fuel shortages."[54] On November 24, 1979, the hostage-taking of U.S. citizens from the American embassy in Tehran by student dissidents revealed just how impotent even the most powerful country on earth could be.

Ongoing tension continued in the U.S. Catholic Church as liberal theologians challenged the conservative hierarchy on a variety of issues. Although the exodus of priests and sisters had slowed from earlier in the decade, the number of men and women entering religious life was only a fraction of what it once had been. Between 1958 and 1962, more than twenty-three thousand women entered American communities; between 1976 and 1980 the number was under twenty-eight hundred.[55]

The culture of the United States continued to change throughout the 1970s. American society became increasingly materialistic, as shown by the explosion of personal credit card usage and the amount of debt incurred by individuals; and a growing secularism began eroding the Judeo-Christian values on which the country had been founded. In 1973, the Supreme Court's Roe vs. Wade decision legalized abortion, laws against pornography were liberalized, and a movement began to permit euthanasia.

Some historians, including Stewart, believe that the shift in culture, influenced by materialism and secularism, contributed to the decline of religious vocations.[56] While these cultural shifts undoubtedly had an impact, numerous other factors were also at work, including the loss of specific identity that occurred in many congregations as they scrambled to modernize, the greater valuation of marriage as a vocation following Vatican II, and the unprecedented opportunities women had educationally and professionally, which began during the 1970s.

Paul VI died during the summer of 1978 after a fifteen-year pontificate that was responsible for numerous accomplishments which embodied the spirit of *aggiornamento*. He had "abolished the Index of Forbidden Books; made Holy Office investigations more modern and humane, ... put the liturgy into modern languages from English to Pidgin; internationalized the Roman Curia; instituted more than fifty national bishops' conferences around the world that would give the Church a more local character than it had known for centuries, ... [and] pushed the ecumenical movement to frontiers undreamed of a decade before...."[57] For most Catholics in America, however, he would always be identified with his 1968 encyclical, which had precipitated so much dissent.

Albino Luciani, patriarch of Venice, succeeded him. The new pope, "a lovable man with an infectious smile who had spent his entire career in pastoral work,"[58] took the name John Paul I. Thirty-three days later he died suddenly of an apparent heart attack. The cardinals had scarcely returned home when they were called back to Rome. Once again, they put their trust in the Holy Spirit, and on October 15, 1978, elected Karol Wojtyla—the first non-Italian pope since 1522, and the first-ever from a Communist country. For more than a quarter of a century, his pontificate would be marked by a unique blend of orthodox theology and overwhelming popularity.

A decade and a half earlier, when John XIII said he wanted to bring a little fresh air into the Church, he could not have imagined the force of the gale that was soon unleashed as traditionalists and progressives clashed over what each believed was a faithful response for updating the Church. Similarly, none of the members of the Little Company of Mary could have anticipated the cultural changes that were about to sweep across America—or how profound the impact of those changes would be on their congregation and others.

CHAPTER FOURTEEN

TRUSTING
IN THE SPIRIT

The 1969 General Chapter of the Little Company of Mary in Rome addressed the challenges and opportunities of post-Vatican II times.

Post-Vatican II changes reshaped many aspects of religious life, from the smallest details of daily living to the overall meaning of consecrated life in the Church. For the members of the Little Company of Mary in the American Province, these changes included a revision of their missions and of the way in which they served.

As 1964 began, the Little Company of Mary celebrated a homecoming. The new monument of the Virgin Mary was completed for the graves of their sisters buried in Holy Sepulchre Cemetery, and on January 4, the remains of those sisters who had been interred at Calvary Cemetery were transferred, prompting one member of the community to write, "Now all are at rest together."[1]

The next several years would be a time of challenge and adjustment for the American Province. By 1965, the sisters in San Pierre had been coping for some time with not having enough physicians to support their new general hospital. The "extreme shortage of doctors in this area [of Indiana]"[2] eventually had unavoidable consequences. The community realized that acute care at the Healthcare Facility would have to be discontinued. In the future, the new building would be used to provide space for a larger number of convalescent patients.

At about the same time, it became evident to the sisters in Syracuse that St. Mary's days were numbered. The facility was not only in need of constant repair but the building's layout was also obsolete. Operating rooms had too little space and patient areas did not meet one of the state's newest standards, which mandated that patient beds be in areas built of fire-resistant materials. [3]

The diocese offered tentative support for the community's plans to relocate and build a new facility, but it was tempered by a cautionary warning, as a letter from Monsignor Daniel Lawler, Director of Diocesan Charities and Welfare to Bishop Foery indicates:

> It is my understanding that the Diocese of Syracuse is willing to cooperate with the Sisters of the Little Company of Mary ... to replace the present St. Mary's Hospital, if funds can be obtained without an appeal to the parishes....
>
> However, I pointed out that the problem of developing a new hospital on a new site would be enormous.... St. Mary's assets are ... limited to its present real estate; also ... community turmoil in

hospital planning is so complex that no one today can predict the decisions that will be made....

[M]y plan [is] to point out to Sister Oliver the pledge of our cooperation ... but also indicate the risks of such a program, and the difficulties we may face in persuading the community to support a new St. Mary's. It would then be up to the Sisters to decide whether they believe they should go forward in this direction....[4]

After considerable thought and prayer, the community decided to proceed with the project—a decision influenced by the American Province's own track record of successful hospitals in Evergreen Park, Jasper, and Torrance. The sisters planned to build in the northern section of the county, where they felt a hospital would benefit most Syracusans.

The Little Company of Mary was highly regarded by those who knew them, as a letter from Justice William E. McClusky of the New York Supreme Court illustrates. Writing to Monsignor Lawler, the judge mentioned that one of his physician friends "was amazed at the work being done at St. Mary's by the staff and the officials.... [that] it was one of the best run hospitals of its size in this area."[5] Unfortunately, that admiration would not affect the New York State Planning Committee's decision.

At the beginning of 1965, the community in upstate New York took initial steps toward expansion. That summer, under the headline, "St. Mary's Plans New Hospital," the [Syracuse] *Herald-Journal* reported:

St. Mary's hospital officials last night announced a proposal to build a new, $7 million hospital in the northern area of Onondaga County to replace its present building [on] Court Street.

The proposed new hospital would boost St. Mary's capacity to 255 beds—about 180 more than the hospital now has. The Rt. Rev. Msgr. Daniel E. Lawler, director of hospitals for the Roman Catholic Diocese of Syracuse ... said a letter of intent —the first step required under state law—has been submitted.... The state council must approve a proposal before the hospital can proceed with planning, hiring an architect or further work....[6]

Midway through 1967, the Community Health Information and Planning Service, Inc. (CHIPS) recommended that the Syracuse area would best be served by having three major health centers and proposed a merger between St. Mary's Hospital and St. Joseph's Hospital.[7] The Little Company of Mary's vision differed critically from the planning commission's, but the sisters in Syracuse continued to hope that the state hospital commission would eventually approve their plans for a new hospital.

Throughout 1968, the Hospital Board at St. Mary's laid out its case for a new general hospital, reasoning that even if St. Joseph's built a new ambulatory center as recommended, the planning commission itself acknowledged that the area would need an additional hospital in the near future. Based on this information, the sisters asked, "Why not build it before costs rise?"[8]

Two state senators sent a joint letter to the Hospital Review and Planning Council urging approval of a new St. Mary's:

> One of the most significant advantages of the St. Mary's proposal, to our minds, is that the hospital itself is administered and staffed by an outstanding order of nursing nuns, "The Little Company of Mary." The administrative talent, which the Sisters provide to staffing the hospital, as well as their nursing ability, will continue in our community an asset, which, if measured in dollars and cents, would total millions over years of service. We should not consider too lightly the possibility of the "Little Company of Mary" leaving Syracuse if St. Mary's is phased out or forced to close without rebuilding their own hospital. A new hospital, on the other hand, could mean more of the nursing sisters coming to Onondaga County.[9]

Before year's end, however, it became obvious that the state would not approve the plan. Not only did this destroy the congregation's hope of expansion in upstate New York, but it also sealed the fate of the sisters who were serving in Syracuse. With no viable options, the community was forced to end the work that they had begun thirteen years earlier.

In mid-May 1969, the Little Company of Mary turned over the operation of St. Mary's to the Third Order of Franciscan Sisters, and on the final day of the month departed from the Diocese of Syracuse after sixteen years of service to the people of upstate New York.[10] Less than a year later, the maternity hospital was phased out. The old structure became a drug rehab facility for a brief period of time and was then

Sister Jean Stickney, L.C.M., brings her nursing skills to the migrant people living in the villas miserias (misery villages) of Buenos Aires.

demolished. The Franciscan Sisters continued to operate the medical hospital until 1975.[11] Today, the building houses an affiliate of the United Cerebral Palsy Association known as "Enable," which offers assessment, therapy, training, and support to disabled children and adults.[12]

As their counterparts in Syracuse were praying and working for a new hospital in the mid-1960s, the community in Buenos Aires was expanding its ministry in small ways. Several years earlier, a health center had opened with government support and private contributions, and one member of the Little Company of Mary and an LCM nurse joined the health team comprised of seven pediatricians, two internists, and one obstetrician who provided care for the medical needs of the area's fifteen thousand homeless residents.[13]

During 1965, the community in Buenos Aires became more involved in working with the immigrants who lived in a shantytown settlement a short walk from their hospital. Two trams, originally used as school buildings by the local parish, were converted into dispensaries, and a pediatrician volunteered part-time. Although the small Little Company of Mary community could only spare one member for this work, the community hoped to eventually increase their service to the country's poor.

When the 1970s began, the four-story, seventy-two-bed Little

Company of Mary Hospital in Buenos Aires had been in operation for almost two decades, and the community was planning to open a four-bed coronary unit in March 1973.[14] The congregation was concerned with the relative costliness of running a small hospital because it meant that most patients were either wealthy or members of the middle-class who had health insurance. The sisters believed that if the facility could be enlarged, it would be more cost-effective and their apostolate could be extended to the less fortunate.

The service that the Little Company of Mary provided in the Argentine foundation was multidimensional. As one sister noted:

> Emphasis in the apostolate within the hospital setting is not only to the patient[s] but [also] to the families, personnel, and medical staff. Sisters visit the patients daily; one Sister distributes Holy Communion whenever the Chaplain is not available. Many patients return to the Sacraments while in our care.[15]

The sisters identified three other apostolates in addition to hospital nursing: public health, which addressed the needs of the poor migrant community; the continuation of their mission to help priests (especially missionaries) recover physically, emotionally, and spiritually from the loneliness and deprivations of assignments by setting aside several hospital rooms for them; and an apostolate of formation to support Argentine women as they prepared to become community members.[16]

While the sisters were planning to expand their ministry, Mother General was giving a great deal of thought to the future of the mission itself. The community there had been stressed by overwork for some time, and she was concerned for both their physical and psychological welfare.

In the fall of 1974, the sisters in Evergreen Park gathered together for three days of discussion, prayer, and "discernment" —a time of listening to and trusting in the Holy Spirit in order to ascertain God's will. For awhile, the American Province had considered the possibility of establishing a mission outside Buenos Aires aimed at helping the poor, but as the sisters went through the process of discernment, they concluded that they should not attempt this new apostolate.

Mother General soon decided that the beleaguered community in Buenos Aires could no longer continue. Although all of the provinces had been asked for volunteers for South America, there had been no appreciable response,

Sister M. Antonieta Benavides, L.C.M., a native of Argentina, teaches a group of children.

and the U.S. community could no longer sustain the apostolate without help.

When the news of their planned departure was made public, an immediate outpouring of sentiment from the Argentine people revealed just how much the sisters were loved and needed. Dozens of letters arrived in Chicago addressed to "Mother General," begging her to reverse her decision. In a five-page letter handwritten on lined paper, a priest from outside Buenos Aires explained:

> I am the pastor of the San Miguel parish in Parana, (Irish by birth), where three priests run a parish of 30,000 souls. All three priests, as well as the neighboring ... community of Dominican[s] have experienced time and again, the kindness, goodness, and the professional know-how of your good nuns, and the thought that they are now due to leave is something we do not like to think about because ... Buenos Aires will never be the same again without this dearly-beloved community....

> Something that should not be overlooked ... the quiet, unobtrusive work [the sisters] did for priests.... [N]o matter what the ailment or sickness, our dear kindly Sister Superior Margaret [Mary] always gave top priority to the ministers of God at no cost to themselves, and they left the Sanatorium always comforted in body and soul and eternally grateful to the community of Blue Nuns.

One aspect of the Blue Nuns work that I greatly admire ... is the number of souls that they cause to return to the sacraments.... [A] mere 7% of the Argentinians [*sic*] are practicing Catholics.... Since the Blue Nuns opened the Sanatorium shortly before World War One, the number of souls that returned to the grace of God under the holy and gentle persuasion of the "Blues" is known only to the Recording Angel. But it is a great number and is among the most precious things that your Congregation performs....[17]

Two members of the family directly responsible for the Little Company of Mary's presence in Argentina wrote of their feelings. One writer accepted the decision somewhat philosophically:

My maiden name is Morgan—a grandchild of the Mrs. Morgan ... you cared for her daughter when she became ill in Chicago and who in gratitude offered them to start a new hospital in San Antonio de Areco.

The Blue Sisters have become so dear to all of us.... It is saddening to learn, so I believe, [that the] Buenos Aires Blue Nuns are being recalled....

Whatever you decide is the best for the Order—we have to abide by it....

Cordially, Margarita Morgan Moore[18]

However, her cousin Moreen Morgan unleashed a passionate plea that revealed her anger and distress:

Dearest Mother General,

It can't be true. [A]fter reading in our English newspaper an article ... I am calling for mercy for the sisters of the Little Company of Mary ... help the nuns stay in Buenos Aires. [I]t was my grandmother Margaret Mooney de Morgan who brought these nuns from [the] United States ... here ... in the early 1900s. My aunt [Maria Clara Morgan] ... was so well looked after ... by the Blue Nuns as they [are] affectionately called here, that even though she died, my grandmother was moved by the way she was cared for, that she moved Heaven and Earth and brought the good nuns down here, built a hospital for them in a town 150 miles from Buenos Aires....

Well, you have no idea [of] the work those nuns do down here as there are so many English-speaking communities; I won't name ... all their activities and their successes because fifty pages ... wouldn't be enough to relate all their doings. [N]ow you want to sever them from those dear to them.... I hope you'll think it over and leave those nuns here, where they belong [with] us....[19]

Many Argentines shared personal memories of the community and offered expressions of gratitude. An elderly woman wrote:

I can remember the days when your Sisters first arrived in this country and stayed with the Passionist Sisters at the convent where I was a student. I am well aware of the struggle and hardships there were to get the Sanatorium started.... I wish ... to let you know that our family, together with many others, appreciate[s] all [that] the Sisters of the Little Company of Mary have done....[20]

Other correspondents voiced their dismay:

There is no other hospital that I know of in Argentina where the spiritual support of our Faith, so important to the healing of the sick, is so well combined with technical proficiency as in the Little Company's Hospital.... [M]ay I and my wife and children beg you to please reconsider...? If they go, something very good ... and very necessary for the American and British communities will be taken away.[21]

No amount of prayer or pleading, however, could change the outcome. In a letter published in the *Buenos Aires Herald,* the American Provincial acknowledged "the many gracious and solicitous letters received" but added, "The predicament in attempting to staff the hospital has been increasing for the past several years, and unfortunately, there have been no vocations. Therefore, the decision to withdraw our Sisters cannot be reversed or reconsidered, as we do not have Sisters to send to Buenos Aires."[22]

The *Hermanas de María de Schönstatt* (Marian Sisters of Schönstatt) quickly offered their support. "They hope their Superior General in Germany will give permission for a period of experimentation in hospital administration under the guidance of the [LCM] community with the intention of assuming eventual ownership and management,"[23] reported one member of the LCM community. "[W]e all feel that our prayers and effort ... are going to be realized in these Sisters [who are] so friendly with the Little Company of Mary.... The Marianas know the sacrifices of the early years...." [24]

The Superior General sent the following message worldwide notifying members that the apostolate in Buenos Aires would end on September 15:

> This will be a sad day for all the Sisters of the Congregation.... It is a consolation to know that the Hospital is being taken over by the Schönstatt Sisters, who are well known to our Sisters in the Argentine. Two of these Sisters have already worked with us some years ago, so they are not strangers. [25]

Several months later, the community of the Little Company of Mary in Buenos Aires turned their hospital over to these sisters, but remained two months longer to provide a smooth transition. The final entry in the Buenos Aires logbook reads:

> This afternoon ... [we] completed the painful farewells to the throng of personnel in the lobby and the hundreds or more friends who accompanied us to the airport. It was a grand tribute to the many Sisters of all the provinces who have given of themselves to the service of the Argentines. To the loving care of our Mother Mary, we entrust the fruits of our labors, our friends, and benefactors throughout the years, the hospital family, our ten sisters in the cemetery at San Antonio de Areco, the families of our three Argentine sisters, and our dear Marian Sisters of Schönstatt. Our mission in Argentina is completed.... [26]

On November 15, 1975, the last "Blue Nuns" left South America after sixty-two years of service. The sisters accepted the leave-taking as God's will, knowing that the people of Argentina would remain in their hearts and in their prayers forever. Thirty years later, the hospital that the Little Company of Mary founded, which the Schönstatt Sisters renamed *Mater Dei* (Mother of God), continues to provide compassionate nursing care to the residents of Buenos Aires. In 2004, Sanatorio Mater Dei served more than 150,000 patients, [27] and like the sisters who preceded them, the *Hermanas de María de Schönstatt* offer a mission of hope and healing to the city's less fortunate.

During the late 1960s and into the mid-1970s, the Sisters of the Little Company of Mary in the American Province experienced the sadness and disappointment of having to leave foundations where they had served those in need and with whom they had established lasting relationships. However, in the midst of this difficult time, they were presented with an opportunity that would allow them to fulfill their founder's wishes more directly than ever before.

At the end of December 1973, Monsignor James P. Cassidy, representing Terrence Cardinal Cooke, the archbishop of New York, contacted the American Province requesting the sisters' nursing and administrative expertise at Calvary Hospital in the Bronx, which was entirely devoted to incurable cancer patients.[28]

The mission of Calvary Hospital dated back to 1899, when a group of Irish Catholic women began caring for indigent advanced cancer patients at the House of Calvary in Greenwich Village. In 1910, the Catholic Archdiocese of New York asked the Dominican Sisters of Blauvelt, New York, to care for the patients,[29] and five years later the hospital relocated to the Bronx. The Dominican Sisters of the Sick Poor took over in 1958 and completely renovated the 111-bed hospital.[30] When they could no longer staff the facility because of a lack of sisters, the Archdiocese turned to the Little Company of Mary.

Sister Mary John Schlax, the Provincial Superior, sent the following message to all members of the community:

> Our active participation in a hospital for the terminally ill would be perpetuating the work and apostolate that our own Mother Foundress desired for us. The care of the sick and the dying has been our goal, and while we have had many opportunities, it seems that this is the "perfect opportunity" to minister to the dying and care for them during their final days.[31]

Each sister was asked to prayerfully consider this potential apostolate. Several sisters were needed, and four immediately volunteered. The following week, the Provincial Superior and two other sisters met with Monsignor Cassidy and Cardinal Cooke to discuss the possibility of working at Calvary Hospital.[32] Afterwards, Sister Mary John advised Mother General M. Madeleine Carrigan, "[W]e have come to the conclusion that the work with the terminally ill at this hospital is the work of Mother Foundress and that we must make every attempt to accept the invitation."[33]

In April, the American Province received word from Rome that Mother General and her Council, "... were happy to give official approval of the acceptance of the invitation of Cardinal Cooke to care for the sick and dying in his diocese." [34]

On May 6, 1974, a small community comprised of Sister Ruth Putnam, Sister Patricia Dooley, Sister Roseann McCarthy, and Sister Virginia O'Brien began their mission in the Bronx. Of their first day, one sister wrote, "As we walked in ... the cleaning crew was making a quick exit out the basement door. We looked around ... all wondering what we were in for? Trying to smile and say, "Oh, how nice, we sensed our poverty—not only of material things but [also] of friends, relatives, and 'secure community.'"[35]

Sister Mary John helped them settle in and sent the following message back to Evergreen Park:

> The sisters commenced work last Monday ... [and] as one would expect, it was a bit tiring simply because everything and everybody was new....
>
> For their orientation, each ... was assigned to an instructor and observed patient care even though all would not be in nursing. [T]he administrator's idea is to have each person know exactly what is done for their patients so that they will have a fuller appreciation of the standard of care and the loving concern shown the patient.[36]
>
> Our convent is ... [three] doors ... from the hospital. Because the sisters who had been at Calvary owned the furnishings, when we arrived the house was quite bare except for very nice new bedroom furniture. Bit by bit we will be getting the furniture, and I am hoping that our oratory [i.e., chapel] can soon be set up.
>
> This last week the Cardinal had a reception here—a farewell to the sisters who had left Calvary and a welcome to us. His Eminence was so gracious and warm ... to each of us. He told two of the sisters that we were a gift from God.
>
> This will give you a little idea of our first days here in New York. Please do keep us in your prayers, as it is wonderful work—really the work of Mother Foundress.[37]

Midway through the 1970s, the LCM was invited to Calvary Hospital in the Bronx.

The New York group, who referred to themselves as "Bronxers," quickly discovered that this borough was not just geographically distant from the other U.S. foundations of the Little Company of Mary. From a sociological perspective, it was light-years away from the comfortable, middle-class setting of Evergreen Park and Torrance or the strong, small-town values of Jasper. The little community found themselves in the midst of one of the most troubled areas of New York City, notorious for its poverty, crime, violence, and drug use.

Their residence required some getting used to. "As we settled in," noted one sister, "we discovered more leaks and cracks that need[ed] repair ... we also had our share of insects and house invaders [i.e., rodents]...."[38] "When the [door] alarm is set off," it sound[s] like an air raid drill," wrote one sister.[39] Another sister added, "The combination of heat and noise prevented us from sleeping except for a few winks. Because the house is so old, it retained the heat. The windows only seemed to let in the noise and dirt ... [and] the streets were alive until 3 or 4 a.m."[40]

The four Bronx sisters (all of Irish heritage), needed to adapt to an inner-city culture that was totally foreign to them. During their hospital welcome, "the all-black Calvary choir sang, 'Jesus is the Light' with enthusiasm,"[41] and the Bronxers soon realized that *they* were the minority because most of their fellow hospital workers were people of color—either black or Hispanic. In addition, the community scrambled to learn a few words in the languages of people they lived among—from

"*Ni Hao ma*" (Chinese for "How are you?") to "*Zay gezunt*" ("Be well" in Yiddish). [42]

Calvary Hospital differed from the other facilities in which the sisters had served. It "was run on a hospice concept, caring for those with six months or less to live. Many of the patients had experienced the gamut of medical/surgical care, and they now faced the news that nothing more could be done.... [At] Calvary ... they experienced excellent pain management, personal dignity, [and] choices in daily living...."[43] Working among people who were all very close to death was a ministry that the sisters in the American Province had never participated in before.

The dying have taught the sisters a number of things about living— the importance of letting those you love know that you love them, of taking time to do some of the things you really want to do in life and doing it "now," and of not living with regrets.[44] One member of the community observed, "Terminal patients face life through the lens of reality. In addition, they would often ask questions about 'the next life' or share past memories of family and friends...."[45]

To their surprise, the LCM community discovered that a number of patients who had come to the hospital expecting to die were later discharged and lived for some months with a "renewed vigor for living," returning only when they felt the end was near. The patients at Calvary were able to wear their own clothes and decorate their rooms according to their personal tastes, and were encouraged to participate in a wide range of activities based upon their individual desires, abilities, and lifestyles. "Children and grandchildren were especially welcome, since life and continuity have dominion at Calvary, not death."[46]

Three of the four members of the Bronx community worked in areas where they did not provide actual nursing care—in Admitting, Pastoral Care, and as a Director of Nursing. However, they had contact in other ways. According to Sister Virginia O'Brien, Thursday night was "Cocktail Night" for patients who were up to enjoying a drink. She recalls helping the volunteer cocktail ladies, who dressed in bright attire, with their cart, which contained a variety of drinks as well as nuts, cheese and crackers, and candy. For a number of patients, the very idea of being able to enjoy a cocktail was amazing, made even more so by the fact that a nun would be serving them.[47] The first time Sister Virginia asked a patient what he would like, he answered, "Oh, nothing, Sister." When the other cart workers heard this, they said, "What? He always has a martini," and one of the lay volunteers made it for him. It was a time of adjustment for both the patient and his blue-veiled server.

Every Friday, a music therapist entertained both patients and staff as she walked from room to room with her guitar and took special requests. The legendary pianist Vladimir Horowitz performed a concert at the hospital, and the actress Cicely Tyson visited and handed out autographs. At Calvary, patients could go to a ballgame at Yankee Stadium or to the Barnum & Bailey's Circus, of which one of the sisters wrote: "En route we drove along the Hudson with Manhattan on one side and New Jersey not far in the distance.... One ninety-four-year-old patient kept saying, 'No wonder they call this the greatest show on Earth.' She couldn't wait to get a bag of popcorn and shared it with all of us.... It was a wonderful afternoon."[48]

Throughout 1974 and 1975, the sisters continued their mission to the incurably ill at Calvary Hospital. The small community became friends with the staff, who were delighted at their attempts to learn Spanish, and they often invited patient visitors to share a meal with them. The sisters were not the only generous ones. In an area rife with crime and drugs, they learned what was important to the good people who happened to be poor—how dedicated they were to their work and their homes; how large-hearted they were with gifts when someone celebrated a birthday or was expecting a baby.[49]

Halfway through 1975, the Provincial Council asked the Bronx community to consider relocating because their house on Grand Avenue in the South Bronx was in a section notorious for its high crime rate. The Council not only felt that living in a better area would be safer but it would also provide a little more space from the hospital atmosphere of Calvary, which took its toll on those who worked there.[50] After weighing the pros and cons of moving, the sisters decided that transportation would be a major problem if they moved, so chose to remain where they were.

The sisters recorded two areas of concern during their mission at Calvary Hospital. The first was that since cancer technicians provided most of the nursing care, the sisters themselves had limited patient contact.[51] It also appears that at least a number of the doctors at Calvary resisted addressing the emotional needs of those facing death by maintaining a hospital environment in which "the new death and dying concepts are taboo...." as well as refusing to have either a psychologist or psychiatrist on staff.[52] Despite its shortcomings, Calvary Hospital was a wonderful training ground for the sisters, and a former Bronxer remarked that she learned more from the cancer technicians in dealing with the terminally ill than from anyone else.[53] In September, the board of Calvary Hospital met to consider building a new facility to replace the existing building, which had been renovated thirteen years earlier but still needed constant repair. In addition, the demand for beds far exceeded available space, and those seeking admission to Calvary were placed on a waiting list. With a gift of land from the Archdiocese of New York, it was hoped that the hospital could expand to two hundred beds within a few years.

The American Province of the Little Company of Mary faced a dilemma. A larger hospital would necessitate more sisters, but the community had no additional members to spare. It was decided that it would be best for all concerned to have a larger congregation of nursing sisters take over the hospital's operation and become familiar with its workings and spirit before the facility almost doubled in size.

The small LCM group departed from the Bronx in June 1977. For the sisters who served there, the three years had been a broadening experience. The Bronx community had learned to live in an urban setting as part of ethnically diverse community unlike any other foundation in the American Province. In one of their Christmas messages, the sisters had written, "The Bronx life has exposed us to the reality of the life of the poor. Sharing in the black and Spanish cultures has opened our eyes to the suffering, yet oftentimes cheerful, people of God. *Feliz Navidad.*"[54]

Two years after the sisters left Calvary Hospital, the Little Company of Mary in Evergreen Park began a ministry to the sick and dying that was very close to what Mary Potter had envisioned for her daughters. Like the first pioneering members of the Little Company, the sisters again began providing home care as part of a team of nurses, social workers, home health aides, and pastoral ministers who offered nursing services to patients during their final days, as well as comfort and emotional support to family members. The new ministry, which had been introduced to America only four years earlier, was called hospice care.[55]

Around that time, several sisters had begun to work in the new field of Pastoral Care as trained chaplains, offering a ministry of care, counseling, and emotional support that deepened their spiritual involvement with their patients and their patients' families. Despite their reduced numbers, the members of the American Province continued to expand their apostolate of healing to include the emotional and spiritual welfare of others.

In 1977, the Little Company of Mary celebrated the centenary of its founding in England and the eighty-fourth year since the congregation extended its healing presence to the United States. On October 8, the community in Evergreen Park was honored with a "Century of Caring" observance as well as by testimonials from various public officials. The Illinois State Assembly passed a Resolution expressing "respect and gratitude for their dedicated efforts,"[56]and the Mayor of Chicago proclaimed August 22, 1977, "Little Company of Mary Day in Chicago."[57] In appreciation of their many contributions, Governor Jim Thompson wrote:

> We are fortunate that you came to the Chicagoland area where you have continued to serve the people for almost a century. With the ingenuity of the pioneering spirit, you have sought excellence in treating, comforting and healing the sick.... Your services have always been underscored by personal kindness, sympathy, hope and cheer for your patients and families.... The world has truly been a better place because the Sisters of the Little Company of Mary passed this way.[58]

The sisters of the American Province also received recognition from the highest office in the land. In a congratulatory letter, President Jimmy Carter offered his praise:

> You serve as a shining example for the entire nursing profession. Guided by a strong faith in God and true to the spirit of humility and love, which inspired the founding of your Company, you have fulfilled a vital need by giving spiritual comfort to the patients in your care and to their families. For this and for all your worthwhile endeavors, you have the deep appreciation of all of your fellow citizens. You have added greatly to the strength of our society, and I know you will continue to do so in the years ahead.[59]

Perhaps more than at any other time in their history, between the mid-1960s and 1980, the Sisters of the Little Company of Mary in the

United States experienced innumerable changes, ranging from the modification of their habit to the reevaluation of what a religious vocation really meant and how it was to be lived. In the face of these transformations, which saw some of their missions end and other healing ministries begin, the sisters in the American Province placed their hope in God and trusted that His Spirit would guide them. During the most trying times, they not only continued their tradition of attending to physical ailments but also extended their apostolate to encompass the healing of their patients' emotional and spiritual wounds. As time went by, the sisters reached out beyond the confines of their hospitals to touch the lives of people in nearby parishes and local communities—ministries that would continue to expand during the last two decades of the twentieth century and beyond.

CHAPTER FIFTEEN

BEARERS OF GOD'S
TENDER COMPASSION

Sister M. Terrence Landini, L.C.M., lends an ear to a patient in Torrance, California.

B y the beginning of the 1980s, the rebellious, defiant tone which had been prevalent throughout the United States since the late 1960s had worn thin. Most Americans were ready for a change. That election year, they responded to an optimistic presidential candidate who saw America as "the last best hope of man on earth."[1] On January 20, 1981, the day Ronald Reagan was sworn into office, Iran released fifty-two American hostages after having held them in captivity for 444 days.

Much of the vocal dissent by liberal Catholics toward the Church had also quieted. But during John Paul II's first visit to the United States in 1979, he discovered just how different "American thinking" could be. Sister Theresa Kane, an American Sister of Mercy and president of the Leadership Conference of Women Religious, urged the Holy Father to be " open to and respond to ... the women ... desirous of serving in and through the Church as fully participating members."[2] The pope did not respond to her call to extend the priesthood to women, however, and the Vatican subsequently rebuked her.[3] John Paul II made it clear that some matters, such as the ordination of women and the possibility of marriage for priests, were no longer open to discussion or debate. By late 1979, he stopped granting virtually all requests for laicizations from priests who wished to leave their active ministry and marry.[4]

For the Little Company of Mary, the early 1980s brought new ministries, particularly an unforeseen mission on the West Coast. In the beginning of March 1983, two members of the community began an apostolate in California at the invitation of Monsignor Otto Sporrer, pastor of St. Nicholas Parish in Laguna Woods. He had learned about the Little Company of Mary from Father Tony Bullen, who was on sabbatical from England and familiar with the "Blue Nuns" in his native Liverpool. The priest knew that the congregation had been founded to provide assistance in homes, and he urged the monsignor to contact the sisters for help in his parish, which included a nearby retirement community called Leisure World.

After reading Monsignor Sporrer's letter, Sister M. Terrence Landini discarded it, thinking that it would be virtually impossible for the small community to respond to his request. She quickly had a change of heart, however. "The Spirit said pull that thing out of the wastebasket," she explained, which she did, and then passed the invitation on to the congregation.[5]

Throughout the history of the American Province, a number of

For twenty years, Sister Mary John Schlax, L.C.M., and Sister Mildred Radziewicz, L.C.M., have brought the presence of the Little Company of Mary to the parishes and homes of people in Laguna Hills California. Here, they celebrate a birthday with a dear friend, Mrs. Patchell.

decisions have been based more on a response to the Holy Spirit than on common sense: establishing a community in remote San Antonio de Areco; choosing a field in Evergreen Park as the site for their first hospital; building a convalescent home in out-of-the way San Pierre. After discussion and prayer, the sisters decided that this ministry was part of the Little Company of Mary's charism, and requested sister volunteers. [6]

Sister Gloria Harper and Sister Nancy Boyle responded enthusiastically and soon formed a community of their own in a rented home in Santa Maria, California, where they began a ministry of Pastoral Care. They helped with Special Sacraments—preparing children who had not received the sacraments at the usual age—and also participated as Eucharistic ministers and lectors; readied adults for the sacrament of Confirmation; worked in bereavement to plan funeral and wake services; and visited nearby hospitals, retirement communities, and individual homes. In addition to offering spiritual comfort and support, they became involved in a number of corporal works of mercy—collecting clothes for the poor and bringing food to the homebound.

Sister Mary John Schlax and Sister Mildred Radziewicz arrived at St. Nicholas a few years later and have continued this work since that time. The two sisters, who have been joined by volunteer Sister Theresa Kim from Korea, open their home and share their table, especially at holidays, with those who have no families. In addition, they often take gifts of homemade soup and bread to those whom they visit. "It is that personal touch," says

Sister Mildred, "that lets people know that someone cares...."[7]

The sisters touch the lives of Catholics, non-Catholics, and non-Christians, and believe that their ministry fulfills the Little Company of Mary's mission " ... [to] respond to contemporary needs by evangelizing in word and deed through the ministries of prayers for the dying, nursing, teaching, and other pastoral activities."[8]

In 1987, Sister Sharon Ann Walsh, the community's Provincial Leader, asked Sister Gloria, Sister Mary John, and Sister Mildred to initiate an "Associates Program"—a concept that had originated with Mother Mary Potter, who had referred to the laypeople who embodied the Little Company's ideals and would assist them in their mission as "The Greater Company of Mary."

The first Associate members in the United States turned the founder's hope into reality when nine women parishioners learned about Mary Potter's vision and the unique charism of the Little Company of Mary and subsequently made a personal commitment, renewed yearly, to pray daily for the dying, vocations, the Holy Souls, and for the beatification of Mary Potter.[9] They provide "a visible sign of Christ's healing presence," similar to what the sisters have been doing for the past 128 years.[10] Associate membership, which began in California, has spread to other areas of the country, and today includes more than 125 dedicated individuals.

During the 1980s, the sisters became more involved in hospice care, which was just taking hold in the United States. The hospice movement, which [had] its roots in the work of two British physicians, Dame Cicely Saunders and Dr. Elisabeth Kübler-Ross, brought the often taboo subject of dying into the open and shed light on the needs of patients during this important passage.[11] The Little Company of Mary had provided a compassionate presence to the dying for more than a century, but now the sisters became familiar with the latest psychological findings that Kübler-Ross had gleaned from interviews with the dying, and learned more about the various stages of grief—denial, anger, depression, bargaining, and acceptance."[12]

As a result, members of the Little Company of Mary have been part of hospice teams for more than twenty-five years, caring for patients in their final days. Sister Renee Cunningham formerly served as a hospice nurse at Memorial Hospital in Jasper, which established a countywide hospice in 1986. She is now involved in "palliative care," a distinction made necessary after new Medicare regulations took effect in Indiana in

The LCM Associate Program, begun in California in 1987, has spread throughout America.

1992. "We're there for the family," she explained. "They know they can call us anytime." About three-quarters of her patients have cancer; the others suffer from end-stage cardiac or renal disease; and in the last three years, she has worked with six patients with ALS (Lou Gherig's disease).

Sister Renee stressed the importance of having a family reminisce about the life of their dying loved one and mentioned how crucial it is for those in their final days to hear their family laughing at memories because then they often don't fight the end. She emphasized, "The biggest thing, without exception, is a life review. Because of our culture, people look at what they didn't do. I try to help them change that, to look at what they did accomplish."

When she speaks of her patients, Sister Renee's face lights up. "Every day they teach me more about living and dying. They entrust me with a very precious gift by allowing me to journey with them in their final days on this earth. I now know that life is meant to be enjoyed."[13]

As a Christian, and particularly in light of the charism of the Little Company of Mary, Sister Renee views death as "a spiritual event," and recalls the days when the sisters prayed for the dying in front of the Blessed Sacrament on Fridays between noon and 3 p.m. She also remembers night watches, which Sister Kathleen McIntyre explained further. In the "early days"—until the late 1950s—the sisters would go to a funeral home and pray all night for a deceased patient or relative of one of the sisters. After keeping vigil, the sisters would attend Mass, then return to the convent.[14] Some of these community traditions have been discontinued, but the sisters still pray the rosary for the dying every day, and those sisters who are part of hospice teams again find themselves called to be present at the bedside of patients during their final hours.

The principal apostolate of the Little Company of Mary has always been concern for the dying, and the very presence of the sisters has often made a difference in the way in which a life has ended, as illustrated by a story that Sister Mary John Schlax and Sister Mildred Radziewicz related:

> Some years ago, an elderly man in his eighties was brought to the Little Company of Mary Hospital in Torrance, unable to speak and partially paralyzed because of a stroke. The young woman in social services, who was assisting him, discovered that he had neither insurance nor Medicare coverage, and most surprising, he did not have a social security number. She quickly brought this to the sisters' attention." We sat with him during his hospitalization and continued to visit him after he was transferred to a nursing home," said Sister Mary John. "One day we asked him if he wanted to see a priest. He shook his head no. When we learned that he was not married, we inquired if he might be a brother. He shook his head, but a change had come over him. Finally, we gently asked, 'Are you a priest?' and his eyes filled with tears. We named several religious orders— Dominican, Jesuit, Benedictine. None elicited a response, but at the mention of 'Franciscan,' he started to cry."

> Why he walked away from his vocation remains a mystery, but shortly before he made that decision he had a falling out with his brother, a fellow priest working in Peru. Soon afterwards, he left the priesthood without requesting to be laicized—the process that would have allowed him to discontinue his active ministry and be dispensed from his vows. Instead, he simply disappeared. His priest brother returned to the States and searched for him at various construction sites, where he thought his brother might be working, but never found him. The missing priest remained "lost" until he was brought to Little Company of Mary Hospital, mute and paralyzed.

> "We got in touch with a local Franciscan chaplain, who visited him and later heard his confession and anointed him," explained Sister

Mary John. The sisters could have stepped away knowing that they had helped someone return to the Lord, but they felt that there was more to be done. "We sought help from our Provincial Leader, Sister Nancy Boyle, who knew the former head of the Franciscan order. She contacted him and he called the current Provincial in New York who flew out to visit his long-lost Franciscan brother." In a moment that the sisters described as wonderful, their patient, who had recently returned to his Faith and to his priesthood, concelebrated Mass with the Franciscan Provincial at their home.

Their weekly visits continued as the months went by. Sister Mary John, acting as his secretary, helped him to get back in touch with his family. She wrote to his relatives for him and then read him their responses. When a lump on his shoulder turned out to be malignant, the sisters provided even more support. "We were always visiting him," added Sister Mildred. "One night we saw him about 10 o'clock and asked his caretaker to be sure to call if he got worse." The two were notified at four in the morning and hurried to his side. They prayed with him until he died at 7 a.m. A few days later his body was flown back to the Provincialate in New York where his funeral was held. He was laid to rest in the monastery's cemetery wearing the habit of the Franciscan order.

The following week the sisters remembered him with a Scripture service in their home. Catholics and non-Catholics attended as well as the Jewish woman who had provided care for him during his final days and the Irish girl who just happened to pick up on the fact that he lacked a social security number.[15]

The prayers and presence of the Little Company of Mary have positively touched innumerable souls during their final hours. But it is the dying themselves who have often taught the sisters great lessons of faith. Decades later, Sister M. Joseph Casey vividly remembers a ten-year-old girl who was responsible for one of the most moving experiences in her many years of nursing service:

I was in pediatrics and there was a beautiful, redhead little girl named Becky who in three days lost almost all of her waist-length hair because of the chemotherapy she was having for bone cancer. At that time, the television program, "Little House on the Prairie," was very popular, and in the show the children wore frilly nightcaps to bed. The girls in surgery wore something like that, so I asked them to make one for Becky, which they did, and she loved it.

One morning I had been with Becky for about an hour and was about to leave the room when she mentioned that she needed to tell me something. "I'm going to see Jesus tonight," she said, "and I'm going to tell Him all about you." I told her, "Oh, no, sweetheart, not tonight—you're still strong." But before I left the hospital, I asked the other sisters to call me at any time if there was any change in Becky's condition.

That night I stayed dressed just in case and slept in a chair. Right before midnight I got a call and was told, "Sister, come right away." Back then we were not supposed to be out by ourselves, but I didn't want to take the time to find someone to go with me, so I just ran down the street. By the time I got to the 9th floor, she was gone. Her parents were with her and said to me, "Sister, look at the beautiful smile on her face." I just felt that the Lord was still present in that room...."[16]

As the understanding of psychology became increasingly important during the latter decades of the twentieth century, the American Province of the Little Company of Mary expanded its focus of healing to include care of the spiritual, emotional, and temporal well-being of the people they serve.

The late 1980s saw triumphs and tragedies. The Berlin Wall came down, and the Communist countries of Eastern Europe enjoyed their first taste of democracy. The space shuttle *Challenger* exploded, and AIDS was discovered. At the beginning of 1991, as a result of Iraq's invasion of Kuwait, the first massive deployment of U.S. troops since Vietnam led an international coalition of thirty-two countries in Operation Desert Storm—the first of two wars in the Persian Gulf.[17]

The final decade of the century also witnessed the birth of the electronic age: computers became household items; the World Wide Web allowed unprecedented access to information; and e-mail and cell phones changed the way millions communicated with each other. The nation experienced a decade of tremendous economic growth and prosperity for many Americans, yet it was also a frustrating time for those involved with government health-related programs and managed care, and the numerous, complex regulations of Medicaid would have serious repercussions for

1. LCM Sisters in a villa miseria
2. Cardinal Bernardin blessing
   LCM Sisters (1993)
3. Counseling Ministry —
   Sister Deborah Conley
4. Sister Jean Stickney, Sister
   Margaret Christina Hoban
5. Announcement card from
   Archbishop Cushing
6. LCM facility at San Pierre, Indiana
7. LCM Sisters in the
   American Province (1993)
8. Sisters with Joseph Cardinal
   Bernardin — 100th Anniversary
   of LCM in America (1993)

The Most Reverend
Richard J. Cushing, D. D.

Archbishop of Boston

is pleased to announce that the Sisters of the Little Company of Mary are now operating the Otis General Hospital, 85 Otis Street, East Cambridge, Massachusetts, and that in the future the hospital will be known as

The Little Company of Mary Hospital

5.

6.

7.

8.

1. LCM Sisters with Francis Cardinal George
2. Sister Magdalen Nolan — Evergreen Park Nursery (1952)
3. Sister Nancy Boyle
4. Sister Adrian Davis with performers including Pat O'Brien (1966)
5. Flowers for Sister Francis Beggan (1987)
6. A class of novices (1965)
7. 100th Anniversary of LCM (1977)
8. Contrast of classic and contemporary at LCMH (1984)

5.

6.

7.

8.

1. Blessing of hospital in Buenos Aires (1953)
2. Memorial Hospital — Jasper, Indiana (2004)
3. LCM Sisters in Buenos Aires (1975)
4. Hannon Tower at LCMH Torrance (2005)
5. Torrance Chapel (2005)

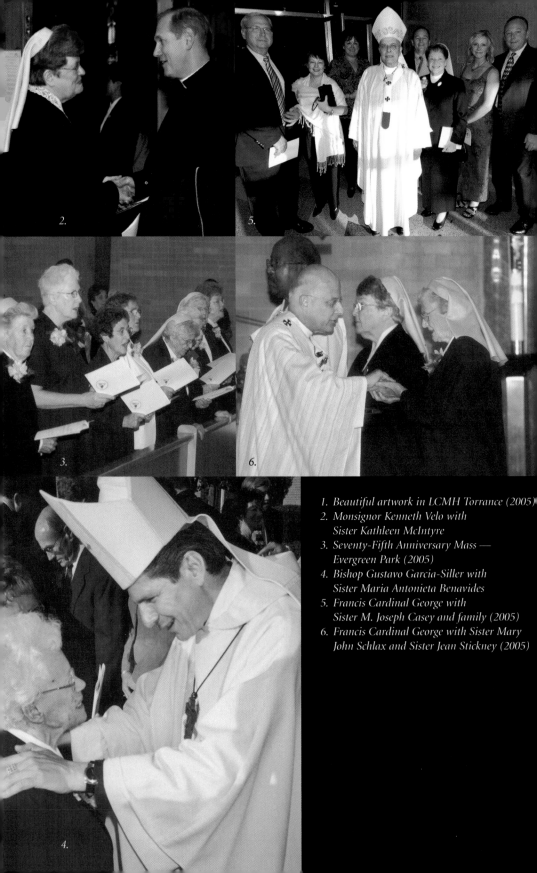

1. Beautiful artwork in LCMH Torrance (2005)
2. Monsignor Kenneth Velo with Sister Kathleen McIntyre
3. Seventy-Fifth Anniversary Mass — Evergreen Park (2005)
4. Bishop Gustavo Garcia-Siller with Sister Maria Antonieta Benavides
5. Francis Cardinal George with Sister M. Joseph Casey and family (2005)
6. Francis Cardinal George with Sister Mary John Schlax and Sister Jean Stickney (2005)

one of the Little Company of Mary's facilities.

By the late 1980s, most patients at the convalescent home in San Pierre were Medicaid recipients. A discrepancy with the rate of reimbursement meant that only a portion of the actual patient cost was covered, and this continued to worsen over time. The only way to remedy the situation was to change ownership.[18] In 1989, the Little Company of Mary leased the convalescent home, which they had built and run since 1952, to the Holy Cross Health System, and the Sisters of the Holy Cross of South Bend assumed the work begun by the blue-veiled sisters.

Not long after the Little Company of Mary stepped away from their mission in northwestern Indiana, their hospital in Torrance entered into a neonatology partnership with nearby San Pedro Peninsula Hospital.[19] In 1992, the two hospitals became part of an integrated regional health care system known as the Little Company of Mary Health Services,[20] which joined Providence Health Systems in a collaborative partnership in 1999.

As the decade progressed, a number of sisters began serving in a myriad of ways—a sort of spiritual multitasking. Sister Gloria Harper, who works in administration in Torrance, California, incorporates the spirituality of Mary Potter during hire orientation as she educates new employees about the history, legacy, and vision of Venerable Mary Potter. This is done at each of the Little Company of Mary Hospitals to provide all who serve there with an understanding of the community's founder and to ensure that Mary Potter's spirit is actively carried on by those who work at the facility.[21]

The sisters who work in Pastoral Care have opportunities to touch the lives of patients in ways that were not possible when they worked in nursing positions. Sister Francis Curran, a volunteer from Ireland, explained, "We have the time to spend with patients and families way beyond what other professionals can give."[22] Freed from the obligations of providing specific nursing services, the sisters can budget their time where it is most needed, whether that means providing a calming presence to help soothe an agitated patient or simply being physically and spiritually present at the bedside of a dying patient, which is at the heart of the Little Company of Mary apostolate.

For the past 128 years, the Sisters of the Little Company of Mary have been there for those in need. The following story, related by Sister Sharon

Ann Walsh, is but one example of this:

> When we were preparing to move into our "new-to-us" house in Evergreen Park two years ago, we met a friendly couple who lived next door. They were gracious, welcoming, and funny, all at the same time.
>
> After we moved into our home, we would often meet them in our daily comings and goings to the hospital. We had countless conversations on the front sidewalk and over the backyard fence. We shared many laughs and treats like rainbow ice cream cones, over the fence.
>
> About a year later, the husband became sick and was admitted to Little Company. It was the first time they had ever been at LCMH. Everything was new and strange. The husband, who was very ill, was diagnosed with cancer.
>
> We offered support and assisted them through the hospital stay and discharge home. Sometimes we brought over hot meals for the two of them and planned little surprises—funny little gifts or a take-out order of ribs so they didn't even have to think about cooking.
>
> As he became more and more ill, we helped them move into the transition home program and then into the LCM Hospice Program. Emotional and spiritual support was all that we could give to both of them as the weeks went on. They were both courageous and an inspiration to us as they lived each day to the fullest in the time they had left together.
>
> We visited them the night before he died and helped his wife change his bed and freshen him up. He opened his eyes and said, "Thank you."
>
> He died the following morning. When his wife phoned us, we went over to be with her and wait for the hospice nurse and her daughter to arrive. We prayed for him with his wife and held her in prayer during the difficult days of the wake and funeral.[23]

Several weeks later, they received the following letter:

Dear Sisters,

I have been reflecting on many things this past week. One uppermost in my mind is how grateful I have been that all of you were there for [my husband] and me throughout his illness, and how you were all there for us at the end when I called to tell you I didn't think [he] was breathing. I knew I should have called hospice, but you were the ones I wanted to be here, and you all came, and I knew everything would be all right....

I was also remembering how very generous you were with your time and your gifts—all the phone calls and visits and words of encouragement, the many flowers for [my husband] and even a Mother's Day card and flowers for me; the beautiful Mary Potter medal, which I shall always cherish; all the food you brought us, even thinking of rainbow ice cream cones while our family was here.... Thank you for the beautiful Mass card and for all of your prayers. And ... for the thoughtfulness of having someone cut our grass. You have brought tears to my eyes many times.

May God grant each of you His special blessings as you continue to carry on your mission. I am so grateful to God for the gift of all of you being present in our lives. He has blessed us abundantly.[24]

After a death occurs, the sisters offer comfort and consolation and conduct memorial services in nursing homes. Sometimes, they even help a bereaved family in an unusual way, as Sister Gloria Harper recalls: "I remember one time when we had two teenagers who lost their widowed mother. They did not want her to be cremated, but they did not have the money to pay for her burial. When some of our sisters learned about this, they contacted the owner of a nearby mortuary whom they knew, and he generously provided the funeral without cost so that the young people could bury their mother."[25]

In addition to their primary apostolate of providing support to the dying and their families, one of the most dramatic changes that has occurred within the Little Company of Mary during the past twenty-five years has been the way in which the unique gifts, special talents, and individual personalities of the members of the community have expanded the congregation's apostolate in new and unusual ways.

In past decades, almost all of the sisters in the American Province were involved in nursing or medical technology. One rare exception is Sister Catherine (Kay) Shalvey, who has contributed her business savvy to the congregation for almost fifty years. The twelve years of experience she had as a legal secretary before entering the Little Company of Mary meant that during the early years of her religious life, she often found herself typing papers for her fellow sisters who were nursing students. This work was not what she felt called to, but as she explained, "I couldn't leave because [I knew] this is where God wanted me."[26] The answer to how Sister Kay's gifts fit into a nursing community came in the person of kindly Australian-born Mother Oliver Carter. The new Provincial Leader quickly recognized her penchant for business, a talent that Sister Kay later developed by earning business degrees and has used well in Evergreen Park for more than four decades.

According to Sister M. Adrian Davis, before Vatican II, "You could say no to an assignment, but you couldn't ask for something."[27] In response to the Church's call to update their service in religious life, however, the community gave each sister the freedom to respond to what she felt God was calling her to within the Little Company of Mary apostolate. Consequently, there are now more diverse ministries of healing in the American Province than ever before.

Sister Maria Antonieta Benavides, a member of the community from Argentina, today volunteers in Pastoral Care in Torrance, a ministry she characterizes as "very, very different from nursing." She understands well the delicate balance between the corporal and the spiritual, explaining, "We come to the soul through the body." In the multicultural environment of southern California, she is often asked to translate because of her fluency in Spanish, Italian, and Portuguese, and says, "I always ask the patient, 'Would you like the prayers in English or Spanish?'"[28]

Sister Deborah Conley serves as the only Little Company of Mary spiritual director in the American Province. Using a holistic approach, she helps those who come to her discover where they are spiritually, emotionally, and physically, and how they can turn to God even more.[29] Some of her clients are seeking crisis counseling; others are involved in the growth process because of an ongoing brokenness in their lives—often the consequence of alcohol or drug abuse. In conjunction with the Twelve-Step Program of recovery, she helps them "to see how God is present and active in their lives, to have courage to look at the 'dark places' and also where God has given grace and energy."[30]

In her multifaceted ministry, Sister Deborah provides HIV/AIDS counseling at St. Sabina's parish in Chicago and also directs spiritual retreats for priests, religious, and lay people. She sees this as "another expression of the ministry of healing"[31] as she helps others reach "a balance and an integration in one's life of all the … gifts that God has given and the chosen development of those gifts"[32]—her definition of spiritual maturity.

One of the hallmarks of the Little Company of Mary has been the kindness of the sisters in matters both big and small. Sister Virginia O'Brien recounted an incident from years ago that changed her way of thinking:

> I was working on the 3–11 shift—a young Sister who thought that being busy and doing were the important things, as I rustled up and down the halls in my white, starched gown. On the floor was a young patient about thirty [who] was married and had a small child. Her room was off the rotunda across from the desk. She had just found out she had cancer. I walked into the room one evening and said, "Can I do anything for you?" She [asked], "What can you do for a broken heart?" All I could do was sit on the edge of the bed and hold her in my arms, while we both cried. I learned that night that "doing" isn't always the important thing. Sometimes there is nothing one can do except just "be present."[33]

The difference that the sisters can make in an individual's life is clear in the following memory that Sister Kathleen McIntyre recalled of a thirty-four-year-old woman who underwent surgery for breast cancer and returned to the hospital nine months later because the cancer had spread:

> In the operating room, she refused general anesthesia until a sister was present, so I stayed with her throughout the surgery, then visited her every day. Despite her grave illness, the woman's main concern was for her husband and two daughters, ages 16 and 12. The 16-year-old was planning to go to her first formal dance and her mother wanted to be with her when she chose her dress, but she was too ill to leave the hospital.

> When a number of the staff on the surgical floor found out about this situation, they decided to bring some of their own party dresses

to the hospital. "We gathered up a variety of formal dresses and put them in storage," said Sister Kathleen. "One night, we brought the mother, the grandmother and the 16-year-old daughter to the Recovery Room so they could choose a dress. The grandmother altered it and it fit the girl perfectly." Sadly, the mother eventually passed on from ovarian cancer, but her daughter will never forget how her mother helped her pick out her dress and later saw her dressed up like a princess for her first formal dance.[34]

Even the sisters' smallest acts of kindness have been special to those who received them. One example of their thoughtfulness was the tradition of providing milk and cookies to the elderly residents of the convalescent home in San Pierre when they invariably awoke in the middle of the night—a practice that Sister Mary Babcock initiated when she served there.[35]

A generous moment, which is second nature to the community, can sometimes last a lifetime, as the following reminiscence of something that occurred more than thirty-five years ago, illustrates:

> We would go out to the *villas* to talk with the mothers, and the kids would be waiting for us," Sister Michael explained. "Back then, every time our family members wrote to us, they would send money, which we saved to buy shoes for the children. One day another sister and I piled seven children into a car. We had a driver, and two of the little ones sat on our laps. First, we stopped at a shoe store. The children went wild trying on high-heeled shoes before we could get them fit for shoes of their own. Before we returned home, we took them to an ice cream parlor and then to the zoo."[36]

In Sister Michael Murray's religious life, which spanned seventy years, the joy and exuberance of a small group of Argentine children endured as one of her most vivid memories.

Members of the Little Company of Mary have brightened the lives of countless children over the decades as well as the lives of youths and adults. Usually the sisters touch a person's life for just a brief moment, but sometimes the encounter has had lasting and unexpected results. Several decades ago, in the middle of the night, Sister Adrian Davis baptized a newborn Rh factor baby named Hurley, who was in danger of death. Thirty-some years later, as she celebrated her Golden Jubilee (fiftieth year of religious profession), Thomas Hurley—now a priest at Old St. Patrick's Church in Chicago—reappeared in her life, offering his prayers and blessings as he concelebrated her anniversary Mass.[37]

For seventeen-year-old Bill Dunne, contact with Little Company of Mary Hospital in Evergreen Park directly contributed to a once-in-a-lifetime honor—being chosen as a torchbearer during the 1996 Olympics. As a high school volunteer, the Palos Heights teenager made a daily contribution of his time at the hospital, spending hours with the elderly and with cancer patients and also helping out at the St. Vincent de Paul Society. Dunne's outstanding community service resulted in his being selected by the United Way/Crusade of Mercy to share the rare honor of carrying the torch in the Chicago leg of the relay, which began in Greece and ended in Atlanta.[38] The young man's generosity is a tangible extension of the spirit of the sisters, which fills their hospital.

Ten years ago, the Sisters of the Little Company of Mary had a vision for a healthier community and performed a community needs assessment. Findings suggested that there were many underlying behaviors that contributed to the poor health of many community members. Sponsored by the hospital, under the leadership of Sister Margaret Christina Hoban, and with the help of a variety of community leaders, Healthier Evergreen was born. This successful organization consists of ten committees and/or focuses, which include developing a community care network; helping the environment; fighting heart disease, cancer, and obesity; restricting tobacco and substance abuse; fighting domestic violence; promoting cultural diversity; and caring for the needy. Each of these ongoing initiatives continues to help create a healthier community.[39] As Sister Margaret Christina points out, "the single greatest contributor to good health is not the health care system, but rather the lifestyle choices of its residents."[40]

In addition to the Laguna Hill ministry, two other sisters in the community have been actively involved in parish work. For the past fourteen years, Sister Jean Marsden has been a parish nurse—first at St. Henry's, and now at St. Margaret Mary's on Chicago's North Side. In her various ministries of care, consolation, and health, and to the poor and to women associates, she does everything from visiting homes, hospitals, and nursing homes and providing physical assessments and blood pressure monitoring to helping the disadvantaged with food and other assistance. For the dying, she plans liturgies, committal services, wakes, and burial services, and offers follow-up grief for family members. Sister Jean also arranges retreats and provides support where needed in her work with women associates.[41] She says that having a "listening ear" is important in assessing the needs of the body, mind, and spirit of those for whom she cares.

As a parish nurse, one of her primary concerns is watching over people and keeping them safe. One day she had a nagging feeling that something was very wrong with one of her elderly parishioners who had severe memory problems. "I went to her home and knocked on the door," said Sister Jean. "At first, there was no answer, but finally the woman came to the door almost naked and covered with blood from a serious head injury. She might have fallen forty-eight hours earlier, and the gas was on in the apartment. I immediately called 911 for her and phoned the gas company to come out right away."

Another time, when Sister Jean's pager went off, she says, "I ran like the dickens" in response to a parishioner who was having a heart attack. "He was experiencing severe arrhythmia, and there was no ambulance. I broke every rule and stuck him in my car and raced to the nearest hospital. He claims I saved his life." The North Side sister has also picked up on lethal hypertension numerous times, and in one instance discovered an abdominal aneurysm that was about to rupture.[42]

Two hundred and forty-five miles east of Chicago is Toledo, Ohio, whose downtown area has been the heart of Sister Kathleen Scott's ministry for almost fifteen years. As the pastoral leader of St. Francis de Sales, the oldest church in the diocese and one-time cathedral, she is responsible for everything except administering the sacraments. Through her multidimensional inner-city witness, she helps provide food, clothing, and resources for assistance with utilities and rent to those in need. She also visits homes and hospitals, takes Communion to the homebound and to those in nursing homes, and prepares individuals for baptism, reception of the Eucharist, confirmation, and marriage.

A primary focus of her ministry is the area's homeless—the "street people"—many of whom are suffering from addictions or mental disorders in addition to being jobless for a variety of reasons. Through St. Francis or in conjunction with social service agencies, Sister Kathy does whatever is possible to put some hope back in their lives as she "helps" them with their job searches, directs them to a medical clinic for treatment, or assists them in finding a place to stay. For some people, all she can do is provide coffee and donuts in the church basement, knowing that at least they will not have to face the day on an empty stomach.[43]

Simply being present for members of her parish is another of Sister Kathy's main concerns. Of the many people whose lives she has touched in her ministry, one of the most memorable is Lena, a ninety-eight-year-old, white-haired widow. Sister Kathy often brought her Communion and offered spiritual, supportive care as she listened to Lena chat about how she marched in support of women's suffrage or was sometimes told by parishioners at several nearby Catholic parishes to, "Go down to St. Francis" because she was black.[44] Until Lena's death at age 103, Sister Kathy was there for her, providing presence, companionship, and a listening heart.

Even when the sisters are no longer participating in the Little Company of Mary's active ministry, Sister M. Terrence Landini explained that they are still engaged in volunteer ministry, either inside or outside the hospital. Virtually all members of the community who are physically able are involved in some type of charitable endeavor.[45] For Sister Mary Jane Feil, this means working in Chicago's inner city. During the past twelve years, besides serving part-time in the Pastoral Care department where she spends time with patients and distributes Holy Communion, her ministry also takes her to "The Port," a shelter started by a Franciscan priest, which provides assistance to homeless families. Sister Mary Jane touches the lives of the disadvantaged by making home visits, taking people to doctors' appointments, and assisting at a food pantry, in addition to helping out with parish nursing one day a week.[46]

Sister Deborah Conley also lends her presence to Chicago's inner city on a regular basis as a volunteer counselor at a health clinic that treats those who have AIDS, are HIV-positive, or are at risk because of substance abuse problems.

Concern for the elderly is another special area to which the Little Company devotes itself. For the past few years, Sister Marianne Herres has dedicated herself to a ministry of Adult Day Care, where she helps with activities, monitors vital signs, and provides a presence to those who are suffering from the devastating effects of Alzheimer's disease as well as from other less serious ailments common to an older population.[47]

In 1995, the Little Company of Mary sold the convalescent home in San Pierre, Indiana. By then, it had been operated by the Sisters of the

Sister Nancy Boyle, L.C.M., and Sister Mary Joy O'Grady, C.S.C., light a unity candle in San Pierre.

Holy Cross for six years. On October 15, sisters from both congregations participated in a special ceremony during which the head of each congregation, Sister Mary Joy O'Grady, C.S.C., and Sister Nancy Boyle, L.C.M., lit a unity candle. During the celebration, in a special "Commitment Prayer at the LCM Facility," the Holy Cross Sisters pledged, "We will strive as sister presence to give compassionate care in our 'ministry of the moment' to all who enter here so that truly the Presence of the Lord is in this place." The following year, Little Company of Mary Convalescent Center officially became Our Lady of Holy Cross Care Center—a name specifically chosen to reflect the contributions of both religious communities.[48]

Sister Marilla Dyer is one Holy Cross Sister who has continued the work started by the Little Company of Mary. She clearly remembers the moment in which she was called to serve:

> I was standing in front of the statue in the foyer at San Pierre waiting for a ride and God said to me, "I don't want you at Saint Mary's." I prayed, "Lord, don't kick me out of the Motherhouse; I love it there," but God told me, "I need you here." I thought to myself, "I don't know beans from buttermilk about this stuff."

After having served as a teacher for forty years, Sister Marilla began her ministry at the age of seventy-four, carrying on the tradition of compassionate care that the Little Company of Mary had started in the 1950s. She has continued the belief of the blue-veiled sisters that "No one dies alone," a motto that her congregation has also adopted. Sister Marilla feels that "The spirit of the Little Company of Mary is in the walls in San Pierre, and we [Sisters of the Holy Cross] were able to build on that."[49]

Midway through the 1990s, Joseph Cardinal Bernardin of Chicago attempted to diffuse some of the tension that still existed between American Catholics by issuing a statement entitled, "Called to be Catholic in a Time of Peril." The following year, he launched the Catholic Common Ground Project, which he hoped would be a forum "where radical, conservative, liberal, and moderate Catholics could discuss issues in the church in a way that was creative and faithful to the Catholic tradition and without the distrust, polarization, and entrenchment ... that made dialogue and real learning from each other impossible."[50]

Many Catholics viewed the project as a positive step, but Bernardin was chastised by some of his fellow cardinals, who thought that it "failed to acknowledge adequately Scripture and Tradition as the actual common ground of the Catholic Church ... [and] placed dissent on the same level as truth...."[51]

In the final days of his battle with pancreatic cancer, Bernardin acknowledged:

A dying person does not have time for the peripheral or the accidental. He or she is drawn to the essential, the important—yes, the eternal. And what is important, my friends, is that we find that unity for which Jesus prayed so fervently on the night before he died. To say it quite boldly, it is wrong to waste the precious gift of time given to us, as God's chosen servants, on acrimony and division.[52]

Three weeks later, Bernardin, who used his last years to teach others how to die, accepted his own death.

The millennium year began in America with celebrations from coast to coast and ended in controversy when the presidential election was determined only after numerous judicial appeals ended with a Supreme Court decision. The following September, Al Qaeda operatives hijacked three U.S. aircraft, and their ensuing acts of terrorism resulted in the deaths of 2,986 people. Subsequent years found the United States at war in Afghanistan and in Iraq, where several hundred thousand American servicemen and women serve in an effort to eliminate terrorism and to aid in those countries' transitions to democracies. The economic boom of the early 1990s, which had faltered late in the decade, was lost in the devastating aftermath of 9/11, leading to a loss of jobs and bankruptcies, and financial hardship for hundreds of thousands of Americans.

The first years of the new millennium posed new challenges for the Catholic Church in the United States. Although the number of American priests declined only slightly from 58,000 in the mid-1960s, the number of parishes without priests jumped from three percent (1965) to fifteen percent in 2002. In 1965, 1,575 priests were ordained compared to 450 in 2002, and the number of seminarians fell from 49,000 in 1965 to 4,700 in 2002. The average age of a Catholic sister in America was sixty-eight years, and Mass attendance had fallen precipitously. While three out of four U.S. Catholics attended Mass weekly in 1958, a Notre Dame University study showed that in 2002 the number was one in four.[53]

During the last decade of the twentieth century, the Catholic Church in the United States found itself confronted by the painful reality of accusations of sexual abuse by a small percentage of American priests. In January 2002, ... revelations about the protection of ... [such] priests rocked the archdiocese of Boston, creating a media firestorm that swept across the country, making the sexual abuse crisis the single most important event in American Catholicism since the Second Vatican Council and the most devastating scandal in American Catholic history.[54]

Five months later, the United States Conference of Catholic bishops met in Dallas and approved a *Charter for the Protection of Children and Young People* designed to initiate a system of reforms that would prevent such abuse from ever occurring again.[55] An all-lay review board headed by former Oklahoma governor Frank Keating, a staunch Catholic, was created in 2003 to oversee that the bishops did what they had pledged. Keating resigned the following year, explaining that while "most of America's bishops are fully supportive," some fell far short, as they attempted "to resist grand jury subpoenas, to suppress the names of offending clerics, to deny, to obfuscate, and to explain away...."[56] Illinois Appellate Court Judge Anne Burke was appointed to replace Keating. After learning that the bishops' forty-six-member Administrative Committee agreed to delay the yearly audits of diocesan compliance, she wrote to Bishop Wilton Gregory (president of the U.S. Conference of Catholic Bishops): "We are very disheartened by this apparent decision to go back to 'business as usual.'"[57] The Catholic Church in America continues to work toward resolving this serious problem.

Just as the Catholic Church in the United States has undergone difficulties in recent decades, so too have all active congregations of religious in America because of the lack of religious vocations, not only in this country but also throughout the western world. Sister Jean Stickney, Vocation Director for the LCM American Province, along with Sister Kathleen McIntyre, Sister Gloria Harper, Sister Sharon Ann Walsh, and volunteer Sister Francis Curran, are part of the "Vocations to Consecrated Life" committee, which is actively working to make the Little Company of Mary and its apostolate more widely known in the United States and beyond through a variety of media, including a vocational Web site (www.lcmglobal.org), a CD-ROM, and an international brochure.[58]

In addition, Sister Elizabeth Gilroy and Sister Tess de Dassel are heading an international effort to foster new vocations. They pointed out that at the present time, young women in Korea and in the African country of Zimbabwe are responding to the Lord's call to enter His service. Cognizant of the need for a global push, they believe that the congregation needs to "take risks in this area, to have hope, and to bear responsibility to preserve the charism of the order."[59]

Sister Elizabeth suggests that part of what is needed is sharing the unique charism of the community—not only praying for the dying but also the gift of staying with people in their need and pain,"[60] modeled after the person of Mary, who stood by her Son and shared His anguish in His last hours.

As a chaplain, Sister Sharon Ann Walsh is very familiar with all sorts of pain—emotional, spiritual, and physical. She recognizes that her ministry allows her "the privilege of really being with people in all the moments of their lives,"[61] whether sharing in the joy of parents after the birth of a child or simply being with a family following a life-altering diagnosis or situation. Sister Sharon Ann values the "energizing" quality of the hospital and the importance of being with people, not simply in serving patients, but also having so much opportunity to be with the staff in Evergreen Park who have "such a heightened awareness of Mary Potter and the missions."

An important part of her ministry takes place at the Cancer Center, the newest center on campus, which offers total cancer treatment to the people of Chicago's southwestern suburbs. For Sister Sharon Ann, oncology work is closely linked with the Little Company of Mary because its charism is prayer for the sick and the dying, and also because the disease has a connection with the congregation's very roots since Mary Potter experienced cancer in her own life.[62]

In January 2005, the Little Company of Mary celebrated the seventy-fifth anniversary of its first hospital in the United States. Three-quarters of a century have elapsed since the sisters first opened its doors. The hospital in Evergreen Park still stands tall and proud, surrounded today by numerous newer buildings which attest to their wise stewardship.

Among the many congratulatory messages that the community received was a letter from James J. Sexton, the Mayor of the Village of Evergreen Park, who wrote, "Little Company's compassion for the sick is deep-rooted and today their commitment to caring for the sick is as strong as ever...."[63] The archbishop of Chicago, Francis Cardinal George, offered his praise, noting, "Not only have your doors been open to those in need, but you have also continued to open your hearts in prayer,"[64] and President George W. Bush recognized the Little Company of Mary's devoted service, acknowledging, "Your efforts reflect the compassionate spirit of our country and help build a healthier future for all."[65]

In mid-March 2005, Sister M. Adrian Davis and Sister Gloria Harper visited Ibadan, Nigeria, at the request of Archbishop F. Ade Job, who had heard of the Little Company of Mary from a Nigerian chaplain in Torrance. The prelate had met with members of the Torrance community some months earlier and invited the congregation into his archdiocese hoping that they might build a small hospital there.

Sister Adrian, who characterized the Nigerians as "very open and gracious, a very joyous people,"[66] saw firsthand the workings of the archdiocesan Justice, Development, and Peace Commission, which was hosting an educational session about AIDS for a group of Muslims. The Rural Health Promotion Program works to develop an increasing sense of responsibility among the tribal peoples and is truly a self-help program —done by Nigerians for Nigerians. One of its critical initiatives has been teaching mothers to make hydrating solutions for children who might otherwise die of dehydration from dysentery, which is commonplace.

The inclusiveness of the program impressed the sisters. One of the parishes had a well-stocked pharmacy on site because of the difficulty of the locals to get into town, and it is open to everyone, not just members of the parish.

This land of searing heat and omnipresent malaria has a wealth of vocations, and Sister Adrian described the unusual sight of seeing hundreds of young, black seminarians, at various stages of training, wearing white cassocks. This is one of the few riches in this impoverished country. Because Nigeria's political instability and difficult climate negate the possibility of any involvement that would require the establishment of a mission or the sisters' constant presence, Archbishop Job has suggested that the role of the Little Company of Mary could be that of animating or "bringing to life." Later this year, the American Province will "consider the possibility of underwriting the expense of a three-year pilot project of the rural health program (with appropriately timed visits from LCM Sisters) ... enabling the Nigerians to carry out the much-needed [Mobile Health Education, Promotion and Prevention] program to a population in great need."[67]

On April 2, 2005, John Paul II, who had guided the Roman Catholic Church for more than a quarter of a century, died of heart failure after enduring the ravages of Parkinson's disease for years. He had logged over 775,000 air miles during his twenty-seven year pontificate, traveling to 129 countries from Azerbaijan to Zaire.[68] As the youngest pope in 132 years and as the most traveled pontiff in history, he had a charismatic appeal to young Catholics. He used the power of the media advantageously as he brought a message of faith and hope to the millions worldwide who turned out to see him while he stressed the efficacy of "redemptive suffering" and the importance of the culture of life, which recognizes the innate dignity and rights of each human being as a child of God.

Vatican journalist Wilton Wynn suggests that John Paul II "promoted ecumenism in his actions more than in words or documents. He was the first pope to enter Canterbury Cathedral [Church of England]; the first to preach in a Lutheran Church; the first to set foot in a synagogue."[69] He enjoyed unprecedented respect and adulation, yet his profound theological conservatism, his penchant for stifling debate, and his willingness to resort to authoritarianism caused difficulty for some U.S. Catholics.

Less than two weeks after celebrating the funeral Mass for John Paul

II, Joseph Cardinal Ratzinger was elected to be his successor. Based on the German cardinal's past words and writing, his pontificate may closely resemble that of his predecessor; however, John XXIII demonstrated that the papacy can dramatically change those who assume it. The new pontiff, known for his theological toughness as a cardinal, has chosen to be called "Benedict," and the last pope to take that name was known for his diplomatic skills and peace-making efforts. His name choice may indicate a slight shift not only in the way the new pope hopes to be perceived but also in the way he will act as Holy Father.

In the spring of 2005, the last two Holy Cross Sisters who had assumed the work of the Little Company of Mary in San Pierre concluded their ministry. Sisters Geralda and Alice Lamping (blood sisters), who themselves needed walkers to get around to visit the elderly and sit with the dying, realized that their days of service at San Pierre were over. These sisters, along with eighty-five-year-old Sister Marilla Dyer, who had been forced to depart last year because of failing health, had served in San Pierre for the past ten years.[70] There is no longer a "sister presence" at the facility, but Sister Marilla continues to hope and pray that if someone will financially support this ministry, perhaps one Holy Cross Sister and one Little Company of Mary Sister can jointly continue this invaluable work.

The entire American Province has faced challenges of its own during the past decade. Sister Carol Pacini, who has served as Provincial Leader in the United States since 1995, has worked with her fellow sisters to help them stay positively focused on the Little Company of Mary's primary mission of praying for the dying, and has also emphasized a deepening awareness of each member's personal vocation.[71]

During the past ten years, the Little Company of Mary Hospitals in the Midwest and on the West Coast have continued to set new standards for health care for the twenty-first century; the history of the American Province has been documented; the community established the Mary Potter Ministry Fund, which shares a small portion of the American Province's resources with needy women and children; and the sisters in the United States, more than ever before, recognize and appreciate their role as part of a global religious institution.[72]

The history of the Little Company of Mary in America, which began when three members of the community arrived in Chicago 112 years ago, has become a heritage to which each sister in the American Province has uniquely contributed. It has been, and still is, a journey of sacrifice and accomplishment, a legacy of witness provided, and, most important, a presence of hope and healing expressed through the care of consecrated women of strong faith whose tender compassion, boundless generosity, and loving kindness have touched countless lives in countless ways.

As the sisters of the American Province look to the future, there will certainly be new challenges, but they will be no more daunting than those encountered by the original pioneering trio when they first set foot in America's heartland. With fidelity to their congregation's distinct charism, determination modeled on that of their own founder, and openness to the guidance of the Holy Spirit, the mission that Mary Potter envisioned will continue for many years to come in the United States and throughout the world.

RECEPTIVE HEARTS FOR
THE CONTINUING JOURNEY

Sisters representing every Province participated in the LCM Congregational Chapter held in Australia during April 2005.

In April 2005, at the same time that the cardinals of the Catholic Church were convening in Rome to elect a new Holy Father, forty members of the Little Company of Mary met in Australia for a Congregational Chapter. Over the course of two weeks, they elected a new congregational leadership team and discussed and prayerfully considered issues that will not only affect the Little Company of Mary during the next six years but will also impact their strategic vision for 2011.

After a welcoming liturgy heralded by the sounds of a didgeridoo, an aboriginal wind instrument, Sister Mark Cornelius set the tone for this momentous chapter. Focusing on the theme, "Awakening to New Life ... Journeying to an Evolving Future," the outgoing Congregational Leader animated her listeners—representatives from every Province—with a memorable introduction:

> ... [W]e have come together attuned in mind and heart to the spirit of the Gospel, to the genuine spirit and original aims of Mary Potter, and to the precious heritage of Little Company of Mary.... To share and express the ... enrichment and transformation that has accompanied the ever-evolving journey of Little Company of Mary....
>
> We are called in these days ahead to give new vitality to the witness of Mary Potter's life and founding insights, at the centre of which the Maternal Heart of Mary occupied a preferential place. It is our mission to incarnate in our lives the legacy, which with her being recognised and declared Venerable, is a gift for the whole Church. In this way, as we commit ourselves and our energies to the spirit that Mary Potter lived, God will continue re-creating the Little Company of Mary through each of us.[1]

During the Chapter, members recommended involving all sisters as well as lay people in Vocation Ministry; strengthening the unity among all sisters; enriching the spirituality of the Little Company of Mary; continuing the development of the Greater Company of Mary, especially by empowering lay leadership; reconfiguring the provinces while preserving each province's heritage and tradition; further developing the LCM Web site; and promoting the LCM mission and ministries through the wise stewardship of the congregation's resources.[2]

The sister representatives also elected a new Congregational Leadership team led by Sister Jeannette Connell of the English Province.

LCM representatives from America included Sister Sharon Ann Walsh, L.C.M., (Councilor); Sister Carol Pacini, L.C.M., (Province Leader); and Sister Kathleen McIntyre, L.C.M., (Councilor).

Sister Carol Pacini from the American Province will serve as one of three Congregational Councilors at the LCM Generalate in London, and Sister Kathleen McIntyre has been elected to replace her as Province Leader in the United States.

Vocations continue to be a focus for the Little Company of Mary, and although almost all active congregations of religious in America and Europe have experienced a lack of vocations during the past few decades, there are several reasons to hope for a reversal of this situation. Vocation Director Sister Jean Stickney believes that there will be a resurgence of vocations among American women in the near future. One of her primary goals is to make the particular vision and spirituality/mission of the Little Company of Mary more widely known both in the United States and globally. Another is to explore an alternative form of religious life with temporary commitment. Sister Jean is an active member of the National Religious Vocation Conference and the National Religious Formation Conference, organizations that promote collaboration among congregations to effectively respond to contemporary trends.

Sister Patricia Wittberg, S.C., a church sociologist who has studied such trends in religious life, notes that in France during and after the

Revolution, religious congregations were either totally disbanded or greatly dispersed, to such a degree that the future of religious life in those countries was in doubt. However, an unexpected reversal took place within seventy years so that during the nineteenth century, "Over 600 new religious communities were founded ... more than had been established in any previous period."[3]

While there are obvious differences between what occurred then and what is happening today, this example illustrates how difficult it is to predict the future of religious life. Since the cultural upheaval that led to the decline of religious vocations was unforeseeable, so too might be its turnaround. Unlike other human endeavors, religious vocations are gifts of God, not simply a matter of individual decision. Consequently, they are beyond the realm of predictability.

According to Sister Rose McDermott, assistant to the vicar for religious in the archdiocese of Philadelphia, "If the charism [the gift of the Spirit embodied within a congregation] is of God, and the efforts at renewal and adaptation are wise and sincere, the gift will surely endure in the hearts of the members, attract others ... and contribute richly to the life and holiness of the church."[4] Indeed, the vitality of the Little Company of Mary is dependent upon each sister's efforts toward renewal and adaptation.

Another consideration for the future of religious life is its evolvement in ways not yet envisioned, something to which Sister Mark alluded:

> History teaches us that at the time of major shifts in ... civilization, a new type of religious life has always emerged. Now, one hundred and twenty-eight years after our foundation, all signs indicate the end of one era and the beginning of a new stage in the history of our world....[5]

Numerous others, both inside and outside the congregation, share this viewpoint. Peg Schneider, a former member of the Little Company of Mary who continues to work as a chaplain in Evergreen Park, offered her perspective, which combines the insight of having been a member of the Little Company of Mary for several decades with the objectivity of being a layperson today. "The vision of Mary Potter is available to the people of the world," she points out, "and her legacy can continue if one is willing to let go, trusting that God will give us courage to work into a future that is not always known." While recognizing that tradition is the foundation, she believes "the future is not about replicating the past but honoring it for its richness...."[6]

One of the most important developments to come out of Vatican II was the new appreciation of laypeople and their role in the Church. In the Council document *Lumen Gentium (Light of nations)*, the Church acknowledged that all members of the Catholic faith, simply by reason of their baptism, have received an equal call "to the fullness of the Christian life and the perfection of charity."[7] Wittberg points out:

> The importance of this seemingly innocuous statement cannot be stressed enough. [I]t nullified the basic ideological foundation of eighteen centuries of ... religious life ... which held that only vowed members of religious orders could achieve true spiritual perfection.... Now ... the Vatican Council was stating that all baptized Catholics were called to holiness, not just the members of religious orders....[8]

From its very beginnings, the Little Company of Mary has recognized the importance of laypeople and especially those who are part of "the Greater Company of Mary"—Associates, Affiliates, and Mary Potter's Volunteers who make a commitment to embody the congregation's charism. In addition, the community in the United States has consciously sought to imbue Mary Potter's vision and spirit to those who operate their hospitals and to all who serve within these institutions.

A dozen years ago, Province Leader Sister Nancy Boyle spoke of Venerable Mary Potter's belief in the importance of laypeople for her congregation:

> She said that although our numbers may be small, the greater Little Company is made up of the laypeople who embrace the Little Company mission. The legacy of the pioneering Sisters who nurtured the mission with unconditional love through its simple beginnings in America, endures today through the empowerment of others.... The few have become thousands. The mission lives through the Little Company family of Sisters, doctors, nurses, caregivers, employees, volunteers, and benefactors.[9]

Last autumn, for the first time, lay leaders from Little Company of Mary Hospitals in the United States and their spouses were invited to accompany three sisters in their Heritage Program—a pilgrimage that members of the community have taken for almost twenty years—retracing and visiting sites in London, Portsea, and Nottingham that were meaningful in Mary Potter's early life and as she founded the Little Company of Mary.

In the United States, there is an emerging trend of individuals requesting closer involvement with the sisters in their spirituality and mission on a temporary basis. This is not surprising in an increasingly mobile society where having three to four careers in a lifetime has become commonplace and permanence is illusive. The Congregation has also recently established a plan for Mary Potter volunteers—individuals who will commit themselves in active ministry to the vision and mission of the Little Company of Mary for a specified period of time, preferably one year, with the possibility for renewal.[10]

Today, the sisters in the United States continue the mission of the Little Company of Mary in a way that closely resembles the work of the original pioneering sisters who lent their presence, their helping hands, and their loving hearts to the homes and neighborhoods of the people of Hyson Green. More than a century and a quarter later, Mary Potter's daughters in America are also going where the need is—to homes and hospitals, to nursing facilities and inner city neighborhoods to serve through a variety of ministries.

Venerable Mary Potter knew firsthand something of the mysterious designs of Divine Providence. Noting the perilous times in which she lived,[11] she reminded her daughters, "Hope is a flower of great beauty in God's sight and can only grow on earth. It blooms best in adversity."[12] The founder of the Little Company of Mary also added, "I have an idea that our Lord sometimes wishes us to imitate His Mother by giving us trying circumstances, that he may perfect our peace and patience...."[13]

Almost two thousand years ago, a small group stood on a hill and looked up at their crucified Lord. For the grieving Mother and the little company who surrounded her, it was the moment of Calvary as they tried to make sense of something that they could not fully comprehend. During that difficult time, Jesus' faithful disciples were unaware of the plan of the Father or the astonishing surprise that the third day would hold—a miracle already in motion through His most energizing Spirit. Today, as both the Catholic Church in the United States and the American Province of the Little Company of Mary face the uncertainties of the future, it is fitting to remember that God's ever-present Spirit continues to work in wondrous and unexpected ways.

In a congratulatory letter recognizing Little Company of Mary Hospital's seventy-fifth anniversary in Evergreen Park, Bishop Gustavo Garcia-Siller reminded the community:

> While a Jubilee is a time for us to look back, it is appropriate for us to look ahead.... Remember that the amazing grace of the Lord has been faithfully guiding and lovingly providing for you all along your journey. Your discipleship and God's Spirit will pave your steps in the future.[14]

By answering the call set forth during the recent Chapter "to make better known in our world the person of Mary Potter, her charism and spirituality, and its relevance in today's world,"[15] those in the American Province, along with all the Little Company of Mary Sisters throughout the globe, "go forth with eagerness ... [to] respond more perfectly to the needs of God's family in our world today."[16] In so doing, they strive to fulfill that which Sister Mark hoped for them at the conclusion of the recent Congregational Chapter when she prayed, "[May] the light of Mary, Mother and Disciple, whose mission we share, always be reflected in each of you as together we continue the great journey begun by Venerable Mary Potter...."[17]

ENDNOTES

CHAPTER ONE—HOMECOMING

1. Patrick Dougherty, *Mother Mary Potter, Foundress of the Little Company of Mary*, p. 43.
2. Ibid., p. 85.
3. *Catholic Encyclopedia*, "St. Francis Xavier," <http://www.newadvent.org/cathen/06233b.htm>.
4. Elizabeth West, L.C.M., *One Woman's Journey: Mary Potter—Founder ~ Little Company of Mary*, p. 12.
5. James Brodrick, S.J., *Saint Francis Xavier (1506–1552)*, p. 67.
6. Elizabeth West, L.C.M., op. cit., p. 18.
7. James Brodrick, S.J., op. cit., p. 85.
8. Mother Mary Potter, *Autobiographical Notes*, p. 45.
9. James Brodrick, S.J., op. cit., p. 83.
10. Ibid., p. 337.
11. *Butler's Lives of the Saints*, Herbert J. Thurston and Donald Attwater, eds., p. 1521.
12. Ibid., p. 1508.
13. Elizabeth West, L.C.M., op. cit., p. 169.
14. Mother Mary Potter, quoted in Patrick Dougherty, op. cit., p. 235.
15. Ibid., p. 273.
16. Mother Mary Potter, *Conferences J*, p. 15.
17. "Ignatius of Loyola (1491–1556)," <http://www.gonzaga.ie/staticpages/index.php/ignatiusofloyola>.
18. James Brodrick, S.J., op. cit., p. 56.
19. Ibid., footnote, p. 105.
20. Elizabeth West, L.C.M., op. cit., p. 23.
21. James Brodrick, S.J., op. cit., p. 472.
22. Ibid., p. 56.
23. Mother Mary Potter, *Conferences A*, p. 33.
24. Mother Mary Potter, *Rule of the Little Company of Mary*, cited in Dougherty, p. 297.
25. Herbert J. Thurston, ed., op. cit., p. 1520.
26. Mother Mary Potter, *Autobiographical Notes*, p. 44.
27. Mother Mary Potter, *Conference on the Confraternity of Calvary*.
28. Mother Mary Potter, *Autobiographical Notes*, p. 44.
29. Elizabeth West, L.C.M., op. cit., p. 125.
30. Patrick Dougherty, op. cit., p. 125.
31. "St. Francis Xavier," <http://www.goacentral.com/Goahistory/St.FrancisXavier.htm>.

CHAPTER TWO—BEGINNINGS

1. John Gardiner, *The Victorians, An Age in Retrospect*, p. 15.
2. Simon Schama, "Wives, Daughters, Widows" in *A History of Britain*, Vol. III, p. 213.
3. Asa Briggs, *Victorian Cities*, p. 101.
4. R. J. Evans, *The Victorian Age (1815–1914)*, p. 74.
5. *Report on the Sanitary Conditions of the Labouring Population of Great Britain*, cited in Schama, op. cit., p. 179.
6. Simon Schama, "Wives, Daughters, Widows" in *A History of Britain*, Vol. III, p. 219.
7. Unattributed quote in R. J. Evans, op. cit., p. 78.
8. Ibid., p. 79.
9. Ibid., p. 148.

10. T. F. Mills, "Crimean War (1853–1856)," *Land Forces of Britain, The Empire and Commonwealth*, published online September 1, 2000.
11. Elizabeth West, L.C.M., *One Woman's Journey*, p. 5.
12. Certificate of Marriage for the District of Adelaide (Australia) between William Norwood Potter and Eliza Jane Harvey, dated 7 January 1867, courtesy of Pamela Fontana.
13. Letter from Thomas Potter to his son Father Francis Potter, March 27, 1910, Generalate Archives of the Little Company of Mary, Tooting Bec, London, England.
14. Patrick Dougherty, *Mother Mary Potter, The Foundress of the Little Company of Mary*, p. 18.
15. Letter from George Potter to Mother Hilda Potter, December 7, 1919, *Letters – Series P*, Generalate Archives, loc. cit.
16. Elizabeth West, L.C.M., op. cit., p. 7.
17. Mother Mary Potter, *Autobiographical Notes*, p. 10.
18. Cited in Dougherty, op. cit., p. 21.
19. Elizabeth West, L.C.M., op. cit., p. 11.
20. Letter from George Potter to Mother Hilda Potter, L.C.M., January 12, 1920, Generalate Archives, loc. cit.
21. Mother Mary Potter, *Motherhood*, p. 25, Generalate Archives, loc. cit.
22. Elizabeth West, L.C.M., op. cit., p. 12.
23. Ibid., p. 12.
24. Ibid., p. 13.
25. Pamela Fontana, "Godfrey King," pp. 7–8, in *Family History Studies as a Tool in Biographical Research: By Reference to the Venerable Mary Potter*, Text of a Talk for the AGM of the Catholic Family History Society, November 2004.
26. Elizabeth West, L.C.M., op. cit., p. 13.
27. Mother Mary Potter, *Autobiographical Notes*, p. 3.
28. Elizabeth West, L.C.M., op. cit., p. 14.
29. Ibid., p. 15.
30. Ibid., p. 21.
31. Ibid., p. 23.
32. Letter from Mary Ann Potter to Father Edward Selley, July 12, 1876, Generalate Archives, loc. cit.
33. Elizabeth West, L.C.M., op. cit., p. 39.
34. Letter from Mary Potter to Monsignor Virtue, Virtue Letters #3, Generalate Archives, loc. cit.
35. Letter from Mary Potter to Monsignor Virtue, cited in Dougherty, op. cit., p. 43.
36. Letter from Mary Potter to Monsignor Virtue, Virtue Letters #10, Generalate Archives, loc. cit.
37. John A. Hardon, S.J., *Pocket Catholic Dictionary*, p. 277.
38. Elizabeth West, L.C.M., op. cit., p. 45.
39. Mary Potter, cited in Dougherty, op. cit., p. 51.
40. Mother Mary Potter, *Autobiographical Notes*, p. 13.
41. Elizabeth West, L.C.M., op. cit., p. 60.
42. Mary Potter to Mary Fulker, Letter #3, June 1876.
43. Letter from Mary Ann Potter to Father Selley, July 12, 1876, Generalate Archives, loc. cit.
44. Selley letters, August 14, 1876, loc. cit.
45. Mother Mary Potter, *Autobiographical Notes*, p. 18.
46. Mother Mary Potter, quoted in Dougherty, p. 101.
47. Mother M. Cecilia Smith, L.C.M., *Personal Reminiscences*, p. 6, Generalate Archives, loc. cit.
48. Elizabeth West, L.C.M., op. cit., p. 100.
49. Ibid.
50. *The Catholic Encyclopedia*, "Diocese of Nottingham," <http://www.newadvent.org/cathen/11133a.htm>.
51. A. N. Wilson, *The Victorians*, p. 139.
52. Elizabeth West, L.C.M., op. cit., p. 115.
53. Eve Healy, *The Life of Mother Potter: Foundress of the Little Company of Mary*, p. 17.
54. Ruth Lindsay, "Mother" (of the "Little Company of Mary"), *The Month* Magazine, Vol. cxxxiv, November 1919, p. 420.
55. Mother M. Cecilia Smith, L.C.M., op. cit., p. 7, Generalate Archives, loc. cit.
56. Elizabeth West, L.C.M., op. cit., p. 136.
57. Mother M. Cecilia Smith, L.C.M., op. cit., p. 20.
58. *The Catholic Encyclopedia*, "Pope Leo XIII," <http://www.newadvent.org/cathen/09169a.htm>.
59. Elizabeth West, L.C.M., op. cit., p. 144.
60. *Annals, 18*, p. 25.
61. Eve Healy, op. cit., p. 28.
62. Ruth Lindsay, op. cit., p. 418.
63. Ibid., p. 417.
64. Ibid.
65. Ibid., p. 420.
66. Ibid., p. 422.
67. Elizabeth West, L.C.M., op. cit, p. 182.
68. John Henry Newman, *Parochial and Plain Sermons*, Vol. VI, p. 22.
69. Ibid., Vol. VII, p. 109.
70. Ian Ker, *Newman: On Being A Christian*, p. 148.

71. Mother Mary Potter, Letter to the Australian pioneers, 1885.
72. Ruth Lindsay, op. cit., p. 422.

CHAPTER THREE—INTO AMERICA'S HEARTLAND

1. "Immigration—Who Lives in America?" <http://teacher.scholastic.com/immigrat/facts.htm>. Between 1891 and 1900, the number of U.S. immigrants was 3,687,564; 439,730 for 1893 alone.
2. Patrick W. Carey, "Toward Americanism: 1866–1899" in *The Roman Catholics in America*, p. 50.
3. Julie Bryne, "Roman Catholics and Immigration in Nineteenth-Century America," National Humanities Center, Texas Christian University, <www.nhc.us/tserve/nineteen/nkey/info/nromcath.htm>.
4. CDC National Center for Infectious Diseases, Travelers' Health Online (2004).
5. Letter from Charles A. Mair to Mother Mary Potter, September 8, 1892, Generalate Archives of the Little Company of Mary, Tooting Bec, London, England.
6. Letter from Charles A. Mair to Mother Mary Potter, October 10, 1892, Generalate Archives, loc. cit.
7. Related by LCM Sisters at the Generalate of the Little Company of Mary (Sister Mark Cornelius, Sister Judith Barwick, Sister Raphael Butler), Tooting Bec, London, England, August 2003.
8. Elizabeth West, L.C.M., *One Woman's Journey*, p. 160, citing C. Clear, *Nuns in Nineteenth Century Ireland*, p. 64.
9. Ibid.
10. Letters "J," #5, undated. Mother Mary Potter to Sister M. Veronica Dowling, L.C.M., Generalate Archives, loc. cit.
11. Ibid.
12. *Lloyds Weekly Shipping Index 1893, Volume 1* (Guildhall Library, London, England) indicates the ship leaving Genoa for New York, April 24, 1893, was the *Kaiser Wilhelm II*, not the *Kaiser Wilhelm* as listed in the Chicago Logbook.
13. Mother M. Veronica Dowling, L.C.M., Chicago Logbook, p. 1, Archives of the Little Company of Mary Sisters, Evergreen Park, Illinois.
14. Ibid., p. 2.
15. Ibid.
16. Sources: *Tenth Census of the United States, 1880; Eleventh Census of the United States, 1890.* (Actual figures were 204,859 and 587,112, respectively)
17. Chicago Historical Society, "The Great Chicago Fire and the Web of Memory," <www.chicagohs.org/fire>.
18. Ibid.
19. John Higham, *Strangers in the Land: Patterns of American Nativism, 1860–1925*, pp. 6–9.
20. Letter from Mother M. Veronica Dowling, L.C.M., Chicago Logbook, p. 6, Archives of the Little Company of Mary Sisters, loc. cit.
21. Letter from Charles A. Mair to Mother M. Catherine Crocker, March 1, 1893, Generalate Archives, loc. cit.
22. Chicago Logbook, pp. 8–9 (Original handwritten Logbook).
23. Letter from Mother M. Veronica Dowling, L.C.M., Chicago Logbook, p. 6, Archives of the Little Company of Mary Sisters, loc. cit.
24. Chicago Logbook, loc. cit., p. 8.
25. Ibid., p. 7.
26. Ibid., p. 8.
27. Ibid., p. 11.
28. Ibid., p. 12.
29. "The Columbian Exposition," <http://ecuip.lib.uchicago.edu/diglib/social/worldsfair_1893/>.
30. Robert Anderton Naylor, *Across the Atlantic*, p. 149.
31. Chicago Logbook, p. 11, Archives of the Little Company of Mary Sisters, loc. cit.
32. Mother M. Veronica Dowling, L.C.M., op. cit., p. 13.
33. Harold M. Mayer and Richard C. Wade, "The White City and the Gray" in *Growth of a Metropolis*, p. 193.
34. Letters "J" #19, undated. Mother Mary Potter to Mother M. Veronica Dowling, L.C.M., Generalate Archives, loc. cit.
35. *Chicago Daily Times* and *Chicago Tribune*, November 26, 1880, cited in Charles Shanabruch, *Chicago's Catholics: The Evolution of an American Identity*, p. 34.
36. Chicago Logbook, p. 15, Archives of the Little Company of Mary Sisters, loc. cit.
37. Letters "J", #36, undated. Mother Mary Potter to Mother M. Patrick Tuohy, L.C.M., Generalate Archives of the Little Company of Mary, loc. cit.
38. Letters "J," #42, undated. Mother Mary Potter to Mother M. Patrick Tuohy, L.C.M., loc. cit.
39. David O. Whitten, (Auburn University), *The Depression of 1893*, <http://www.eh_net/encyclopedia/whitten.panic.1893.php>.
40. Thayer Watkins, San Joss State University Economics Department, <www.2sjsu.edu/faculty/watkins/dep1893.htm>.
41. Chicago Logbook, p. 16, Archives of the Little Company of Mary Sisters, loc. cit.
42. Ibid., p. 17.
43. Ibid., p. 21.
44. Ibid., p. 24.
45. A discrepancy exists in the actual date of the reception of the habit. One source shows clothing date as April 26, 1898; another source, May 23, 1898.
46. Chicago Logbook, p. 29, Archives of the Little Company of Mary Sisters, loc. cit.
47. Ibid., p. 25.

48. Ibid., p. 26.
49. Ibid.
50. John A. Hardon, S.J., *Pocket Catholic Dictionary*, p. 16.
51. Patrick W. Carey, "Americanism," in *Catholics in America*, p. 65.
52. Chicago Logbook, p. 28, Archives of the Little Company of Mary Sisters, loc. cit.
53. Ibid., p. 29.
54. Ibid.

CHAPTER FOUR—A BLUE VEIL AMONG DIAMONDS AND PEARLS

1. Ishbel Ross, *Silhouette in Diamonds—The Story of Mrs. Potter Palmer*, p. 32.
2. Brenda Warner Rotzoll, "The Other Bertha Palmer," *Chicago Sun-Times*, March 16, 2003.
3. Paul Gilbert and Charles Lee Bryson. *Chicago and Its Makers—A Narrative of Events from the Day of the First White Man to the Inception of the Second World's Fair*, p. 882.
4. Ishbel Ross, op. cit., p. 9.
5. Brenda Warner Rotzoll, op. cit.
6. "The Women's Building at the 1893 Exposition," <http://members.cox.net/academia/cassatt5.html#hayden>.
7. Ibid.
8. Barbara Haber, Book Review in *Women's History Review*, Volume 12, Number 3, 2003, page 518.
9. Erik Larson, *The Devil in the White City—Murder, Magic, and Madness at the Fair that Changed America*, p. 235.
10. Bertha Honoré Palmer, Speech on Opening Day of the Women's Building at the World's Columbian Exposition, May 1, 1893.
11. Sister M. Dunstan Kelleher, L.C.M., "Our Superior—Sister Stanislaus," History of the Chicago Foundation, p. 32, Archives of the Little Company of Mary Sisters, Evergreen Park, Illinois.
12. Florence Logbook, January 23, 1902, Generalate Archives of the Little Company of Mary, Tooting Bec, London, England.
13. *Chicago Daily News*, Last Edition, January 23, 1902, p. 9.
14. *New York Times*, Front page (page 1, column 6), January 26, 1902.
15. *Chicago Tribune*, January 1, 1902, p. 4.
16. Ishbel Ross, op. cit. pp. 13–22.
17. Ibid., p. 140.
18. Patrick Dougherty, *Mother Mary Potter—Foundress of the Little Company of Mary*, p. 216.
19. Ishbel Ross, op. cit., p. 141.
20. Ibid.
21. Sister M. Dunstan Kelleher, L.C.M., op. cit., p. 32, Archives of the Little Company of Mary Sisters, Evergreen Park, Illinois.
22. Ibid.
23. Ishbel Ross, op. cit., p. 56.
24. Ibid., pp. 54–55.
25. Sister M. Dunstan Kelleher, L.C.M., op. cit., p. 32, loc. cit.
26. Marguerite B. Williams, "Open Potter Palmer Paintings to Public," *Chicago Daily News*, January 11, 1922.
27. Sister M. Dunstan Kelleher, L.C.M., op. cit., p. 33.
28. Ibid.
29. Minutes of the Generalate Council, March 6, 1902, Generalate Archives, loc. cit.
30. Ishbel Ross, op. cit., p. 137.
31. Chicago Historical Society, <http://www.chicagohs.org/treasures/cost6.html>.
32. Ibid.
33. Jen Aronoff, "The place to be (for a long, long time)," *The Daily Northwestern*, Evanston, Illinois, October 18, 2001.
34. Ibid.
35. *The Dubois County Daily Herald*, July 31, 1961, p. 1.

CHAPTER FIVE—NO LONGER MISSION TERRITORY

1. Kathy Young, Archivist at Loyola University Chicago, Archives, Chicago, Illinois, April 26, 2005.
2. Letter from John Dill Robertson, M.D., President of the Board of Trustees to Sister Patricia [*sic*], L.C.M., May 31, 1910, Archives of the Little Company of Mary Sisters, Evergreen Park, Illinois.
3. Phone conversation with Kathy Young, Archivist at Loyola University, Chicago, Illinois, April 25, 2005.
4. Loyola University Chicago, Archives, <http://www.luc.edu/archives/loyolahistory.shtml>.
5. Letter from the Reverend Henry S. Spalding, S.J., to Mother M. Patrick Tuohy, L.C.M., June 12, 1910, Archives of the Little Company of Mary Sisters, loc. cit.
6. Directory of Deceased American Physicians (1804–1924), p. 353.
7. "Thomas Stanley Crowe," in *The Book of Chicagoans—A Biographical Dictionary of Leading Living Men and Women in the City of Chicago*, p. 163.
8. Letter from Dr. Thomas S. Crowe to Mother M. Patrick Tuohy, L.C.M., June 13, 1910, Archives of the Little Company of Mary Sisters, loc. cit.
9. Based on information for Chicago, Illinois, provided by *Microsoft Streets & Trips*.

10. Robert Leckie, *American and Catholic*, p. 270. (Catholic population listed as 14,618,000.)

11. John Tracy Ellis, *American Catholicism*, p. 124.

12. Paul M. Angle, *Crossroads—1913*, p. 7.

13. Ibid.

14. Ibid.

15. "Benedict XV," <http://www.cfpeople.org/Books/Pope/POPEp256.htm>.

16. "Pope Benedict XV," <http://www.firstworldwar.com/bio/popebenedict.htm>.

17. R. R. Palmer and Joel Colton, *A History of the Modern World*, p. 677.

18. Ibid., pp. 684–685.

19. "Statistical Summary—America's Major Wars," <http//www.cwc.Isu.edu.cwc/other/stats/warcost.htm>.

20. Elizabeth West, L.C.M., *One Woman's Journey*, p. 179.

21. Ibid.

22. Ann Carey, "Rome Calls for Renewal," in *Sisters in Crisis, The Tragic Unraveling of Women's Religious Communities*, p. 40.

23. Notes from a Little Company of Mary Corporation Meeting, June 1917, Archives of the Little Company of Mary Sisters, loc. cit.

24. Notes from a Little Company of Mary Corporation Meeting, June 1918, loc. cit.

25. Ibid.

26. John M. Barry, *The Great Influenza: The Epic Story of the Deadliest Plague in History*, p. 171.

27. Ibid., pp. 454–455.

28. Susan Cook, "Illinois and the 1918 Spanish flu Epidemic," Illinois Trails History and Genealogy, <http://www.iltrails.org/flu1918.htm>.

29. "The Influenza Epidemic," Special to *The Henry Republican*, October 15, 1918, loc. cit.

30. *East Saint Louis Journal*, 16 October 1918, as cited by Susan Cook (endnote 28 above).

31. John M. Barry, op. cit., p. 337.

32. Ibid., p. 396.

33. Ibid., p. 239.

34. Transcription of a taped interview (1974) with Sister M. Solace Hannigan, L.C.M., Archives of the Little Company of Mary Sisters, loc. cit.

35. Sisters Register (1909–1925), Archives of the Little Company of Mary Sisters, loc. cit.

36. Charles Shanabruch, *Chicago's Catholics—The Evolution of an American Identity*, p. 230.

37. Council Notes—Roma (1921), Generalate Archives of the Little Company of Mary, Tooting Bec, London, England.

38. Council Notes—Roma (1922), Generalate Archives, loc. cit.

39. Ibid.

40. Letter from Mother General M. Hilda Potter, L.C.M., to Mother Rita Carroll, L.C.M., August 16, 1922, Generalate Archives, loc. cit.

41. Sisters Register (1909–1925), Archives of the Little Company of Mary Sisters, loc. cit.

42. Letter from Mother Mary Potter to Mother M. Catherine Crocker, L.C.M., February 26, 1889, Generalate Archives, loc. cit.

43. Council Meeting—Roma, October 7, 1923, Generalate Archives, loc. cit.

44. "A Short History of the Early Days" (written by an unidentified member of the Chicago Foundation), 1923, Archives of the Little Company of Mary Sisters, loc. cit.

45. "Wide Range of Stocks Shown In Lewis Estate—Five Charities to Be Benefitted," unidentified newspaper clipping (1925), Archives of the Little Company of Mary Sisters, loc. cit.

CHAPTER SIX—PROMISES TO KEEP

1. Guillermo MacLoughlin, "The Forgotten People: The Irish in Argentina and other South American Countries," Irish Centre for Migration Studies, University College Cork, <http://migration.ucc.ie/>.

2. Edmundo Murray, "Researching the Irish in Argentina," Irish Migration Studies in South America, <www.irishargentine.org/intro/researching.htm>.

3. Patrick McKenna, "Irish Migration to Argentina," in *Patterns of Migration—The Irish World Wide: History, Heritage, Identity*, Vol. 1, Patrick O'Sullivan, ed., p. 65.

4. David Barnwell, Ph.D., "19th-Century Irish Emigration to Argentina." Text of a lecture at the Columbia University Irish Studies seminar, <http://www.irishargentine.org/intro/ bibliography.htm>.

5. Patrick McKenna, op. cit., p. 72.

6. Pat Nally, "*Los Irlandeses en la Argentina*" translated and published online, <http://scripps.ireland.com/ancestors/magazine/articles/uhf_argentina2.htm>.

7. James R. Scobie, *Argentina: A City and a Nation*, p. 85, cited in Wanda A. Velez, South American Immigration: Argentina, p. 5.

8. Guillermo MacLoughlin, op. cit.

9. Eduardo "Edward" Morgan y O'Farrell *in Arbol Genealogico de Edward Morgan & Catherine O'Farrell y Gariff* (grandparents of Mary Clare Morgan), Online version, pp. 4–7.

10. History of the South American Foundation, p. 42, Archives of the Little Company of Mary Sisters, Evergreen Park, Illinois.

11. Patrick McKenna, op. cit., p. 71.

12. Chicago Logbook, p. 11, Archives of the Little Company of Mary Sisters, loc. cit.
13. Residence listed on Death Certificate. (endnote 14.)
14. Physician's Certificate of Death for Mary C. Morgan, Certificate #11664, State of Illinois, Cook County, August 1, 1893.
15. *Cook County Death Index*, ID # 0000011664, Newberry Library, Chicago, Illinois.
16. Mount Olivet Cemetery Record of Interments, Chicago: Lot W174, Block Section 7.
17. History of the Foundation at San Antonio de Areco, Archives of the Little Company of Mary Sisters, loc. cit.
18. Letter from Margaret Morgan to Mother Mary Potter, May 25, 1912, Generalate Archives of the Little Company of Mary, Tooting Bec, London, England.
19. Letter from Margaret Morgan to Mother Mary Potter, December 26, 1898, Generalate Archives, loc. cit.
20. Letter from Margaret Morgan to Mother Mary Potter, July 1899, Generalate Archives, loc. cit.
21. History of the San Antonio de Areco Foundation, Archives of the Little Company of Mary Sisters, loc. cit.
22. Letter from Margaret Morgan to Mother Mary Potter, May 25, 1912, Generalate Archives, loc. cit.
23. Ibid.
24. Letter from Margaret Morgan to Mother M. Patrick Tuohy, L.C.M., September 14, 1912, Generalate Archives, loc. cit.
25. Letter from Margaret Morgan to Mother Mary Potter, December 18, 1912, Generalate Archives, loc. cit.
26. According to terms laid out in a letter from Margaret Morgan, cited in endnote 17.
27. Amount of time mentioned in a letter from Margaret Morgan to Mother M. Patrick Tuohy, L.C.M., December 12, 1912, Generalate Archives, loc. cit.
28. Quote from a letter of an unidentified sister, History of the Foundation at San Antonio de Areco, p. 3, Archives of the Little Company of Mary Sisters, loc. cit.
29. Letter from Sister M. Rita Carroll, L.C.M., to Mother M. Philip Coleridge, L.C.M., (et al.), December 26, 1913, Generalate Archives, loc. cit.
30. Letter from Mother M. Hilda Potter, L.C.M., to Sister M. Rita Carroll, L.C.M., January 15, 1919, Archives of the Little Company of Mary Sisters, loc. cit.
31. History of the South American Foundation, p. 4, Archives of the Little Company of Mary Sisters, loc. cit.
32. "Sisters Who Had Formed Part of the San Antonio and Buenos Aires Communities," Archives of the Little Company of Mary Sisters, loc. cit.
33. Memorandum from F. B. O'Grady to Mother M. Ambrose O'Donnell, L.C.M., September 30, 1938, indicating name change of the Congregation by the Governor of the Province of Buenos Aires, Generalate Archives, loc. cit.

CHAPTER SEVEN—FIELD OF DREAMS

1. Chicago Logbook, p. 30, Archives of the Little Company of Mary Sisters, Evergreen Park, Illinois.
2. Ibid., p. 31.
3. Obituary for Monsignor Charles A. O'Hern, *New York Times*, 14 May 1925.
4. Chicago Logbook, p. 31, Archives of the Little Company of Mary Sisters, loc. cit.
5. "Elizabeth Ann Seton," <www.catholic-forum.com/saints/sainte04.htm>.
6. John O'Grady, *Catholic Charities in the United States* (Washington, D.C., National Conference of Bishops, 1930; rpt. New York: Arno, 1971), p. 183.
7. John Tracy Ellis, *American Catholicism*, rev. ed., pp. 54–56.
8. Sister Mary Denis Maher, *To Bind Up the Wounds: Catholic Sister Nurses in the U.S. Civil War*, p. 33.
9. John Fialka, *Sisters: Catholic Nuns and the Making of America*, p. 38.
10. Ibid., p. 45.
11. Ann Doyle, "Nursing by Religious Orders in the United States," *American Journal of Nursing 29* (July 1929): 782–783.
12. Sister Mary Denis Maher, op. cit., p. 70.
13. Ibid., p. 69.
14. Ibid., p. 39.
15. John Fialka, op. cit., p. 72.
16. Carol K. Coburn and Martha Smith, *Spirited Lives: How Nuns Shaped Catholic Culture and American Life, 1836–1920*, p. 2.
17. Mary Potter, Copy of the First Rule, Handwritten MS, Chapter II.
18. Conversation with Sister Kathleen McIntyre, L.C.M., May 12, 2005.
19. Joel D. Howell, *Technology in the Hospital: Transforming Patient Care in the Early Twentieth Century*, p. 3.
20. Adrian Feldhusen, "The History of Midwifery and Childbirth in America," <http://www. midwiferytoday.com/article/timeline.asp>.
21. Francis Cardinal George, "The Cardinal I Never Knew: George Mundelein," <www.catholicnewworld.com/archive/cnw2000/0305/card_0305.htm>.
22. Chicago Logbook, p. 32, Archives of the Little Company of Mary Sisters, loc. cit.
23. Ibid.
24. Ibid., p. 36.
25. Edward R. Kantowicz, *Corporation Sole—Cardinal Mundelein and Chicago Catholicism*, p. 167.
26. Chicago Logbook (transcribed version), Part One—The Foundation in Chicago, Archives of the Little Company of Mary Sisters, loc. cit.
27. Ibid.

28. Petition from John H. McGeary representing the Little Company of Mary to the River Forest Board of Trustees, September 25, 1926.
29. Report to the President and Board of Trustees—Village of River Forest by Charles F. Durland, A. B. Gates, Geo. L. Meyer, and Edward Probst, November 8, 1926.
30. Conversation with Sister Jeanne Crapo, O.P., archivist, Dominican University, River Forest, Illinois, May 17, 2005.
31. Phone conversation with Diane Hansen, Historical Society of Oak Park and River Forest, May 19, 2005.
32. Chicago Logbook, p. 41, Archives of the Little Company of Mary Sisters, loc. cit.
33. *The Village of Evergreen Park 75th Anniversary Album 1893–1968*, p. 4.
34. Ibid., pp. 8 and 11.
35. Letter from Mother Mary Potter to Mother M. Patrick Tuohy, L.C.M., March 4, 1894, Letter #31, Generalate Archives of the Little Company of Mary, Tooting Bec, London, England.
36. *Official Catholic Directory for 1929*, Archdiocese of Chicago, p. 59.
37. Chicago Logbook, p. 43, Archives of the Little Company of Mary Sisters, loc. cit.
38. Ibid.
39. Charles Shanabruch, *Chicago's Catholics—The Evolution of an American Identity*, p. 160.
40. Chicago Logbook, p. 47, Archives of the Little Company of Mary Sisters, loc. cit.
41. Ibid., p. 48.
42. Ibid.
43. *New World*, September 9, 1928.
44. Charles Shanabruch, *Chicago's Catholics: The Evolution of An American Identity*, p. 231.
45. Ibid., p. 232.
46. Chicago Logbook, p. 53, Archives of the Little Company of Mary Sisters, loc. cit.
47. Sanabruch, op. cit., p. 231.
48. Edward R. Kantowicz, op. cit., p. 3.
49. Jay P. Dolan, *The American Catholic Experience: A History from Colonial Times to the Present*, p. 355.
50. Chicago Logbook, p. 58, Archives of the Little Company of Mary Sisters, loc. cit.
51. Quoted in Patrick Dougherty, *Mother Mary Potter—Foundress of the Little Company of Mary*, p. 216.

CHAPTER EIGHT—LIGHT AMID THE DARKNESS

1. *United States Bureau of the Census* statistics from 1929 to 1935.
2. "American Cultural History (1930–1939)," <http://kclibrary:nhmccd.edu/decade30/html>.
3. Emma Lazarus, "The Colossus" (Poem inscribed on the Statue of Liberty), 1883.
4. *A Healing Presence … The story of Little Company of Mary Hospital's Journey of Unconditional Love*, Maurice Possley, ed., p. 8.
5. Mother M. Dunstan Kelleher, L.C.M., History of the Chicago Foundation, p. 20, Archives of the Little Company of Mary Sisters, Evergreen Park, Illinois.
6. Record of Corporation Meetings for the Little Company of Mary (June 1893 to June 22, 1937), p. 27.
7. Chicago Logbook (Part Two), p.1, Archives of the Little Company of Mary Sisters, loc. cit.
8. Ibid., no page number, entry for June 5, 1932.
9. Ibid., no page number, entry for June 21, 1932.
10. Ibid., p. 21.
11. Ibid., p. 22.
12. Ibid., p. 27.
13. Ibid., p. 34.
14. Letter from Archbishop-Elect John J. Cantwell to Mother General, October 29, 1936, Generalate Archives of the Little Company of Mary, Tooting Bec, London, England.
15. Letter from Louis E. Mahoney to Mother M. Stanislaus Madigan, L.C.M., May 7, 1937, Generalate Archives, loc. cit.
16. Letter from Mother M. Stanislaus Madigan, L.C.M., to Mother Ambrose O"Donnell, L.C.M., May 13, 1937, Generalate Archives, loc. cit.
17. Agreement for the Extension of Time for the Payment of Principal and for the Reduction of the Interest Rate of Obligations of the Little Company of Mary, May 2, 1932, Archives of the Little Company of Mary Sisters, loc. cit.
18. *A Healing Presence … The Story of Little Company of Mary Hospital's Journey of Unconditional Love*, Maurice Possley, ed., p. 8.
19. T. H. Watkins, *The Great Depression: America in the 1930s*, p. 309.
20. Chicago Logbook, Part Two, p. 49, Archives of the Little Company of Mary Sisters, loc. cit.
21. Memorandum from Francis B. O'Grady to Little Company of Mary—Buenos Aires, January 5, 1938, Generalate Archives, loc. cit.
22. Letter from Francis B. O'Grady to Mother M. Ambrose O'Donnell, L.C.M., September 30, 1938, loc. cit.
23. Ibid., August 5, 1938.
24. Announcement of the opening of the hospital on Avenida Alvear 3576, Archives of the Little Company of Mary Sisters, loc. cit.
25. Ibid.
26. Letter from Francis B. O'Grady to Mother M. Ambrose O'Donnell, L.C.M., October 22, 1938, Generalate Archives, loc. cit.

27. Ibid.
28. Letter from Francis B. O'Grady to Mother M. Ambrose O'Donnell, L.C.M., September 17, 1938, loc. cit.
29. Letter from Sister M. Rita Carroll, L.C.M., to the Superior of the Chicago Foundation, August 16, 1939, Generalate Archives, loc. cit.
30. "List of Sisters Serving in the San Antonio and Buenos Aires Communities," Archives of the Little Company of Mary Sisters, loc. cit.
31. Logbook (Part Two), p. 54, Archives of the Little Company of Mary Sisters, loc. cit.
32. Sisters Register, Archives of the Little Company of Mary Sisters, loc. cit.

CHAPTER NINE—A TIME OF UNIMAGINABLE DEVASTATION

1. *Mit Brennender Sorge* (*On the Church and the German Reich*), Encyclical of Pope Pius XI, March 14, 1937, <http://www.papalencyclicals.net/all.htm>.
2. *Divini Redemptoris* (*On Atheistic Communism*), Encyclical of Pope Pius XI, March 19, 1937, loc. cit.
3. Ibid.
4. Chicago Logbook (January1940–January1948), p. 63, Archives of the Little Company of Mary Sisters, Evergreen Park, Illinois.
5. Ibid., p. 64.
6. "The Influenza Pandemic of 1918," <www.stanford.edu/group/virus/uda/>.
7. Ibid.
8. Ibid.
9. Sister M. Solace Hannigan, "The Saga of an Indiana Farm and Its Aging and Only Occupant," and taped recollections (January 1974), Archives of the Little Company of Mary Sisters, loc. cit.
10. Chicago Logbook (1940–1948), p. 75, Archives of the Little Company of Mary Sisters, loc. cit.
11. Ernie Pyle, "Ernie Pyle in England" (1941), reprinted in *The Story of the Second World War*, Henry Steele Commager, p. 90.
12. "The London Blitz, 1940," Eyewitness to History, <www.eyewitnesstohistory.com>.
13. "The Logbooks" in Mary Campion, *Place of Springs—The story of the first 100 years of the Province of the Maternal Heart (English Province of the Little Company of Mary)*, pp. 34–35.
14. Ibid.
15. Ibid., p. 39.
16. Frederick Taylor, "Blitz," in *Dresden, Tuesday, February 13, 1945*, p. 102.
17. Ibid., p. 70.
18. Mother M. Dunstan Kelleher, L.C.M., "History of the L.C.M. Community," pp. 45–47, Archives of the Little Company of Mary Sisters, loc. cit.
19. Chicago Logbook (1940–1948), p. 78, Archives of the Little Company of Mary Sisters, loc. cit.
20. James Holland, *Fortress Malta: An Island Under Siege (1940–1943)*, quote from front book flap.
21. Sister Philippina Becket, L.C.M., cited in Mary Campion, *Place of Springs—The story of the first 100 years of the Province of the Maternal Heart (English Province of the Little Company of Mary)*, p. 50.
22. James Holland, op. cit.
23. Chicago Logbook (1940 – 1948), p. 82, Archives of the Little Company of Mary Sisters, loc. cit.
24. "Jewish Historian Praises Pius XII's Wartime Conduct," Interview with Michael Tagliacozzo, Beth Lohamei Haghetaot (Center of Studies on the Shoah and Resistance), <http://academics.smcvt.edu/pcouture/jewish_his torian_praises_pius_xi.htm>. (Note to reader: "pius xi instead of pius xii in address.")
25. Chicago Logbook (1940 – 1948), p. 87, Archives of the Little Company of Mary Sisters, loc. cit.
26. Ibid., p. 89.
27. <http://www.ddaymuseum.co.uk/faq.htm#whichtroop>.
28. Chicago Logbook (1940–1948), p. 90, Archives of the Little Company of Mary Sisters, loc. cit.
29. Ibid., p. 93.
30. "Battle of the Bulge: December 16, 1944 to January 25, 1945," <http://www.com/user/jpk/battle/htm>.
31. Mother M. Dunstan Kelleher, L.C.M., op. cit., p. 49, Archives of the Little Company of Mary Sisters, loc. cit.

CHAPTER TEN—A SMALL BUT SPLENDID BAND

1. Williamson Murray and Allan R. Millett, *A War To Be Won: Fighting the Second World War*, p. 480.
2. Letter from Mother M. Hilda Potter, San Stefano Rotondo, Rome, April 1945, Archives of the Little Company of Mary Sisters, Evergreen Park, Illinois.
3. William L. O'Neill, "Surrender of Japan" in *The Oxford Essential Guide to World War II*, p. 194.
4. Minute Book of the Foundation in Buenos Aires, p. 13, Archives of the Little Company of Mary Sisters, loc. cit.
5. Ibid., p. 14.
6. Ibid., p. 23.
7. Written account by Mother M. Dunstan Kelleher, L.C.M., p. 49, Archives of the Little Company of Mary Sisters, loc. cit.
8. Council Notes, July 6, 1946, Archives of the Little Company of Mary Sisters, loc. cit.
9. Council Notes, April 3, 1947, Archives of the Little Company of Mary Sisters, loc. cit.

10. Written account by Mother M. Dunstan Kelleher, L.C.M., p. 51, Archives of the Little Company of Mary Sisters, loc. cit.
11. History of the Little Company of Mary in Argentina, Archives of the Little Company of Mary Sisters, loc. cit.
12. J. Ronald Oakley, *God's Country: America in the Fifties*, p. 111.
13. Ibid., p. 112.
14. Written account by Mother M. Dunstan Kelleher, L.C.M., Archives of the Little Company of Mary Sisters, loc. cit., pp. 52–53.
15. Council Notes, March 3, 1949, Archives of the Little Company of Mary Sisters, loc. cit.
16. "Inventions of the Fifties," <http://www.fiftiesweb.com/pop/ inventions.htm>.
17. David Halberstam, *The Fifties*, p. 195.
18. Written account by Mother M. Dunstan Kelleher, L.C.M., pages 53–54, Archives of the Little Company of Mary Sisters, loc. cit.
19. *A Healing Presence ... The Story of Little Company of Mary Hospital's Journey of Unconditional Love*, Maurice Possley, ed., p. 33. Please note: In 1950, doctors were unaware of the autoimmune system. Dr. Lawler's pioneering surgery was successful because the kidney functioned for some months before it failed due to rejection. Four years later, Dr. Joseph E. Murray performed a similar transplant at Peter Bent Brigham Hospital in Boston. Because the surgery involved identical twins, the problem of rejection was avoided.
20. Ben Wattenberg, "How the Suburbs Changed America," <http://www.pbs.org/fmc/segments/progseg9.htm>.
21. Ibid.
22. David Halberstam, op. cit., p. 77.
23. Written account by Mother M. Dunstan Kelleher, L.C.M., p. 53, Archives of the Little Company of Mary Sisters, loc. cit.
24. U.S. Census Bureau, *1950 Census of Dubois County*, Indiana.
25. Historic Jasper, Inc., *Jasper Area History*, p. 24.
26. Sheryl D. Vanderstel, "Roman Catholics in 19th Century Indiana, <http://www.connerprairie.org/HistoryOnline/catholics.html>.
27. Ibid.
28. Edward W. Schmidt, S.J., "The Jesuits—History of the Chicago Province," <http://www.jesuits-chi.org/history/>.
29. Annemarie Springer, Ph.D., "Southern Indiana," *in Nineteenth Century German-American Church Artists*, <http://www.ulib.iupui/edu/kade/springer/Ch5/ch5_p4.html>.
30. Ibid.
31. Aurele J. Violette, "Pioneer Priests of Indiana: Joseph Kundek and August Bessonies," in *Cathedral Museum Reflections* XV, 1 (Fall 1995), <http://www.ipfw.edu/ipfwhis/cathchur/kundek.htm>.
32. "Dubois County," <http://www.duboiscounty.org/DuboisCo.htm>.
33. "Jasper, Indiana," <http://www.city-date.com/city/Jasper-Indiana.html>.
34. Historic Jasper Inc., *Jasper Area History*, p. 24.
35. Phone conversation with Sister Margaret Norris, S. P., (Jasper, Indiana), September 22, 2004.
36. "Jasper Hospital Association Is Incorporated," in *Memorial Hospital and Health Care Center, Jasper, Indiana, 50th Anniversary (1951–2001)*, p. 4.
37. "Jasper Mfg. Assn. Underwrites the Balance Needed," Dubois County *DAILY HERALD* (Jasper, Indiana), (no date included), cited in *Memorial Hospital and Healthcare Center, Jasper, Indiana, 50th Anniversary (1951–2001)*, p. 13.
38. Wayne Guthrie, "Jasper Feels Like Million Over Hospital," *Indianapolis News*, Thursday, July 19, 1951, cited on p. 21.
39. Jasper Diary of the Sisters of Providence at St. Joseph's Convent, Archives of the Sisters of Providence, Saint-Mary-of-the-Woods, Indiana.
40. Sisters of Providence, op. cit.
41. Ibid.
42. Jasper Logbook, p. 11, Archives of the Little Company of Mary Sisters, Evergreen Park, Illinois.
43. Ibid., p. 17.
44. Ibid., p. 22.
45. Ibid.
46. Ibid., p. 24.
47. Dubois County *DAILY HERALD* (Jasper, Indiana), July 8, 1951.
48. "Answering Your Questions about Memorial Hospital for Dubois County," cited in *Memorial Hospital and Health Care Center, Jasper, Indiana, 50th Anniversary (1951–2001)*, p. 6.
49. Jasper Logbook, p. 39, Archives of the Little Company of Mary Sisters, loc. cit.
50. Sisters of Providence, op. cit.
51. Jasper Logbook, p. 43, Archives of the Little Company of Mary Sisters, loc. cit.
52. Ibid., p. 47.
53. Ibid., p. 49.
54. Ibid., cited in *Memorial Hospital and Healthcare Center, Jasper, Indiana, 50th Anniversary (1951–2001)*, p. 29.
55. Ibid.
56. San Pierre Logbook, p. 3, Archives of the Little Company of Mary Sisters, Evergreen Park, Illinois.
57. Sister M. Solace Hannigan, L.C.M., "The Saga of An Indiana Farm and Its Aging and Only Occupant," Archives of the Little Company of Mary Sisters, loc. cit.
58. San Pierre Logbook, p. 5, Archives of the Little Company of Sisters, loc. cit.
59. Ibid.
60. David Halberstam, op. cit., Preface.

61. Martin E. Marty, *A Short History of American Catholicism*, p. 170.
62. *A Healing Presence ... The Story of Little Company of Mary Hospital's Journey of Unconditional Love*, Maurice Possley, ed., p. 34.
63. Ibid.
64. J. Ronald Oakley, op. cit., p. 46.
65. "Munificentissimus Deus," <http://www.papalencyclicals.net/Pius12/P12MUNIF.HTM>.
66. "Ad Caeli Reginam," <www.newadvent.org/library/docs_pi12ac.htm>.
67. The Reverend Matthew R. Mauriello, "Pope Pius XII and Our Lady," <www.udayton.edu/mary/meditations/may98.html>.
68. "The Story of the Pledge of Allegiance," <http://www.flagday.org/Pages/StoryofPledge.html>.
69. J. Ronald Oakley, op. cit., p. 323.
70. Ibid.
71. "The Korean War," <http://college.hmco.com/history/readerscomp/reah/html/ah050900_Koreanwar.htm>.
72. David Halberstam, op. cit., p. 62.
73. History of the Little Company of Mary in Argentina, (no page number), Archives of the Little Company of Mary Sisters, loc. cit.
74. *The Standard* (Buenos Aires, Argentina), December 13, 1953.

CHAPTER ELEVEN—CALLED TO CRADLE AND CONSOLE

1. Martin E. Marty, *A Short History of American Catholicism*, p. 170.
2. *Official Catholic Directory* (1960).
3. Conversation with Sister M. Joseph Casey, L.C.M., November 30, 2004.
4. Council Notes, January 25, 1955, Archives of the Little Company of Mary Sisters, Evergreen Park, Illinois.
5. Chronology of the Province of the Immaculate Conception, p. 2, Archives of the Little Company of Mary Sisters, loc. cit.
6. Phone conversation with Monsignor Lawrence McGrath, Librarian, St. John's Seminary, Brighton, Massachusetts, January 3, 2005.
7. Information source: <http://www.sanctasusanna.org/ourUniqueHistory/cardinals.html>.
8. "Sister-Founded Hospitals," Appendix C in *Marvels of Charity: History of American Sisters and Nuns*, George C. Stewart Jr., pp. 516–548.
9. "A Brief History of Cambridge, Massachusetts, USA," <www.ci.cambridge.ma.us/info/ history.html>.
10. Information contained in a Building Permit, per phone conversation with Susan Maycock, Cambridge Historical Commission, Cambridge, Massachusetts, November 1, 2004.
11. *Hospital Administrators Guide Issue* of the *Journal* of the *American Hospital Association*, June 1954, vol. 28, part II, p. 125.
12. Document provided by Brian Youmans, Cambridge Historical Society, Cambridge, Massachusetts.
13. Cambridge Historical Commission, op. cit.
14. East Cambridge Logbook, p. 1., Archives of the Little Company of Mary Sisters, Evergreen Park, Illinois.
15. Meeting with former East Cambridge community members, October 27, 2004.
16. East Cambridge Logbook, p. 5., Archives of the Little Company of Mary Sisters, loc. cit.
17. Ibid., p. 4.
18. Conversation with Sister Jean Stickney, L.C.M., October 27, 2004.
19. Conversation with Sister M. Maura Tangney, L.C.M., October 27, 2004.
20. East Cambridge Logbook, p. 9., loc. cit.
21. Meeting with former East Cambridge community members, October 27, 2004.
22. East Cambridge Logbook, p. 11, loc. cit.
23. Ibid., p. 13, Archives of the Little Company of Mary Sisters, loc. cit.
24. Morris J. Vogel, *The Invention of the Modern Hospital—Boston (1870–1930)*, p. 127.
25. Ibid.
26. Ibid.
27. Letter from Sister Isabel, D.C. to Walter A. Foery, Bishop of Syracuse, December 12, 1955, Daughters of Charity Archives, Emmitsburg, Maryland.
28. Letter from Sister Isabel, D.C. to Monsignor Joseph B. Toomey, Diocesan Director of Hospitals, April 11, 1955, Archives of the Daughters of Charity, Emmitsburg, Maryland.
29. Letter from Sister Isabel, D.C. to Bishop Walter A. Foery, December 12, 1955, Archives of the Daughters of Charity, loc. cit.
30. Letter from Bishop Walter A. Foery to Sister Isabel, D.C., January 28, 1956, Archives of the Daughters of Charity, loc. cit.
31. Syracuse Logbook, p. 5, (March 7, 1956), Archives of the Little Company of Mary Sisters, Evergreen Park, Illinois.
32. Letter from Sister Genevieve, D.C., Superior of St. Mary's Maternity Home and Children's Hospital, October 30, 1955, to Sister Isabel, D.C., Emmitsburg, Maryland, Archives of the Daughters of Charity, loc. cit.
33. Ibid.
34. Mary Campion, *Place of Springs* (The story of the first 100 years of the Province of the Maternal Heart (English Province) of the Little Company of Mary), pp. 39–40.
35. From the *History of St. Mary's Maternity Hospital and Children's Home*, Archives of the Daughters of Charity, loc. cit.
36. Syracuse Logbook, p. 6, (March 7, 1956), Archives of the Little Company of Mary Sisters, loc. cit.

37. Ibid.
38. Conversation with Sister M. Teresa Oleniczak, L.C.M., September 15, 2003.
39. Conversation with Sister M. Joseph Casey, L.C.M., November 30, 2004.
40. Conversation with Sister M. Teresa Oleniczak, L.C.M., September 15, 2003.
41. Ibid.
42. "High Hopes for Future of St. Mary's Hospital," *Syracuse Herald-American*, November 4, 1956, p. 52.
43. Conversation with Sister M. Teresa Oleniczak, L.C.M., September 15, 2003.
44. Phone conversation with Sister M. Joseph Casey, L.C.M., November 23, 2004.
45. Conversation with Sister M. Teresa Oleniczak, L.C.M., September 15, 2003.
46. Syracuse Logbook, p. 8, (May 24, 1956), Archives of the Little Company of Mary Sisters, loc. cit.
47. Letter from Mother Genevieve Canty, L.C.M., to the community at St. Mary's, February 26, 1957, Archives of the Little Company of Mary Sisters, loc. cit.
48. "St. Mary's Hospital Given National Board Accreditation," *Syracuse Herald-American*, Date missing, (1959).
49. Information from Sister M. Raphael, L.C.M., Archivist, regarding documents contained in the Archives at the Little Company of Mary Generalate, Tooting Bec, London, England.
50. Information and quote from "Foundations in the City of Buenos Aires," (unknown author), Archives of the Little Company of Mary Sisters, Evergreen Park, Illinois.
51. Information furnished by a nursing sister at Hospital Morgan, San Antonio de Areco, Argentina, September 10, 2005.
52. Information provided in "Little Company of Mary Community Development Team," Archives of the Little Company of Mary Sisters, loc. cit.
53. San Pierre Logbook (June 1952 – January 1960), p. 12, Archives of the Little Company of Mary Sisters, Evergreen Park, Illinois.
54. "General Hospital To Be Built At San Pierre, Little Co. of Mary," *North Judson News*, May 2, 1957.
55. Telegram from Vatican Secretary of State, Domenico Cardinal Tardini to Reverend Mother General at San Stefano Rotondo, forwarded to the community at San Pierre, Archives of the Little Company of Mary Sisters, Evergreen Park, Illinois.
56. Telegram from Mayor Richard J. Daley to the Sisters of the Little Company of Mary, San Pierre, Indiana, Archives of the Little Company of Mary Sisters, loc. cit.
57. Sister M. Solace Hannigan, L.C.M., "I Walked Through a Dream," undated recollection, Archives of the Little Company of Mary Sisters, loc. cit.
58. <http://www.sanctasusanna.org/ourUniqueHistory/cardinals.html>.
59. "Archdiocese of Boston" in *The Official Catholic Directory 1956*, p. 28.
60. Phone conversation with Robert Lally-Johnson, archivist, Archives of the Catholic Archdiocese of Boston, November 3, 2004.
61. Phone conversation with Monsignor Lawrence McGrath, Librarian, St. John's Seminary, Brighton, Massachusetts, January 3, 2005.
62. Information provided by Dr. William Kevin Crawley, Archivist and Curator of Manuscripts, Archives of the University of Notre Dame, January 6, 2005.
63. Letter from the Reverend Edward L. Heston, C.S.C., to his Superior, the Reverend Theodore Mehling, C.S.C., March 26, 1958, Indiana Province Archives Center.
64. Letter from Archbishop Richard J. Cushing to the Reverend Edward L. Heston, C.S.C., Congregazione di Santa Croce, Rome, Italy, March 10, 1958, Archives of the Catholic Archdiocese of Boston.
65. East Cambridge Logbook, p. 22, Archives of the Little Company of Mary Sisters, loc. cit.
66. Conversation with Sister Virginia O'Brien, L.C.M., October 27, 2004.
67. East Cambridge Logbook, p. 30, Archives of the Little Company of Mary Sisters, loc. cit.
68. "Massachusetts Hospitals: Closures, Merger, Acquisitions and Affiliations," <http://www.mhalink.org/public/mahospitals/maa.shtml>.
69. "Otis Street," Document provided by the Cambridge Historical Commission.
70. Martin E. Marty, op. cit., p. 170.
71. George C. Stewart Jr., *Marvels of Charity—History of American Sisters and Nuns*, p. 415.
72. Ibid., p. 414.

CHAPTER TWELVE—SEASONS OF HOPE

1. Evergreen Park Logbook, p. 21, Archives of the Little Company of Mary Sisters, Evergreen Park, Illinois.
2. Ibid., p. 34.
3. Letter from the Right Reverend Monsignor Thomas J. O'Dwyer to Mother M. Genevieve Canty, L.C.M., January 4, 1956, Generalate Archives of the Little Company of Mary, Tooting Bec, London, England.
4. <http://www.la-archdiocese.org/english/history.html>.
5. "History of the Los Angeles Catholic Archdiocese," <http://www.losangelesalmanac.com/topics/Religion/re02.htm>. (Source cited: Catholic Almanac and the Los Angeles Archdiocese)
6. *A Journey of Unconditional Love: Creating a Healing Environment—The Story of Little Company of Mary Hospital*, p. 13.
7. Ibid.
8. Torrance Logbook, p. 3, Archives of the Little Company of Mary Sisters, Evergreen Park, Illinois.

9. Ibid.
10. Ibid., p. 6.
11. Ibid., p. 8.
12. Ibid., p. 19.
13. Ibid., p. 20.
14. Ibid., p. 21.
15. Ibid., p. 22.
16. *A Journey of Unconditional Love: Creating a Healing Environment*, p. 18.
17. Cited in *A Healing Presence … The Story of Little Company of Mary Hospital's Journey of Unconditional Love*, p. 40.
18. Torrance Logbook, p. 26 (January 16, 1958), Archives of the Little Company of Mary Sisters, loc. cit.
19. Ibid., p. 29.
20. Ibid., p. 14.
21. Ibid., p. 40.
22. Ibid.
23. Ibid., p. 50.
24. Ibid., p. 59.
25. Ibid., p. 55.
26. "A New Generation," in "Establishing the Peace Corps,"
    <http://www.peacecorpswriters.org/pages/1999/9911/911pchist.html>.
27. Alden Hatch, *A Man Named John—The Life of Pope John XXIII*, p. 157.
28. Thomas Cahill, *Pope John XXIII*, p. 180.
29. Ibid.
30. Alden Hatch, op. cit., p. 163.
31. Ibid., p. 173.
32. *Time*, January 4, 1963, p. 53.
33. Monsignor Loris Capovilla, *The Heart and Mind of John XXIII—His Secretary's Intimate Recollections*, translated by Patrick Riley, p. 5.
34. Thomas Cahill, op. cit., p. 175.
35. Henri Fesquet, op. cit., p. 72.
36. Alden Hatch, op. cit., p. 183.
37. Wilton Wynn, *Keepers of the Keys: John XXIII, Paul VI, and John Paul II—Three Who Changed the Church*, p. 103.
38. Ibid., p. 105.
39. Torrance Logbook, p. 56, Archives of the Little Company of Mary Sisters, loc. cit.
40. Ibid.
41. Ibid., p. 59.
42. Conversation with Sister Kathleen McIntyre, L.C.M., May 12, 2005.
43. Torrance Logbook, p. 39, loc. cit.
44. Conversation with Sister Kathleen McIntyre, L.C.M., May 12, 2005.
45. Sister Jean Stickney, L.C.M., *A Journey of Unconditional Love: Creating a Healing Environment—The Story of Little Company of Mary Hospital*, p. 23.
46. Sister Kathleen McIntyre, L.C.M., *A Journey of Unconditional Love: Creating a Healing Environment—The Story of Little Company of Mary Hospital*, p. 31.
47. *A Healing Presence … The Story of Little Company of Mary Hospital's Journey of Unconditional Love*, p. 51.
48. Transcribed Logbook entry for mid-April 1960, in Part II—The Foundation in Evergreen Park (unpaged), Archives of the Little Company of Mary Sisters, loc. cit.
49. Letter from Francis X. O'Grady to Mother General M. Dominick Foley, L.C.M., March 15, 1960, Generalate Archives of the Little Company of Mary, Tooting Bec, London, England.
50. Transcribed Logbook entry for August 15, 1960, in Part II—The Foundation in Evergreen Park, (unpaged), Archives of the Little Company of Mary Sisters, loc. cit.
51. Ibid.
52. Council Notes (Syracuse), August 23, 1960, Archives of the Little Company of Mary Sisters, loc. cit.
53. Robert Dallek, *An Unfinished Life—John F. Kennedy (1917–1963)*, p. 294. (Kennedy's plurality was 118,574 votes.)
54. F. Michael Perko, S.J., *Catholic & American—A Popular History*, p. 288.
55. John Cogley, "More Stately Mansions," in *Catholic America*, p. 91.
56. John F. Kennedy, *Inaugural Address*, January 20, 1961.
57. Gerard T. Rice, *The Bold Experiment: JFK's Peace Corps*, p. ix.
58. Robert Dallek, op. cit., p. 590.
59. Letter from Mother General M. Dominic Foley, L.C.M., to Mother Provincial M. Oliver Carter, L.C.M., April 20, 1961, Archives of the Little Company of Mary Sisters, loc. cit.
60. Letter from Bishop Walter A. Foery to Mother M. Teresa Oleniczak, L.C.M., April 3, 1961, Archives of the Little Company of Mary Sisters, loc. cit.
61. Wilton Wynn, op. cit., p. 50.
62. *Our American Century: Turbulent Years—The 1960s*, p. 23, Editors of Time-Life Books.
63. Ibid.
64. Léon Joseph Cardinal Suenens, *The Nun in the World—New Dimensions in the Modern Apostolate*, p. 9.

65. Ibid., p. 36.
66. John XXIII's Letter to Religious (July 2, 1962), cited in Léon Joseph Cardinal Suenens, *The Nun in the World—New Dimensions in the Modern Apostolate*, p. 145.
67. Transcribed Logbook entry in Part Two—The Foundation in Evergreen Park, Archives of the Little Company of Mary Sisters, loc. cit.
68. Sister M. Joseph Casey, L.C.M., quoted in Norma Stone's, "Nurse-Nuns Happy With S.U. Campus," *The [Syracuse] Post-Standard*, March 10, 1963. (unpaged)
69. *Newsweek*, "The Ecumenical Council," October 22, 1962, p. 71.
70. John XXIII, Opening Speech of the Second Vatican Council, October 11, 1962.
71. Wilton Wynn, op. cit., p. 176.
72. Henri Fesquet, op. cit., p. 183.
73. Ibid., p. 186.
74. Ibid., p. 175.
75. Ibid., p. 171.
76. Léon Joseph Cardinal Suenens, op. cit., p. 131.
77. Elizabeth Kuhns, *The Habit—A History of the Clothing of Catholic Nuns*, p. 15.
78. Ibid., p. 16, citing the Little Company of Mary Constitution.
79. Syracuse Logbook, entry for August 15, 1963, Archives of the Little Company of Mary Sisters, Evergreen Park, Illinois.
80. Transcribed Logbook entry for December 8, 1963, Part II—The Foundation in Evergreen Park (unpaged), Archives of the Little Company of Mary Sisters, loc. cit.
81. Robert Dallek, op. cit., p. 707.
82. John F. Kennedy, "Radio and Television Report to the American People on Civil Rights," June 11, 1963.
83. Robert Dallek, op. cit., p. 604.
84. Lawrence Elliott, *I Will Be Called John—A Biography of Pope John XXIII*, p. vii.
85. Transcribed Logbook entry for November 25, 1963, Part II—The Foundation in Evergreen Park, loc. cit.
86. Thomas Cahill, op. cit., p. 236.

Chapter Thirteen—Winds of Change

1. Quote of Mother Mary Potter, cited in *Place of Springs*, Mary Campion, p. 22.
2. F. Michael Perko, S.J., op. cit., p. 293.
3. Introductory Statement to the Pastoral Constitution on *The Church in the Modern World* (*Gaudium et Spes*) [The Joys and the Hopes] promulgated by His Holiness, Pope Paul VI on December 7, 1965.
4. George C. Stewart Jr., "20th-Century Sister Population" in *Marvels of Charity: History of American Sisters and Nuns*, p. 565. (The actual number of priests was 58,632. Seminarians numbered 48,992.)
5. Ibid., p. 449.
6. John Cogley, *Catholic America*, p. 114.
7. Chester Gillis, *Roman Catholicism in America*, p. 93.
8. Ibid.
9. Robert McClory, *Faithful Dissenters: Stories of Men and Women Who Loved and Changed the Church*, pp. 8-9.
10. Ibid., p. 13.
11. Ibid., p. 19.
12. Ibid., p. 20.
13. Chester Gillis, op. cit., p. 93.
14. Robert McClory, op. cit., pp. 22–23.
15. John Cogley, op. cit., p. 123.
16. John C. McWilliams, "Chronology of Events," in *The 1960s Cultural Revolution*, p. xxxii.
17. "Watts Riot," <http://college.hmco.com/history/readerscomp/gahff/html/ff_190000_wattsriot.htm>
18. John C. McWilliams, op. cit., p. 65.
19. Wilton Wynn, op. cit., p. 110.
20. Father Bernard Häring, quoted in Peter Steinfels, *A People Adrift—The Crisis of the Roman Catholic Church in America*, p. 255.
21. "Responsible Parenthood," *The Majority Report of the Birth Control Commission*, authors: the Rev. Joseph Fuchs, the Rev. Raymond Sigmond, the Rev. Paul Anciaux, the Rev. A. Auer, the Rev. Michel Labourdette, O.P., and the Rev. Pierre de Locht, included in Robert McClory, *Turning Point: The Inside Story of the Papal Birth Control Commission*, Appendix 1, pp. 171–187.
22. Pope Paul VI, *Sacerdotalis Caelibatus*, issued June 24, 1967.
23. *The Changing Nun*, ed., Sr. Charles Borromeo (Mary Ellen Muckenhirn), p. 74.
24. Ann Carey, *Sisters in Crisis—The Tragic Unraveling of Women's Religious Communities*, p. 33.
25. Ibid., based on information in the *Official Catholic Directory* (for each year).
26. George C. Stewart Jr., op. cit., p. 463.
27. Transcribed Logbook entry in Part II—The Foundation in Evergreen Park (undated, early 1972), Archives of the Little Company of Mary Sisters, Evergreen Park, Illinois.
28. Memorandum from Sister Mary John Schlax, L.C.M., Provincial Superior, March 23, 1977, based on records of the American Province of the Little Company of Mary, Archives of the Little Company of Mary Sisters, loc. cit.

29. List of Former LCM members, Archives of the Little Company of Mary Sisters, loc. cit.

30. George C. Stewart Jr., op. cit., p. 460.

31. Ibid.

32. Sr. Eleace King, IHM, *CARA Formation Directory for Men and Women Religious 1993* (Washington, D.C: CARA /Center for Applied Research in the Apostolate, Georgetown University, 1993), p. 2.

33. Ann Carey, op. cit., p. 33.

34. *2004 Official Catholic Directory*, reported by Sister Rita Stalzer, C. S. J. Cudahy Library, Loyola University, Chicago, Illinois.

35. Christopher J. Kauffman, *Ministry and Meaning: A Religious History of Catholic Health Care in the United States*, p. 273.

36. *2004 Official Catholic Directory*, <http://www.catholicnews.com/data/stories/cns/0403934.htm>.

37. George C. Stewart Jr., op. cit., p. 463.

38. Appendix: Let Us Remember in *A Journey of Unconditional Love: Creating a Healing Environment—The Story of Little Company of Mary Hospital*, pp. 85–86.

39. Interview with Sister Sheila Brosnan, L.C.M., April 18, 2005.

40. House Meeting (San Pierre), November 27, 1972, Archives of the Little Company of Mary Sisters, loc. cit.

41. Conversation with Sister Sheila Brosnan, L.C.M., April 18, 2005.

42. Ibid.

43. Ibid.

44. Letter from Bishop Edward Bagshawe to Mother Mary Potter, June 26, 1891, in Patrick Dougherty's *Mother Mary Potter—Foundress of the Little Company of Mary*, p.183.

45. Patrick Dougherty, op. cit., footnote, p. 184.

46. Letter from Mother Fintan Kealy, L.C.M., to Mother General, June 2, 1939, Generalate Archives of the Little Company of Mary, Tooting Bec, London, England.

47. Memorandum from Sister Ruth Putnam, L.C.M., Provincial Superior to Sisters M. Adrian Davis, Virginia Luebke, and Josephine Keblusek, L.C.M., October 1, 1975, Archives of the Little Company of Mary Sisters, loc. cit.

48. Letter of Sister Deborah Conley, L.C.M., Sister M. Terrence Landini, L.C.M., and Sister Margaret Ann Schneider, L.C.M., to Sister Mary John Schlax, L.C.M., and members of the Provincial Council, June 22, 1976, Archives of the Little Company of Mary Sisters, loc. cit.

49. Memo of Sister Mary John Schlax, L.C.M., to members of the Holy Redeemer group, August 25, 1976, Archives of the Little Company of Mary Sisters, loc. cit.

50. Ibid.

51. Conversation with Sister M. Terrence Landini, L.C.M., April 11, 2005.

52. Memorandum from the Most Holy Redeemer Group, Summer 1976, Archives of the Little Company of Mary Sisters, loc. cit.

53. Conversation with Sister M. Adrian Davis, L.C.M., October 25, 2004.

54. Bruce J. Schulman, *The Seventies: The Great Shift in American Culture, Society, and Politics*, p. 140.

55. Chester Gillis, *Roman Catholicism in America*, p. 97.

56. George C. Stewart Jr., op. cit., p. 459.

57. Wilton Wynn, op. cit., p. 241.

58. Ibid., p. 34.

Chapter Fourteen—Trusting in the Spirit

1. Transcribed Logbook entry for January 4, 1964, in Part II—The Foundation in Evergreen Park, Archives of the Little Company of Mary Sisters, Evergreen Park, Illinois.

2. San Pierre Logbook, December 1965, Archives of the Little Company of Mary Sisters, Evergreen Park, Illinois.

3. Joseph A. Porcello, "St. Mary's Plans New Hospital," in [Syracuse] *Herald-Journal*, August 21, 1966, Archives of the Little Company of Mary Sisters, loc. cit.

4. Letter from Monsignor Daniel E. Lawler to Walter A. Foery, Bishop of Syracuse, October 20, 1965, Archives of the Little Company of Mary Sisters, loc. cit.

5. Letter from Justice William E. McClusky to Monsignor Daniel Lawler, February 28, 1964, Generalate Archives of the Little Company of Mary, Tooting Bec, London, England.

6. Ibid.

7. Community Health Information and Planning Service, Inc., "The Hospitals of Onondaga County: 1967–1975—A Look Ahead—With Recommendations," p. 5, Archives of the Little Company of Mary Sisters, loc. cit.

8. Supplementary Presentation by St. Mary's Hospital to Hospital Review and Planning Council of Central New York, Inc., (Spring 1968), p. 6, Archives of the Little Company of Mary Sisters, loc., cit.

9. Letter from Senator Tarky Lombardi, Jr. and Senator John H. Hughes to Charles Hall, Chairman of the Board, Hospital Review and Planning Council of Central New York, Inc., April 5, 1968, Archives of the Little Company of Mary Sisters, loc. cit.

10. Syracuse Logbook, p. 145, Archives of the Little Company of Mary Sisters, Evergreen Park, Illinois.

11. Phone conversation with Sister Mary Obrist, O.F.M., March 30, 2005, St. Joseph's Hospital Health Center, Syracuse, New York.

12. Phone conversation with Sarah Kozma, March 31, 2005, Research Center, Onondaga Historical Association, Syracuse, New York.

13. Apostolic Activities of the Buenos Aires Community (December 1972), p. 1, Archives of the Little Company of Mary Sisters, loc. cit.
14. Ibid.
15. Ibid.
16. Ibid.
17. Letter from Father John F. O'Malley to Mother General, January 21, 1975, Generalate Archives, loc. cit.
18. Letter from Margarita Morgan Moore to Mother General, December 14, 1974, Generalate Archives, loc. cit.
19. Letter from Moreen Morgan to Mother General, December 16, 1974, Generalate Archives, loc. cit.
20. Letter from [Mrs.] Emily Bell to Mother General, December 20, 1974, Generalate Archives, loc. cit.
21. Letter from Richard E. C. DeRidder to Mother General, December 20, 1974, Generalate Archives, loc. cit.
22. Letter from Sister Mary John Schlax, L.C.M., Provincial Superior, published in the *Buenos Aires Herald*, January 31, 1975, Generalate Archives, loc. cit.
23. Letter from Sister Mary John Schlax, L.C.M., to Mother M. Madeleine Carrigan, L.C.M., Superior General, March 12, 1975, Generalate Archives, loc. cit.
24. Letter from Sister Jean Stickney, L.C.M., to Sister Mary John Schlax, L.C.M., Provincial Superior, April 5, 1975, Generalate Archives, loc. cit.
25. Circular Letter from Mother M. Madeleine Carrigan, L.C.M., Superior General, to Province/Regions, (Summer 1975), Generalate Archives, loc. cit.
26. Buenos Aires Logbook (written by Sister Jean Stickney, L.C.M.), pp. 82–83, loc. cit.
27. Information provided by Sister M. Isabel Tejade. This figure includes outpatients and those treated in the Emergency Room at Sanatorio Mater Dei.
28. Letter from Sister Mary John Schlax, L.C.M., to sisters in the American Province, January 2, 1974, Generalate Archives, loc. cit.
29. "Calvary Hospital Online," <http://www.calvaryhospital.org/index/Welcome+To+Calvary+Hospital/ Where+Life+Continues.htm>.
30. Based on an informational pamphlet entitled "Calvary Hospital," Archives of the Little Company of Mary Sisters, loc. cit.
31. Letter from Sister Mary John Schlax, L.C.M., Provincial Superior to all members of the American Province, January 2, 1974, Generalate Archives, loc. cit.
32. Provincial Council Notes for January 23–25, 1974, Generalate Archives, loc. cit.
33. Letter from Sister Mary John Schlax, L.C.M., Provincial Superior to Mother M. Madeleine Carrigan, L.C.M., Superior General, dated January 30, 1974, Generalate Archives, loc. cit.
34. Letter from the Generalate of the Little Company of Mary to Sister Mary John Schlax, L.C.M., Provincial Superior, April 17, 1974, Generalate Archives, loc. cit.
35. Bronx Logbook, May 5, 1974, Archives of the Little Company of Mary Sisters, Evergreen Park, Illinois.
36. Letter to the LCM community from Sister Mary John Schlax, L.C.M., May 19, 1974, Generalate Archives, loc. cit.
37. Letter from Sister Mary John Schlax, L.C.M., Provincial Superior to Mother M. Madeleine Carrigan, L.C.M., Superior General, May 12, 1974, Generalate Archives, loc. cit.
38. Bronx Logbook, May 21, 1974, Archives of the Little Company of Mary Sisters, loc. cit.
39. Ibid., May 5, 1974.
40. Ibid.
41. Ibid.
42. Ibid.
43. Text provided by Roseann C. Keller, June 30, 2005.
44. Ibid.
45. Ibid.
46. "Calvary Hospital" Informational brochure, no author, Archives of the Little Company of Mary Sisters, loc. cit.
47. Bronx Logbook, May 1974, Archives of the Little Company of Mary Sisters, loc. cit.
48. Letter from the Bronx community to the sisters in Evergreen Park, May 17, 1974, Archives of the Little Company of Mary Sisters, loc. cit.
49. Text provided by Roseann C. Keller, June 30, 2005.
50. Memorandum from Sr. Mary John Schlax, L.C.M., to members of the Bronx community, August 15, 1975, Archives of the Little Company of Mary Sisters, loc. cit.
51. Notes from a House Meeting of the Bronx community, March 19, 1976, Archives of the Little Company of Mary Sisters, loc. cit.
52. Notes from a meeting between Sister Mary John Schlax, L.C.M., and Sister Ruth Putnam, L.C.M., with Terrence Cardinal Cooke and Monsignor James P. Cassidy, November 19, 1976, Generalate Archives of the Little Company of Mary, loc. cit.
53. Phone conversation with Roseann C. Keller, former member of the Bronx community, June 2005.
54. Letter from the Bronx community to sisters in the American Province, Christmas 1975, Archives of the Little Company of Mary Sisters, loc. cit.
55. *A Healing Presence ... The Story of Little Company of Mary Hospital's Journey of Unconditional Love*, p. 72.
56. House Resolution 647, State of Illinois, Eightieth General Assembly, March 1, 1978.
57. Proclamation from Michael A. Bilandic, Office of the Mayor, City of Chicago, July 22, 1977.
58. Letter from James R. Thompson, Office of the Governor, State of Illinois, September 22, 1977.
59. Letter from Jimmy Carter, President of the United States to the Little Company of Mary in Evergreen Park, June 28, 1977.

CHAPTER FIFTEEN—BEARERS OF GOD'S TENDER COMPASSION

1. Ronald Reagan, "City Upon a Hill" speech, originally delivered January 25, 1974.
2. Sister Theresa Kane, R.S.M., Welcome Address to Pope John Paul II at the National Shrine of the Immaculate Conception, Washington, D.C., October 7, 1979.
3. Peter Steinfels, *A People Adrift: The Crisis of the Roman Catholic Church in America*, p. 293.
4. "Pope Rejects Laicization Trend: Strongly Reaffirms Priestly Celibacy," *The Remnant*, April 30, 1979, <http://www.sspxasia.com/Documents/Archbishop-LeFebvre/Apologia/Vol_three/Chapter1.htm>.
5. Meeting with Sister M. Terrence Landini, L.C.M., April 5, 2005.
6. Ibid.
7. Sister Mildred Radziewicz, originally quoted in "In the Potter's Hands," Volume 4, Issue 3, p. 1, Fall 2004.
8. Based on the Constitution of the Little Company of Mary, as explained by members of the Laguna Hills community, February 18, 2005.
9. Sister Mildred Radziewicz, L.C.M., "Our LCM Associates," 1993.
10. Conversation with Sister Mary John Schlax, L.C.M., and Sister Mildred Radziewicz, L.C.M., February 18, 2005.
11. "Brief History of the Hospice Movement," <http://www.hom.org/movement.asp>.
12. Elisabeth Kübler-Ross, M.D., *On Death and Dying*.
13. Sister Renee Cunningham, L.C.M., originally quoted in "In the Potter's Hands," Volume 3, Issue 2, p. 3, May 2003.
14. Conversation with Sister Kathleen McIntyre, L.C.M., May 12, 2005.
15. Meeting with Sister Mary John Schlax, L.C.M., and Sister Mildred Radziewicz, L.C.M., September 24, 2003.
16. Phone conversation with Sister M. Joseph Casey, L.C.M., June 22, 2005.
17. "Persian Gulf Wars," <http://www.infoplease.com/ce6/history/AO838511.html>.
18. Information furnished by Sister Carol Pacini, L.C.M., February 3, 2005, and Sister Catherine (Kay) Shalvey, L.C.M., April 5, 2005.
19. *Creating a Healing Environment—The Story of Little Company of Mary Hospital*, p. 52.
20. Ibid., p. 54.
21. Conversation with Sister Gloria Harper, L.C.M., February 18, 2005.
22. Related by Sister Francis Curran, L.C.M., February 18, 2005.
23. Text provided by Sister Sharon Ann Walsh, L.C.M.
24. Letter to the Sisters of the Little Company of Mary in Evergreen Park from a grateful friend (name omitted to protect the family's privacy), May 22, 2005.
25. Conversation with Sister Gloria Harper, L.C.M., February 18, 2005.
26. Meeting with Sister Catherine (Kay) Shalvey, L.C.M., September 15, 2003.
27. Discussion with Sister M. Adrian Davis, L.C.M., October 25, 2004.
28. Meeting with Sister Maria Antonieta Benavides, L.C.M., September 24, 2003.
29. Conversation with Sister Deborah Conley, L.C.M., April 18, 2005.
30. Ibid.
31. Ibid.
32. Ibid.
33. Sister Virginia O'Brien, L.C.M., quoted from *A Healing Presence—The Story of Little Company of Mary Hospital's Journey of Unconditional Love*, p. 102.
34. Sister Kathleen McIntyre, L.C.M., cited in *A Journey of Unconditional Love: Creating a Healing Environment—The Story of Little Company of Mary Hospital*, p. 42.
35. Conversation with Sister Mary Babcock, L.C.M., February 18, 2005.
36. Shared by Sister M. Michael Murray, L.C.M., September 15, 2003.
37. Story related in a phone conversation with Sister M. Adrian Davis, L.C.M., June 25, 2005.
38. Jack Beary, "Olympic Torch Will Shine on Teen Volunteer," *Daily Southtown*, April 27, 1996.
39. Text courtesy of Kelly Wood, PR & Marketing, Little Company of Mary Hospital, Evergreen Park, Illinois.
40. Sister Margaret Christina Hoban, L.C.M., "A Healthier Evergreen Park—Working Toward a Healthier Community," in *Market Plan for a Healthier Evergreen Park*, p. 2.
41. Meeting with Sister Jean Marsden, L.C.M., May 12, 2005.
42. Phone conversation with Sister Jean Marsden, L.C.M., June 22, 2005.
43. Discussion with Sister Kathy Scott, L.C.M., May 12, 2005.
44. Phone conversation with Sister Kathy Scott, L.C.M., June 28, 2005.
45. Conversation with Sister M. Terrence Landini, L.C.M., May 2005.
46. Discussion with Sister Mary Jane Feil, L.C.M., April 18, 2005.
47. Phone conversation with Sister Marianne Herres, L.C.M., May 7, 2005.
48. Phone conversation with Sister Marilla Dyer, C.S.C., June 21, 2005.
49. Ibid.
50. Patrick W. Carey, *Catholics in America—A History*, p. 156.
51. Ibid.
52. Joseph Cardinal Bernardin, "Faithful and Hopeful: The Catholic Common Ground Project," October 24, 1996, <http://www.geocities.com/pharsea/CommonGround.html>, p. 16.
53. Statistics based on *Leading Catholic Indicators*, Kenneth C. Jones, cited in "The Incredible Shrinking Catholic Church," <http://www.cwnews.com/news/viewstory.cfm?recnum=22821>.

54. John T. McGreevy, Catholicism and American Freedom—A History, p. 289.
55. <http://www.uscob.org/bishops/charter.htm>.
56. Governor Frank Keating, "Keating blasts bishops as he departs from post," reported by Cathy Lynn Grossman, USA TODAY, <http://www.usatoday.com/news/nation/2003-06-13-Keating_x.htm>.
57. Justice Anne Burke letter to Bishop Wilton Gregory, March 29, 2004, quoted in "Head of Review Board: Catholic Bishops Blocked Reform," Richard N. Osling, Associated Press, <http://www.telegram.com/statistic/crisisinthechurch/051304.html>.
58. Meeting with Sister Jean Stickney, L.C.M., June 24, 2005.
59. Conversation with Sister Elizabeth Gilroy, L.C.M., and Sister Tess de Dassel, L.C.M., London, England, December 6, 2004.
60. Ibid.
61. Conversation with Sister Sharon Ann Walsh, L.C.M., May 12, 2005.
62. Ibid.
63. Proclamation from James J. Sexton, Mayor of the Village of Evergreen Park, to the Little Company of Mary in Evergreen Park, November 1, 2004.
64. Letter from Francis Cardinal George, O.M.I., archbishop of the Archdiocese of Chicago, to the Little Company of Mary in Evergreen Park, October 20, 2004.
65. Letter from George W. Bush, President of the United States, to the Little Company of Mary in Evergreen Park, December 21, 2004.
66. Phone conversation with Sister M. Adrian Davis, L.C.M., June 25, 2005.
67. Summary of the visit to Ibadan, Nigeria, from Sister M. Adrian Davis, L.C.M., Sister Gloria Harper, L.C.M., and Sister Bridget Kelly, L.C.M., to Sister Carol Pacini, L.C.M., Provincial Leader and Provincial Councilors, April 26, 2005.
68. "Overview of Foreign Apostolic Trips by Pope John Paul," Vatican Information Service, <www.archdiocese-chgo.org/documents/pope/foreign_trips.pdf>.
69. Wilton Wynn, op cit., p. 249.
70. Phone conversation with Sister Gabriella Doran, C.S.C., June 17, 2005.
71. Conversation with Sister Carol Pacini, L.C.M., June 1, 2005.
72. Ibid.

EPILOGUE—RECEPTIVE HEARTS FOR THE CONTINUING JOURNEY

1. Sister Mark Cornelius, L.C.M., Congregational Leader, Presentation at the Sixteenth Congregational Chapter, April 2005.
2. Acts of the Sixteenth Congregational Chapter, April 8 – April 25, 2005.
3. Patricia Wittberg, S.C., The Rise and Fall of Catholic Religious Orders—A Social Movement Perspective, p. 39.
4. Sister Rose McDermott, S.S.J., "A Canonical Perspective," in The Crisis in Religious Vocations—An Inside View, Laurie Felknor, ed., pp. 225–226.
5. Sister Mark Cornelius, L.C.M., Opening Presentation to the Sixteenth Congregational Chapter, April 2005.
6. Conversation with Peg Schneider, June 9, 2005.
7. The Dogmatic Constitution on the Church, Lumen Gentium, Solemnly Promulgated by His Holiness Pope Paul VI, November 21, 1964.
8. Patricia Wittberg, S.C., op. cit., p. 214.
9. Sister Nancy Boyle, L.C.M., 100th Anniversary of the Founding of the Little Company of Mary, 1993, cited in A Healing Presence —The Story of Little Company of Mary Hospital's Journey of Unconditional Love, p. 99.
10. "Mary Potter's Volunteers," pamphlet within Little Company of Mary's International Vocational Brochure, 2005.
11. Mary Potter, Path of Mary, p. 23.
12. Mary Potter cited in Mary Campion, Place of Springs, p. 15.
13. Mary Potter, 1879.
14. Congratulatory Letter from Gustavo Garcia-Siller, M.Sp.S., Auxiliary Bishop of the Archdiocese of Chicago, to the Little Company of Mary in Evergreen Park, January 2005.
15. Acts of the Sixteenth Congregational Chapter, p. 4.
16. Acts of the Sixteenth Congregational Chapter, p. 8.
17. Sister Mark Cornelius, L.C.M., Closing of the Sixteenth Congregational Chapter, April 24, 2005.

LITTLE COMPANY
OF MARY—APPENDIX

In life, the Sisters of the Little Company of Mary brought their faith, hope, and love to each person they encountered. The splendid example of their lives, as well as their prayers, continue even though they are no longer with us.

REMEMBERING THE LCM SISTERS
WHO HAVE GRACIOUSLY SERVED IN AMERICA

Chicago Foundation (1893-1955)
Province of the Immaculate Conception (1955-2005)

LCM SISTERS WHO HAVE GONE TO THE LORD

Sister M. Veronica Dowling, March 4, 1896
Sister M. Elizabeth Ryan, August 8, 1898
Sister M. Lucy Ambrose, October 26, 1913
Sister M. Columba Kealy, November 21, 1918
Sister M. Charles Madigan, November 3, 1921
Sister M. Barbara Crowe, August 22, 1923
Sister M. Colette Harper, August 25, 1930
Sister M. Raphael McCarthy, September 21, 1932
Sister M. Cecilia Burgert, May 11, 1939
Sister M. Evangelist Touhey, December 27, 1939
Sister M. Rosarii Hassett, October 26, 1940
Sister M. Philomena Haslem, July 16, 1944
Sister M. Stanislaus Casey, September 18, 1943
Sister M. Joseph Sullivan, November 25, 1945
Sister M. Dionysius Touhy, December 13, 1946
Sister M. Raphael Dwyer, December 24, 1951
Sister M. Colette Morrissey, July 15, 1953
Sister M. Helena Johnston, November 26, 1953
Sister M. Christopher Collins, July 11, 1954
Sister M. Fintan Kealy, November 4, 1958
Sister M. de Lourdes Lee, January 3, 1960
Sister M. Stanislaus Madigan, July 30, 1961
Sister M. Dunstan Kelleher, November 17, 1962
Sister M. Callista O'Donoghue, September 10, 1963
Sister M. Dorothea Dwight, March 23, 1964
Sister M. Juliana Callan, September 4, 1964
Sister M. Carmel Nolan, December 18, 1964
Sister M. Thaddeus Brennan, February 3, 1965
Sister M. Mercedes Sorensen, April 22, 1965
Sister M. Camille Plotzke, October 23, 1965
Sister M. Rita Carroll, June 6, 1966
Sister M. Felix Barrett, December 20, 1968
Sister M. Regina Powell, September 12, 1969
Sister M. Ruth Manning, July 27, 1972
Sister M. Ignatius Dooley, March 10, 1973

Sister M. Columba Brady, March 11, 1973
Sister Mary Anne Kohler, January 26, 1974
Sister M. Catherine Barrett, September 25, 1975
Sister M. Lucy Colgan, February 12, 1976
Sister M. Joseph Harrison, May 29, 1976
Sister M. Leo Lang, June 12, 1976
Sister M. Veronica Henneberry, June 19, 1976
Sister M. Barbara Snyder, October 1, 1977
Sister M. William Scott, July 24, 1978
Sister M. Hilda O'Halloran, September 28, 1978
Sister M. Fidelis Ward, October 11, 1978
Sister M. Louis Bertrand, November 21, 1978
Sister M. Teresa Mahon, January 10, 1979
Sister Mary Grace King, February 5, 1979 (M. Virginia*)
Sister M. Solace Hannigan, March 21, 1979
Sister M. James Beaupré, August 30, 1980
Sister Ruth Putnam, April 2, 1981 (M. Charles*)
Sister M. Imelda Durkin, June 4, 1981
Sister Alice Besançon, January 20, 1983 (M. Anastasia*)
Sister Mary Rose Solano, July 17, 1983 (M. Perpetua*)
Sister M. Elizabeth Hough, November 27, 1983
Sister M. Bernadette O'Hara, February 26, 1984
Sister M. Peter Flaherty, December 21, 1985
Sister Rita Ann Rooney, May 20, 1987 (M. Paula*)
Sister M. Regina Marshon, October 9, 1987
Sister M. Francis Thompson, December 20, 1989
Sister M. Agnes O'Neill, January 17, 1990
Sister M. Benedicta Mahoney, September 19, 1990
Sister M. Paul Hurtubise, July 15, 1991
Sister Margaret Mary Doherty, January 30, 1992
Sister M. Francis Beggan, December 14, 1993
Sister M. Helen Burke, May 8, 1994
Sister M. Rita Bracken, December 9, 1994
Sister M. Eugene Trenner, July 8, 1995
Sister M. Dominica Cekolin, June 17, 1997
Sister Nancy Boyle, February 10, 1998 (M. Gerard*)
Sister Peter Marie McCormack, October 5, 1998
Sister M. Damian Young, January 27, 2000
Sister M. Carmelita Hoban, December 9, 2001
Sister M. Magdalen Nolan, January 24, 2002
Sister M. Patricia Dooley, October 1, 2002
Sister M. Michael Murray, May 27, 2004

LCM Sisters serving in America
who were later transferred to other Provinces:

Sister M. Bon Consilio Sullivan, transferred to England (1898)

Sister M. Patrick Tuohy, transferred to Rome (1921)

Sister M. Xavier Roarty, transferred to Italy (1927)

Sister M. Laurence Delaney, transferred to Ireland

Sister M. Veronica Killeen, transferred to Florence

Sister M. Patrick Merriman, transferred to Malta

Sister M. Bernadette O'Neill, transferred to England

Sister M. Padua O'Neill, transferred to England (1927)

Sister M. Natalie Gillen, transferred to Carmelite Monastery (1938)

Sister Paul Hoban, (M. Vincent*) transferred to Rome (1958)

Members of the Little Company of Mary – 2005

Sister Mary Babcock, L.C.M. (M. Raymond*)

Sister Maria Antonieta Benavides, L.C.M.

Sister Sheila Brosnan, L.C.M. (M. David*)

Sister M. Joseph Casey, L.C.M.

Sister Deborah Conley, L.C.M. (M. Edward*)

Sister Renee Cunningham, L.C.M.

Sister M. Adrian Davis, L.C.M.

Sister Mary Jane Feil, L.C.M. (M. Lawrence*)

Sister Gloria Harper, L.C.M.

Sister Marianne Herres, L.C.M. (M. Bonaventure*)

Sister Margaret Christina Hoban, L.C.M. (M. Assumpta*)

Sister M. Terrence Landini, L.C.M.

Sister Jean Marsden, L.C.M.

Sister Kathleen McIntyre, L.C.M. (M. Robert*)

Sister Virginia O'Brien, L.C.M. (M. Augustine*)

Sister M. Teresa Oleniczak, L.C.M.

Sister Carol Pacini, L.C.M.** (M. Bartholomew*)

Sister Mildred Radziewicz, L.C.M. (M. de Montfort*)

Sister Mary John Schlax, L.C.M.

Sister Kathleen Scott, L.C.M. (M. Louis*)

Sister Catherine Shalvey, L.C.M. (M. Colette*)

Sister Jean Stickney, L.C.M. (M. Gemma*)

Sister Maura Tangney, L.C.M. (M. Patrick*)

Sister Sharon Ann Walsh, L.C.M. (M. Bernard*)

*Original name in religious life
** Elected to LCM Congregation Team, 7/2/05, London, England

The Sisters of the Little Company of Mary lovingly remember and with gratitude give thanks to God for those women who shared their way of life and journeyed with them in ministry for a time—and then responded to the Lord's call in another way.

ACKNOWLEDGMENTS

This book could not have been written without the kind and gracious cooperation of many people. First and foremost, my heartfelt thank you to each and every Sister of the Little Company of Mary in the American Province for generously sharing their time, thoughts, and memories with me. In addition to their lives, the sisters' recollections and suggestions have contributed a wealth of richness to these pages. A special recognition to Sister Carol Pacini, who set in motion the plan to get this history written and to Sister Kathleen McIntyre, who wisely guided this book to completion. Thanks to Sister Jean Stickney for her perceptive advice and helpful suggestions, and to Sister Margaret Christina Hoban for organizing the archival materials in Evergreen Park, which were essential for an accurate retelling of this incredible story.

My sincere appreciation to the sisters in London and Nottingham for their information and insight, and especially to Sister Raphael Butler for her patience with my seemingly endless questions, for the hours she spent searching through the archives, and for the many cups of tea that she thoughtfully set before me. Charlotte Karlsson's assistance in relaying my numerous emails and phone calls was most helpful.

A special thank you to Mary Jo May for managing this project with grace and enthusiasm, and to the readers who provided feedback and caught my errors: Sisters Kathleen, Carol, and Jean (all mentioned above), as well as Sister Terrence Landini, Sister Sharon Ann Walsh, Mary Jo May, Denise Stillman, and Mary Jo Quick. Thanks to Mary Lou Durkin for her organizational expertise, which lent order to this endeavor, and to all in the LCM Province Office in Evergreen Park whose warmth made me feel at home, especially Bernadette Wodke, Jocelyn Mesina, and

Suzanne Petrouski. Nora O'Malley and Peg Schneider offered their unique perspectives of the LCM community, and I appreciate the time and effort Roseann C. Keller took to write her recollections of Calvary Hospital, which added colorful detail to the account of that ministry.

I am particularly grateful to Elizabeth West, L.C.M. Her scholarly yet immensely readable work, *One Woman's Journey: Mary Potter—Founder ~ The Little Company of Mary* provided much of the framework and detail of Mary Potter's life and a substantive portion of Chapter II. And an appreciative thank you to His Excellency, Patrick Dougherty, Bishop of Bathurst, for the extensive research and insights that his biography, *Mother Mary Potter—Foundress of the Little Company of Mary* offered.

Thank you to the following archivists, researchers, and reference librarians who lent their assistance and expertise to this project: Julie A. Satzik, Assistant Research Archivist, Archdiocese of Chicago, Joseph Cardinal Bernardin Archives and Records Center; John Brady, Reference Librarian; Jack Simpson, Curator of Local and Family History; Kathleen McMahon, Reference Librarian; Matt Rutherford, Reference Librarian and Grace Dumelle, Assistant—Newberry Library; Olivia Chen, Erin Tikovitch, and Rob Medina—Chicago Historical Society; The Reverend John Paul Salley, Sister Rita Stalzer, C.S.J., Reference Librarian/Bibliographer; Kathy Young, Archivist; Professor John Makowski, and Christopher Walker, Reference Librarian—Loyola University of Chicago; Professor Antoinette Brazouski, Northern Illinois University; Monsignor Lawrence McGrath, Librarian, St. John's Seminary, Brighton, Massachusetts; Susan Maycock, Cambridge Historical Commission; Brian Youmans, Volunteer Research Docent, Cambridge Historical Society, Cambridge, Massachusetts; Robert Lally-Johnson, Archivist, Archives of the Catholic Archdiocese of Boston; Irena Balgalvis, Reference Librarian, Boston Public Library; Dr. William Kevin Crawley, Archivist and Curator of manuscripts, Archives of the University of Notre Dame; Sister Rita King, D.C., Archivist, Emmitsburg, Maryland; Sister Margaret Ahl, D.C., Provincial Archivist, Daughters of Charity DePaul Provincial House, Albany, New York; Carl H. Roesch, Diocesan Archivist, The Chancery Office, Syracuse, New York; Darrol Pierson, Librarian, Indiana State Library; Steve Gutierrez, Assistant Manager, Village of River Forest; Diane Hansen, Historical Society of Oak Park and River Forest; Phyllis Newquist, Mount Olivet Cemetery,

Chicago; and Sarah Kozma, Onondaga Historical Association, Syracuse; Peggy Tate Smith, Rights and Reproductions, Mystic Seaport; Tina Ward, Oak Lawn Library. A very special thank you to Pamela Fontana for opening her Portsmouth home to me, for generously sharing her knowledge of Mary Potter's family, and for providing a personal tour of the town where Mary Potter once lived. Lauryn Toczylowski's creativity and expertise transformed a simple manuscript into a beautifully designed book. Thanks to all who prayed for this endeavor. If I have failed to acknowledge anyone—the omission is a lapse of mind, not of heart.

Thank you to those religious who shared information or personal recollections of the Little Company of Mary: Sister Gabriella Doran, C.S.C., Sister Marilla Dyer, C.S.C., Notre Dame, Indiana; Sister Margaret Norris, S.P., Jasper, Indiana; Sister Marie Esther Sivertsen, S.P., Archivist Assistant, St.-Mary-of-the-Woods, Indiana; Sister Mary Obrist, O.S.F., Syracuse, New York; Sister Jeanne Crapo, O.P. Dominican College, River Forest, Illinois; Sister Victoria Heiderscheidt and Sister Elizabeth Dingbaum, Marian Schönstatt Sisters, Madison, Wisconsin. *Muchas gracias* to Maria Luisa de la Reiga at Sanatorio Mater Dei and to the *Hermanas de María de Schönstatt*, especially to Sister M. Teresa Buffa, Sister M. Isabel Tejade, Sister M. Clarisa Ferrer, and Sister M. Elena Lugo for the kindness and warm hospitality they extended to my husband and me during our visit to Buenos Aires and Florencio Valera. Thanks to Father F. William Etheredge for his encouraging response to my tentative first chapter and to Monsignor Glenn Nelson and Fathers Steven Knox, Michael Black, Addison Hart, and Godwin Asuquo whose homilies at NIU's Newman Center provided spiritual sustenance and sometimes inspired the preceding pages.

I am deeply indebted to a number of people who have influenced me more than I probably even realize: Walter Serbent, my fifth/sixth-grade teacher who demonstrated the importance of striving for excellence; Sister Andrea Naples, ASCJ, my high school English teacher who nurtured my love of literature; NIU professors James Giles and Gustaaf van Cromphout, who taught me a thing or two about writing. The Medical Mission Sisters of Philadelphia who had such an impact on me and with whom I was privileged to share religious life for a while. My father, Anthony Kish, who worked so hard to provide me with so much and my mother, Joann Kish, who imparted to me her deep devotion to our faith and her love of reading.

A special thank you to my children: Kimberly, Carolyn, Jon, Abigail, Christina, Katherine, and Andy for their loving encouragement during the past two years. I am also grateful to each of my five grandchildren who were so understanding when "Gran'mama" could not come out and play as often as usual. Unending thanks to Christina Noel Nall for giving me the chance to take this wondrous journey and for lending her unique vision and creative talents to this project and to Abigail Nall for helping reshape my thoughts and words. This history is all the better because of their editorial contributions. Carolyn Anne Gerard oversaw every detail of design and production needed to turn these pages into the book that it has become. Last, but certainly not least, thanks to my husband for being with me, at least in spirit, every step of the way. Vincent's technical assistance, computer know-how, and willingness to take on the role of my "Executive Assistant" without being asked will long be remembered—as will the many miles we shared as I researched and wrote this book. In spite of my numerous self-doubts, he always believed that I could do this. His unwavering faith in me is etched into my memory and heart forever.

Merrie Ann Nall
DeKalb, Illinois
September 15, 2005

Photo Credits

Page 35: Photo of S.S. *Kaiser Wilhelm II.* (Print #58.931.44) Courtesy of Mystic Seaport—The Museum of America & The Sea, Mystic, Connecticut.

Page 39: Photo of Chicago, State Street, 1893. (ICHi #13914) Courtesy of Chicago Historical Society.

Page 45: Photo of the View across West end of the Main Basin—CWE 1893. (ICHi #02520) Courtesy of Chicago Historical Society.

Page 55: Photo of Bertha Honoré Palmer. (ICHi #12030) Courtesy of Chicago Historical Society.

Page 60: Photo of Residence of Mrs. Potter Palmer, 1350 Lake Shore Drive, Chicago. (ICHi #38947) Courtesy of Chicago Historical Society.

Page 87: Photo of statue of Mary Clare Morgan, Maria Clara Morgan Hospital, San Antonio de Areco. Courtesy of Vincent Nall.

Page 87: Photo of inscription on statue of Mary Clare Morgan, Maria Clara Morgan Hospital, San Antonio de Areco. Courtesy of Vincent Nall.

Page 139: Photo of Maria Clara Morgan Hospital, San Antonio de Areco. Courtesy of Vincent Nall.

Page 179: Photo of Little Company of Mary Hospital, Torrance, California. Courtesy of Vincent Nall.

Page 194: Photo of young postulants and novices enjoying a songfest during recreation. Courtesy of Chicago Photographers, Chicago.

Page 244: Photo of ceremony held on October 15, 1995 at San Pierre. Lighting of the unity candle. Courtesy of Sister Marilla Dyer, C.S.C., Notre Dame, Indiana.

Photo Insert Pages—Group 1:

Page 1: Photo of newborn nursery—Little Company of Mary Hospital—Evergreen Park (1964). Courtesy of Joe Casey Photography, Beverly, Illinois.

Page 7: Photo of sister & newborn (1964). Courtesy of Chicago Photographers, Chicago.

Page 7: Photo of religious profession (1964). Courtesy of Chicago Photographers, Chicago.

Page 7: Photo of the final resting place of Venerable Mary Potter—St. Barnabas Cathedral – Nottingham, England. Courtesy of Merrie Ann Nall.

Page 8: Photo of Maria Clara Morgan Hospital, San Antonio de Areco. Courtesy of Vincent Nall.

Photo Insert Pages—Group 2:

Page 2: Photo of LCM Sisters in the American Province (1993). Courtesy of Wm. H. Cramp.

Page 4: Photo of a class of novices (1965). Courtesy of Chicago Photographers, Chicago.

Page 5: Photo of blessing of hospital in Buenos Aires (1951). Courtesy of the *Hermanas de María de Schönstatt.*

Page 5: Photo of Memorial Hospital, Jasper, Indiana (2004). Courtesy of Vincent Nall.

Page 5: Photo of Hannon Tower at Little Company of Mary Hospital, Torrance, California (2005). Courtesy of Merrie Ann Nall.

Page 6: Photo of Little Company of Mary Hospital chapel, Torrance, California (2005). Courtesy of Merrie Ann Nall.

Page 7: Photo of artwork at Little Company of Mary Hospital, Torrance, California (2005). Courtesy of Merrie Ann Nall.

Page 8: Photo of Monsignor Kenneth Velo with Sister Kathleen McIntyre. Courtesy of Sandy Bertog.

BIBLIOGRAPHY

A Healing Presence … The Story of Little Company of Mary Hospital's Journey of Unconditional Love. Edited by Maurice Possley. Willard, Ohio: RR Donnelly & Sons Company, 2000.

Angle, Paul M. *Crossroads—1913.* Chicago: Rand McNally, 1963.

Barry, John M. *The Great Influenza: The Epic Story of the Deadliest Plague in History.* New York: Penguin Books, 2004.

Book of Chicagoans: A Biographical Dictionary of Leading Living Men and Women in the City of Chicago. Edited by Albert Nelson Marquis. Chicago: A. N. Marquis & Company, 1917.

Briggs, Asa. *Victorian Cities.* Harmondsworth, Middlesex, UK: Penguin Books, Ltd., 1990.

Brodrick, James, S.J. *Saint Francis Xavier (1506–1552).* New York: The Wicklow Press, 1952.

Butler, Rev. Alban. *The Lives of the Fathers, Martyrs, and Other Principal Saints.* Edited by Rev. Bernard Kelly. Vol. IV. Chicago: The Catholic Press, 1959.

Butler's Lives of the Saints. Edited by Herbert J. Thurston and Donald Attwater. Allen, Texas: Thomas More Publishing, 1956.

Cahill, Thomas. *Pope John XXIII.* New York: Viking, 2002.

Campion, Mary. *Place of Springs—The story of the first 100 years of the Province of the Maternal Heart (English Province) of the Little Company of Mary.* Merseyside, Great Britain: Print Origination, 1977.

Capovilla, Loris F. *The Heart and Mind of John XXIII—His Secretary's Intimate Recollection.* Translated by Patrick Riley. New York: Hawthorne Books, 1964.

Carey, Ann. *Sisters in Crisis: The Tragic Unraveling of Women's Religious Communities.* Huntington, Indiana: Our Sunday Visitor Publishing, 1997.

Carey, Patrick W. *The Roman Catholics in America.* Westport, Connecticut, and London: Praeger, 1996.

Coburn, Carol K. and Smith, Martha. *Spirited Lives: How Nuns Shaped Catholic Culture and American Life, 1836–1920.* Chapel Hill and London: The University of North Carolina Press, 1999.

Cogley, John. *"Aggiornamento—And Beyond,"* in *Catholic America.* New York: Dial Press, 1973.

Currey, Sister Catherine Ann, PVBM. "Sister-Population Statistics, 1830–1990," in Stewart, George C., Jr., *Marvels of Charity—History of American Sisters and Nuns.* Huntington, Indiana: Our Sunday Visitor Publishing, 1994.

Cushing, Richard Cardinal. *Call Me John—A Life of Pope John XXIII.* Boston: St. Paul Editions, 1963.

Dallek, Robert. *An Unfinished Life—John F. Kennedy (1917–1963).* Boston: Little, Brown, and Company, 2003.

Dolan, Jay P. *The American Catholic Experience: A History from Colonial Times to the Present.* Garden City, New York: 1985.

Dougherty, Patrick. *Mother Mary Potter—Foundress of the Little Company of Mary*. Whitchurch, Hampshire (UK): Portia Press Ltd., 1961.

Ellis, John Tracy. *American Catholicism*. Second Edition, Rev. Chicago: University of Chicago Press, 1969.

Evans, R. J. *The Victorian Age (1815–1914)*. Second Edition. New York: St. Martin's Press, 1968.

Fesquet, Henri, *The Wit and Wisdom of Good Pope John*. Translated by Salvator Attanasio. New York: P. J. Kenedy, 1964.

Fialka, John. *Sisters: Catholic Nuns and the Making of America*. New York: St. Martin's Press, 2003.

Gardiner, John. *The Victorians: An Age in Retrospect*. New York and London: Hambledon and London, 2002.

Gibson, David. *The Coming Catholic Church—How the Faithful are Shaping a New American Catholicism*. Revised and updated. New York: HarperCollins Publishers, 2003.

Gilbert, Paul and Bryson, Charles Lee. *Chicago and Its Makers: A Narrative of Events from the Day of the First White Man to the Inception of the Second World's Fair*. Chicago: F. Mendelsohn, 1929.

Gillis, Chester. *Roman Catholicism in America*. New York: Columbia Press, 1999.

Goodwin, Richard N. *Remembering America: A Voice from the Sixties*. Boston: Little, Brown and Company, 1988.

Halberstam, David. *The Fifties*. New York: Villard Books, 1993.

Hardon, John A., S.J. *Pocket Catholic Dictionary*. Abridged edition of *Modern Catholic Dictionary*. New York: Image Books/Doubleday, 1985.

Hatch, Alden. *A Man Named John—The Life of Pope John XXIII*. New York: Hawthorn Books, 1963.

Healy, Eve. *The Life of Mother Mary Potter: Foundress of the Congregation of the Little Company of Mary*. London: Sheed and Ward, 1938.

Higham, John. *Strangers in the Land: Patterns of American Nativism, 1860–1925*. Second Edition. New York: Atheneum, 1963.

Holland, James. *Fortress Malta: An Island Under Siege, 1940–1943*. New York: Miramax Books/Hyperion, 2003.

Howell, Joel D. *Technology in the Hospital: Transforming Patient Care in the Early Twentieth Century*. Baltimore: Johns Hopkins University Press, 1995.

Kantowicz, Edward R. *Corporation Sole—Cardinal Mundelein and Chicago Catholicism*. South Bend: University of Notre Dame Press, 1983.

Ker, Ian. *Newman: On Being a Christian*. Notre Dame: University of Notre Dame Press, 1990.

Kübler-Ross, Elisabeth, M.D. *On Death and Dying*. New York: Macmillan, 1969.

Kuhns, Elizabeth. *The Habit: A History of the Clothing of Catholic Nuns*. New York: Doubleday/Random House, 2003.

Larson, Erik. *The Devil in the White City—Murder, Magic, and Madness at the Fair the Changed America*. New York: Crown Publishers, 2003.

Leckie, Robert. *American and Catholic*. Garden City, New York: Doubleday, 1970.

Maher, Sister Mary Dennis. *To Bind Up the Wounds: Catholic Sister Nurses in the U.S. Civil War*. Baton Rouge: Louisiana State University Press, 1989.

Marty, Martin E. *A Short History of American Catholicism*. Allen, Texas: Thomas More/Tabor Publishing, 1995.

Mayer, Harold M. and Wade, Richard C. "The White City and the Gray," in *Chicago: Growth of a Metropolis*. Chicago: University of Chicago Press, 1969.

McClory, Robert. *Faithful Dissenters: Stories of Men and Women Who Loved and Changed the Church*. Maryknoll, New York: Orbis Books, 2000.
—. *Turning Point: The Inside Story of the Papal Birth Control Commission, and How* Humana Vitae *Changed the Life of Patty Crowley and the Future of the Church*. New York: Crossroad Publishing, 1997.

McDermott, Rose, S.S.J. "A Canonical Perspective" in *The Crisis in Religious Vocations: An Inside View*. Edited by Laurie Felknor. New York: Paulist Press, 1989.

McGreevy, John T. *Catholicism and American Freedom—A History*. New York & London: W. W. Norton & Company, 2003.

McKenna, Patrick. "Irish Immigration to Argentina," in *Patterns of Migration: The Irish World Wide—History, Heritage, Identity*. Edited by Patrick O'Sullivan. Vol. 1. Leicester: University of Leicester Press, 1992.

McWilliams, John C. *The 1960s Cultural Revolution*. Westport, CT: Greenwood Press, 2000.

Morris, Charles R. *American Catholic: The Saints and Sinners Who Built America's Most Powerful Church*. New York: Times Books/Random House, 1997.

Murray, Williamson and Millett, Allan R. *A War To Be Won: Fighting the Second World War*. Cambridge, Massachusetts, and London: The Belknap Press of Harvard University Press, 2000.

Naylor, Robert Anderton. *Across the Atlantic*. Westminster: Roxburghe Press, 1894.

Newman, John Henry. *Parochial and Plain Sermons*. Volume 6. London & New York: Longmans, Green and Company, 1900–02.

Oakley, J. Ronald. *God's Country: America in the Fifties*. New York: Dembner Books, 1986.

Official Catholic Directory for 1929. New York: P. J. Kenedy & Sons, 1930.

O'Neill, William L. *The Oxford Essential Guide to World War II*. New York: Oxford University Press (Berkley Books), 2002.

Our American Century: Turbulent Years—The 1960s. Editors of Time-Life Books. Alexandria, Virginia: Time-Life Books, 1998.

Palmer, R. R. and Colton, Joel. *A History of the Modern World*. Third Edition. New York: Alfred A. Knopf, 1965.

Perko, F. Michael, S.J. *Catholic & American—A Popular History*. Huntington, Indiana: Our Sunday Visitor, 1989.

Potter, Mary. *Autobiographical Notes*.
—. *Mary's Conferences* "J."
—. *Motherhood: Instructions on Marriage*, 1885.
—. *Path of Mary*. London: Washbourne & Company, 1876.

Pyle, Ernie. "Ernie Pyle in England," in Henry Steele Commager, *The Story of the Second World War*. Boston: Little, Brown and Company, 1945.

Rice, Gerard T. *The Bold Experiment: JFK's Peace Corps*. Notre Dame, University of Notre Dame Press, 1985.

Ross, Ishbel. *Silhouette in Diamonds—The Story of Mrs. Potter Palmer*. New York: Harper, 1960.

Schama, Simon. *A History of Britain: The Fate of the Empire, 1776–2000*. Volume III. New York: Hyperion, 2002. (DPL)

Schlossberg, Herbert. *The Silent Revolution & the Making of Victorian England*. Columbus: Ohio State University Press, 2000.

Schulman, Bruce J. *The Seventies: The Great Shift in American Culture, Society, and Politics*. New York: The Free Press, 2001.

Shanabruch, Charles. *Chicago's Catholics: The Evolution of an American Identity*. Notre Dame, Indiana, and London: University of Notre Dame Press, 1981.

Steinfels, Peter. *A People Adrift: The Crisis of the Roman Catholic Church in America*. New York: Simon & Schuster, 2003.

Stewart, George C., Jr. *Marvels of Charity: History of American Sisters and Nuns*. Huntington, Indiana: Our Sunday

Visitor Publishing, 1994.

Stourton, Edward. *Absolute Truth: The Struggle for Meaning in Today's Catholic Church*. New York: TV Books, 2000.

Suenens, Léon Joseph. *The Nun in the World: New Dimensions in the Modern Apostolate*. Translated from the French by Geoffrey Stevens. Westminster, Maryland: Newman Press, 1962.

Taylor, Frederick. *Dresden: Tuesday, February 13, 1945*. New York: HarperCollins Publishers, Inc., 2004.

Vogel, Morris J. *The Invention of the Modern Hospital—Boston (1870–1930)*. Chicago: University of Chicago Press, 1980.

Watkins, T. H. *The Great Depression: America in the 1930s*. Boston: Little, Brown, and Company, 1993.

West, Elizabeth, L.C.M. *One Woman's Journey: Mary Potter—Founder ~ Little Company of Mary*. Richmond, Victoria (Australia): Spectrum Publications, 2000.

Wilson, A. N. *The Victorians*. London: Random House, 2002.

Wittberg, Patricia, S.C. *The Rise and Fall of Catholic Religious Orders—A Social Movement Perspective*. Albany, New York: The State University of New York Press, 1994.

Wynn, Wilton. *Keepers of the Keys: John XXIII, Paul VI, and John Paul II—Three Who Changed the Church*. New York: Random House, 1988.

"We all have the power
within us for doing good."

~ Venerable Mary Potter ~

"God awaits our acts of love
and confidence in Him."

~ Venerable Mary Potter ~

Sister M. Joseph Casey, L.C.M., in Evergreen Park pediatrics, 1960s.

"Stand with Mary
at the foot of the Cross,
and with your eyes on Jesus,
think what she thought;
and see what she saw."

~ Venerable Mary Potter ~

"Yes, it is our mission
to make known
and to honor
the magnificence of that
marvelous work of God,
the Maternal Heart of Mary."

~ Venerable Mary Potter ~

"May we, children
of the Maternal Heart,
indeed possess her heart,
and be mothers to all those
who are brought to us
that we may show them love
and win them to God."

~ Venerable Mary Potter ~

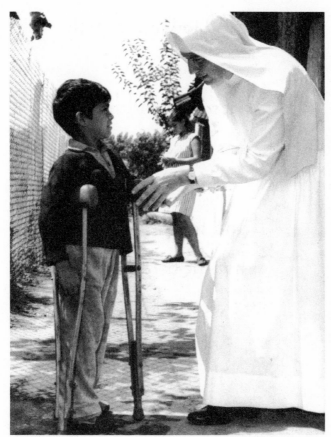
Sister and child in Buenos Aires, Argentina, 1960s.

"Ah! How our Mother

rejoices to see

her own children

take her place at the bedside

of the dying

and to do for them

what she could not do

for Jesus in his agony."

~ Venerable Mary Potter ~

"Finish the life
you have begun for God.
It will be a pleasing,
perfect work,
if you live it in accordance
with your spirit, your vocation . . .
Mary on Calvary."

~ Venerable Mary Potter ~

"Go forth, my children,
on your grand mission.
I hope to watch you from Heaven
and pray for you,
and even in Heaven,
I hope to look with delight
on the work God planted
in His church on earth,
the Little Company of Mary."

~ Venerable Mary Potter ~

Little Company of Mary Sisters and Associates in Evergreen Park, 1990s.

"In the spirit of
Mary on Calvary
our vocation impels us to enter
into the sufferings of others,
to bring about equality and dignity
for all and to collaborate
with others to create a world of justice,
love and peace.
In this way we make visible
the healing presence of Jesus."

~ Venerable Mary Potter ~